MORTGAGE-BACKED SECURITIES

SECURITIES

Investment Analysis & Advanced Valuation Techniques

Andrew S. Davidson
Michael D. Herskovitz

PROBUS PUBLISHING COMPANY
Chicago, Illinois
Cambridge, England

ISBN 1-55738-440-1

Printed in the United States of America

BB

1 2 3 4 5 6 7 8 9 0

■

Table of Contents

■

___

■ **CHAPTER 4**

■ **CHAPTER 5**

■ **CHAPTER 6**

Acknowledgements

This book synthesizes ideas that we have developed in the course of our involvement in the mortgage market. These ideas were refined and enhanced through innumerable discussions with colleagues, traders, clients, investors, competitors and critics. We would like to thank all of you for your contributions to our understanding of the market. We would also like to thank Lan-Ling Milo Wolff for her invaluable assistance in the production of this book.

CHAPTER ONE

■

Innovation in the Mortgage Market

■

Tuesday, 8 a.m. The Fixed-Income Investment Strategy Committee. Bill Stone is discussing the portfolio's performance. The portfolio is invested in treasuries and investment-grade corporate bonds. The same nagging problems keep resurfacing. Performance has been acceptable but lackluster. Competitive pressures and regulatory concerns are mounting. Treasuries offer the necessary liquidity and have low regulatory risk weights, reducing capital demands, but they don't offer the yield necessary to support the liabilities in the current competitive environment. Corporate bonds offer more yield, but event risk coupled with limited supply and lack of liquidity makes it difficult to allocate a significant portion of the portfolio to the sector.

Susan Spring suggests they reconsider investing in the mortgage market. The old objections flow from the group. The market is too complicated. They don't have any experience. While some of their competitors have done well with mortgages, just as many have run into severe problems. Susan is determined not to let the opportunity get away. She outlines the advantages of mortgages: liquidity, high credit quality, a wide range of investment choices, and the opportunity to earn additional yield. She acknowledges the risks and presents a plan for developing the necessary expertise in-house, so they can invest in mortgages with the same confidence as the other markets. Bill and the others realize that to compete, they need to explore the mortgage market further.

The mortgage-backed securities market has grown in ten years from the backwater of fixed-income investing to a core sector. From a narrow market, dominated by the savings and loan industry and offering few products, mortgage-backed securities (MBS) are now a dynamic and varied investment market. The MBS market is unique because of its size and complexity. Mortgage-backed securities can be a blessing or a curse to the investment manager. The market offers so many opportunities, that almost every investor can find a bond that fits his or her needs. Unfortunately, the market also poses many challenges to the investor, and many mortgage investments have turned sour. This book is designed to help the investor better understand and analyze mortgage-backed securities. With MBS, it is impossible to totally eliminate risk or completely account for all potential problems. Nevertheless, with a good framework and the right tools in hand, it is possible to avoid the pitfalls of MBS investing, while reaping the rewards.

The mortgage market has been an area of innovation over the past few years. The continual changes in the market are a result of the explosive growth of the mortgage market and the revolution in technology. The growth in the mortgage market created the raw material for financial engineering, and the revolution in technology has made these complex financial structures feasible. Figure 1-1 shows the growth in mortgage debt outstanding.[1] This represents secured borrowing of individuals to finance home purchases. Total mortgage debt is about $3 trillion dollars. The amount of mortgage debt is approximately equivalent to the amount of government debt.

Nearly one-half of all mortgage debt outstanding has been securitized. Mortgage-backed securities total almost $1.5 trillion. Ten years ago, the entire mortgage-backed securities market was only a few hundred million dollars of securities and represented a small share of the total mortgage market. Similarly, CMO/REMIC issuance has exploded.

---

[1]The data from Figures 1-1 through 1-7 are from *The Mortgage Market Statistical Annual for 1993*, Inside Mortgage Finance Publications, Inc., Washington DC.

Innovation in the Mortgage Market

Figure 1-1

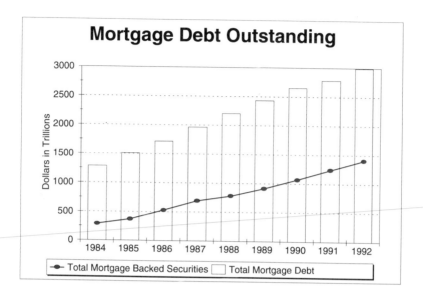

Following the first CMO issuance by the Federal Home Loan Mortgage Corporation (FHLMC) in 1983, the CMO market has grown rapidly. Total CMOs outstanding exceed $700 billion and account for about half of all mortgage-backed securities.

■ MORTGAGE CONTRACTS

In addition to the amount of mortgage debt outstanding, there has also been growing diversity in mortgage contracts. While at one time the vast majority of mortgages were thirty-year, fixed-rate fully amortizing loans, now borrowers are offered a wide variety of terms and contracts. The most common forms of loans are the traditional thirty-year, fixed-rate mortgages and fifteen-year, fixed-rate mortgages. Borrowers may also take out adjustable-rate mortgages (ARMs). ARMs typically have a thirty-year amortization, but their coupons adjust to an index periodically. ARMs indexed to treasury rates, CD rates, and various cost-of-funds indices are available. More recently, balloon mortgages and so-called "two-step" or reset loans have been developed. These typically offer a fixed rate of interest for five to seven years and then float to a new rate at the end of the initial period. The growth in these products can be seen in Figure 1-2, which details the 1992 loan purchases by the FHLMC, which is also known as Freddie Mac.

Figure 1-2

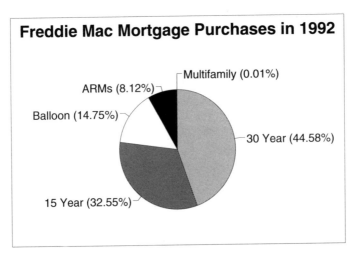

Freddie Mac Mortgage Purchases in 1992

Multifamily (0.01%)
ARMs (8.12%)
Balloon (14.75%)
30 Year (44.58%)
15 Year (32.55%)

■ MORTGAGE ORIGINATORS

As the mortgage market has grown, the composition of the originators has shifted substantially. Up until the 1980s, the mortgage market was dominated by the Savings and Loans, (S & L). Interest-rate deregulation, the growth in the mortgage secondary market, and the all-too-familiar thrift crisis have served to reduce the share of savings institutions in the mortgage market. Now, mortgage companies, which originate loans for sale to the secondary market, are the dominant issuers. Moreover, many of the commercial banks and savings institutions still involved in mortgage originations operate primarily as mortgage banks, selling a substantial portion of their originations. Figures 1-3a and 1-3b show this shift. Savings institutions, which made up nearly half of the originations in 1983, dropped to a one-quarter share in 1991. Mortgage companies grew to over one-half of all mortgage originations.

Figure 1-3a

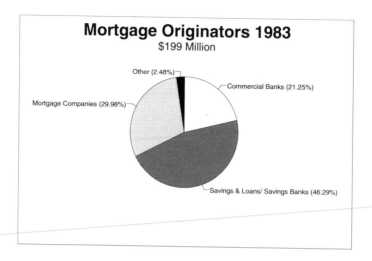

Mortgage Originators 1983
$199 Million

- Other (2.48%)
- Commercial Banks (21.25%)
- Mortgage Companies (29.98%)
- Savings & Loans/ Savings Banks (46.29%)

Figure 1-3b

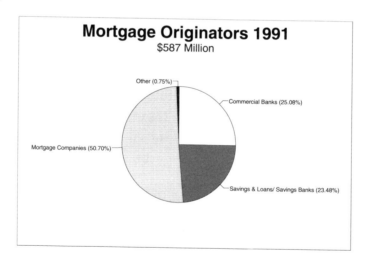

Mortgage Originators 1991
$587 Million

- Other (0.75%)
- Commercial Banks (25.08%)
- Mortgage Companies (50.70%)
- Savings & Loans/ Savings Banks (23.48%)

■ MORTGAGE SECURITIZATION

The growth in the mortgage market and the shift in origination patterns are closely linked to the development of the mortgage secondary market. The main engine for the growth of the secondary market was the government agencies responsible for mortgage securitization. The Government National Mortgage Association, GNMA, is responsible for the securitization of loans guaranteed by the federal government under Federal Housing Authority, FHA, and Veterans Administration, VA, programs. GNMA is a part of the Department of Housing and Urban Development, HUD. The Federal National Mortgage Association, Fannie Mae (FNMA), and Freddie Mac (FHLMC), are private companies chartered by the federal government. They are now called Government Sponsored Enterprises or GSEs. Fannie Mae and Freddie Mac are responsible for the securitization of conventional mortgages that conform to certain size guidelines. Currently, they can securitize loans with face amounts up to about $200,000. Loans for securitization by the agencies must also fit the underwriting guidelines of the agencies.

Figure 1-4 shows the annual securities issuance of the agencies. Fannie Mae and Freddie Mac have grown faster than GNMA over the past few years due to changes in loan sizes and aggressive program development by Fannie Mae and Freddie Mac. There has also been substantial growth in private MBS activity in the past few years, as originators have sought a secondary market outlet for loans that do not meet the GSE requirements.

The success of the secondary markets can be seen by looking at the securitization rates for various mortgage types. In 1992, almost two-thirds of all loans originated were securitized. (Source: *Inside Mortgage Securities*)[2] The securitization rate was the highest for FHA/VA loans, where securitization actually exceeded issuance, due to the securitization of prior years' production. FNMA/FHLMC issuance totaled over 60% of conventional conforming originations. Private MBS issuance totaled almost half of nonconforming mortgage originations.

---

[2]Market-share information based on *The Mortgage Market Statistical Annual for 1993.* Washington D.C.: Inside Mortgage Finance Publications, Inc., 1993.

Figure 1-4

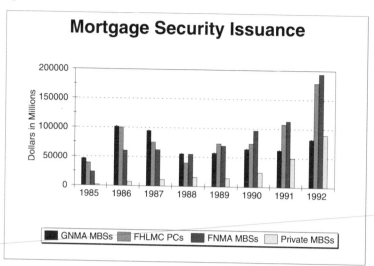

One of the engines powering the growth of the MBS market is the collateralized mortgage obligation (CMO). CMOs allow mortgage-backed securities to be transformed into a variety of instruments with differing investment characteristics. The CMO has served to expand the base of investors in the mortgage market. Figure 1-5 shows the growth of the CMO market.

Figure 1-5

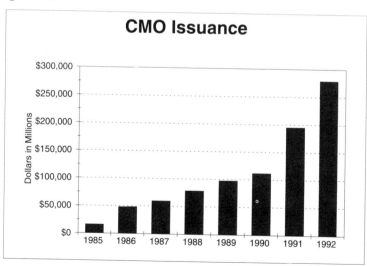

CMOs are now the dominant form of securitization for conforming, fixed-rate mortgages. CMO issuance is limited more by available supply, than by available demand. CMOs have been used to create a wide variety of bond types. Figures 1-6a and 1-6b show some of the more common bond types and their percentage of issuance in 1987 and 1992. The figure shows the growing complexity of CMOs. Another measure of complexity is the number of classes in CMO deals. In 1985, most deals had four or five classes. By 1992, most CMOs had over 20 classes, with some deals even reaching triple digits.

Figure 1-6a

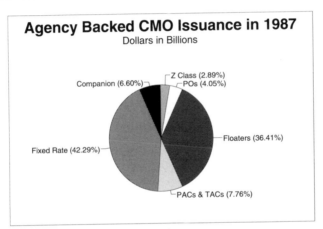

Figure 1-6b

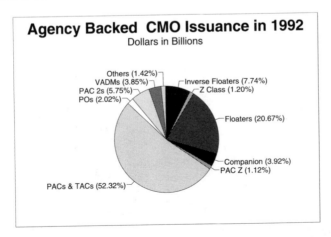

■ MORTGAGE INVESTORS

The net result of the combination of the size of the mortgage market and the variety of investment instruments available is that mortgages are important investments for a wide variety of investors. Figure 1-7 shows the allocation of mortgage-backed securities among investors. S&Ls make up only 11% of the mortgage security investors. Banks, insurance companies, mutual funds, and pension funds are all important investors in the market.

Figure 1-7

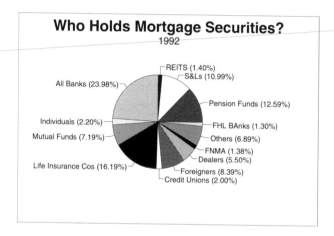

Each type of investor, indeed each individual firm, faces a unique set of investment requirements. Each has its own regulatory structure and its own set of investment objectives. This diversity of demand is one of the causes for the success of the mortgage market. It is also the source of great difficulty. Given the range of products available and the range of investment requirements, general prescriptions about mortgage investing are of little use to the investor with specific needs.

■ ANALYTICAL TOOLS

As the mortgage market has grown, investors have learned some of the complexities of mortgage investing. This complexity stems largely from the borrower's right to prepay his loan at any time without penalty. Prepayments can drastically alter the cash-flow characteristics of a mortgage investment. Figures 1-8a, 1-8b, and 1-8c show the cash flows of a $100 million mortgage-backed security under three different prepayment assumptions. These assumptions will be described in more detail. The first panel shows the cash flows assuming no prepayments. This is an unrealistic assumption, but these cash flows reflect the cash flows of the underlying mortgage contract. Notice that the payment is constant, with the bulk of the payments in the early months coming from interest and the principal payments coming in the later years. The second panel shows prepayments at a 150% PSA (Public Securities Association). This is a reasonable prepayment assumption for loans at a discount, with little refinancing incentive. Here prepayments provide about as much cash flow as interest, and scheduled principal payments become much less important. The third panel assumes a 50% CPR (conditional prepayment rate). This is a typical pattern for a security where the borrowers have a great incentive to refinance. Virtually all of the payments are principal repayments, with bulk of the cash flows coming before the end of the fifth year (month 60).

Figure 1-8a MBS Cash Flows, No Prepayments

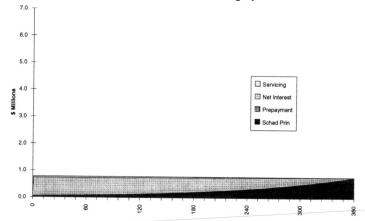

Figure 1-8b MBS Cash Flows, 150 PSA

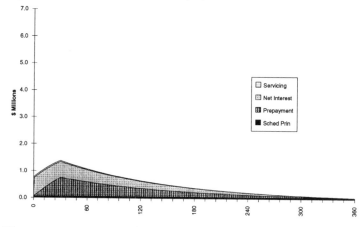

Figure 1-8c MBS Cash Flows, 50% CPR

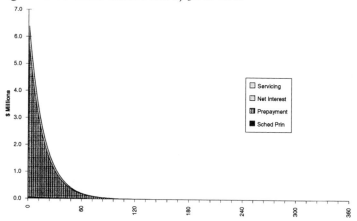

A wide variety of analytical tools have been developed to help investors deal with the potential variability of MBS cash flows. Each tool can be used or misused depending on the circumstances. The table below shows some of these tools. The tools used to analyze mortgages have grown in complexity and variety as the market has grown and as investors have faced a variety of investment environments. As CMO structures have learned to segment the risks of mortgage securities, it has become more important to be able to assess those risks. Often investors have chosen investments because they looked attractive based on historical performance or using current analysis approaches. Often, new instruments require new tools that are able to capture risk more effectively. These tools are listed in Table 1-1.

Table 1-1 Analytical tools for MBS

Type	Value	Risk	Income
Static	Yield Spread	Average life Cash-flow duration	Net margin
Scenario	Total rate of return	Effective duration	Return on equity
Monte Carlo	Option-adjusted spread	OAS duration OAS convexity	Asset/liability optimization

In this book, we will provide a framework for analyzing mortgages, mortgage-backed securities and CMOs. With this tool kit in hand, investors will be able to tailor analysis of the market to meet the specific needs of their institutions. The tool kit also provides a basis for learning. Even as new products are developed, the same basic tools can be used to formulate an investment strategy that identifies opportunity, while controlling risk.

CHAPTER TWO

Overview of
the Method

■

FHLMC Gold 7s are being offered at 100-8 while Gold 7.5s are being offered at 101-10. Not wanting to make the wrong choice, Joe decides that he should analyze the impact of the purchase on the portfolio. Joe analyzes the expected return of the portfolio up and down 300 basis points using both bonds. He tests for prepayment sensitivities and runs an optimization analysis to choose the best bond. The next day he calls back to buy the 7.5s, having determined that they would be a good value even if they cost 2 points and 1 thirty-second more than the 7s. Unfortunately, the market has rallied and the 7s are now trading at 101-2 and the 7.5s are at 102-20. Joe turns back to the computer hoping to analyze the new levels before the market moves again, wondering if there is a better and faster way to evaluate these bonds.

■ PRINCIPLES OF
MORTGAGE-BACKED SECURITIES
Warm-Blooded Securities

Mortgage-backed securities present unique requirements. The mortgage market presents investors with complications not found in other markets. These complications are a source of opportunity and a source of difficulty. The main difficulty arises from the combination of the complexity of the underlying security coupled with the unpredictability of human behavior.

From a purely academic standpoint, a mortgage-backed security can be viewed as a pool of loans with a specific set of imbedded options. The value and performance of these individual loans could be calculated based on optimal exercise of the imbedded options and the results for each loan could be combined to produce overall value and performance measures for the security. To evaluate the security, one would only need to examine the underlying loan documents to determine the contractual obligations of the borrower.

Unfortunately, this procedure would fall far short. Borrower behavior is driven by the interaction of a number of complex factors; many are not directly observable since a mortgage is debt secured by real estate, and for most MBS, this real estate is the primary residence of the borrower, as well as the borrower's most valuable asset. The borrower's decisions on when and how to exercise his or her options are driven by many factors, in addition to the pure mathematics of optimal exercise. For this reason, we like to think of MBS as warm-blooded securities, securities for which the dynamics of human life interplay with the mechanisms of the financial markets.

Choosing the Right Solution

For many years, market participants have struggled with the idea of finding the perfect model to analyze all investment decisions. They hoped to find one method whereby they could input all securities currently available and the correct choice would pop up on the computer screen. This model would somehow take into account all the risks and the likely performance of all securities. The model would analyze the current holdings and the desired outcomes and find the bond or bonds that would make everything right. The model would review history and forecast the future. The model would produce the perfect portfolio.

For better or for worse, such a model does not exist. Some people thought that simulation based option-adjusted spread (OAS) would be the answer. Since OAS considers hundreds of future possibilities, they thought that OAS would definitively answer the question of which bond to buy. However, even OAS, with its broad exploration of the future, cannot by itself provide a clear investment recommendation. OAS analysis, if performed well, can tell you which bonds are cheap, but it doesn't tell you which bonds are right.

Some market participants turned to optimization methods to find the perfect black box. Optimization methods involve setting up an objective and a set of constraints and then finding the bonds that maximize the objective function. While optimization often leads to good solutions to simple portfolio problems, when applied to complex problems, optimization is more likely to demonstrate the shortcomings of your assumptions than a viable prescription for investing.

Given the complexity of the investment decision and the variety of methods of analysis, how should an investor determine which method is appropriate? The answer is a bit unsatisfying if you are looking for a quick solution, but is something like the following: Choose an analysis method that reflects your investment objectives and the complexity of the instruments you are considering. A few examples may demonstrate this point.

It is easy to see that the nature of your investment objectives is important in determining the appropriate level of analysis, for example, if you have a targeted income level and duration. The income and duration of each investment are at least minimum requirements in any analysis. The complexity of these requirements may increase if, as portfolio manager, you are also required to evaluate based on periodic earnings and portfolio market value. Also, more and more portfolio managers are being asked to manage more complex investment targets that more closely reflect the nature of the liabilities. For example, many insurance products contain imbedded options and the investment portfolios need to be structured to offset these risks.

The complexity of the assets also determines the level of analysis. Suppose you are evaluating two single-A-rated corporate bonds. Both are five-year, non-call, bullet-maturity bonds. To determine which is cheaper, you need only calculate the yield and affirm that they both bear the same amount of credit risk. If they both have the same coupon, you need only compare their prices. No amount of scenario analysis, total-return analysis, or OAS analysis could change the result.

On the other hand, suppose you are comparing a callable agency bond with a CMO support bond. Comparing the yields of the two securities will give you only limited information about the relative value of the two securities. Some type of option analysis will be required to distinguish between the two bonds. In this case, the option analysis may become quite complex because the methods typically used for evaluating callable agencies and the methods used for evaluating CMOs are usually different and not always compatible. Table 2-1 outlines some examples of bond comparisons of increasing complexity.

Table 2-1 Analytical Problems of Increasing Complexity

Bond:	vs. Bond:	Description:
High-grade, non-callable corporate	High-grade, non-callable corporate	Same market, bullet maturity, same maturity, same coupon
High-grade, non-callable corporate	High-grade, non-callable corporate	Different maturities, coupons, types of companies
MBS passthrough	MBS passthrough	Callable (prepayments), same market
Callable corporate	MBS passthrough	Callable (prepayments), different market
CMO inverse floater	MBS passthrough	Leveraged, same markets
ARM + IO	Perpetual floater	Leveraged, different markets

In addition, even if you determine that the agency bond is cheaper than the CMO, you might still choose the CMO if it produces better performance in certain environments. For example, you may be

Choosing The Right Solution

more interested in higher income if rates are stable or the prepayment behavior of the support bond reduces the risk of other bonds in your portfolio.

It might seem like the safest course is to perform the most complex analysis to ensure that the risks of the securities are captured and that the investments match the objectives. While appealing, this approach is dangerous. More complex analysis generally requires more assumptions. In a complex analysis these assumptions are hidden from the decision maker. It becomes very difficult to evaluate the impact of changing assumptions on the result. A slight change in assumptions could produce a significant change in investment decisions. Therefore, it is advisable to keep the analysis as simple as possible while addressing all of the relevant risks.

A corollary to the rule that the investment analysis should reflect your investment objectives and the complexity of the instruments you are considering is that the judgment of the investment manager is an important ingredient in the investment process. In this book we are not attempting to provide prescriptions that eliminate the need for judgment, but instead, we are alerting the manager to issues to consider and providing an outline of the tools that are available to assist in these complex decisions.

The performance of mortgage-backed securities can be affected by a variety of factors. In addition to call risk or convexity, there are other factors than can affect your MBS investments. These factors include the shape of the yield curve, path of interest rates, credit risk, economic effects, demographic effects, and statistical variations. In subsequent chapters we will discuss these various sources of risk in more detail.

The complexity of analyzing MBS is compounded by the wide variety of investor objectives. Each investor faces a unique investment environment created by the particular set of client requirements, regulatory limitations, tax status, and accounting rules. Because of the myriad combinations and permutations, each investor must, to some extent, custom tailor its analysis to its circumstances. In this book we provide a framework for analysis that will empower investors to develop analytical tools that adequately address the risks of MBS and simultaneously reflect their unique requirements.

■ FRAMEWORK FOR ANALYSIS

There are many ways to analyze MBS. Each security and application demands a different approach. Approaches to different problems can vary greatly. We have found a common framework that provides consistency across the different approaches. Our framework has four phases. Different approaches take different steps in each phase. Table 2-2 shows the framework of mortgage analysis that will be followed in this book.

Table 2-2   Phases of Mortgage Analysis

Phase of Analysis	Components	Discussed in Chapters
Environment	Interest Rate Economy Supply/Demand Regulatory/Tax/Accounting	Chapter 4
Prepayments	Environmental Factors Modeling Approach	Chapter 5
Cash-Flow Structures	Mortgage Mortgage-Backed Securities CMO/REMIC Portfolio	Chapter 6
Analysis	Valuation Risk Income	Chapter 11
Full Process of the Four Phases	Environment Prepayment Cash Flow Analysis	Chapters 3,7,8,9,10

The four phases are environment, prepayment, cash flow, and analysis. In the environment phase, the range of possible states of the world that affect the analysis are considered. In other words, various scenarios are created. In the prepayment phase, the prepayment rates of the MBS are estimated for the various states or scenarios. In the cash-flow phase, the cash flows of the securities are calculated for each scenario using the prepayment estimates and any other relevant factors. Finally, in the analysis phase, various calculations are performed to summarize the cash-flow results.

Different analyses reflect different choices for the four phases. A relatively simple analysis, yield calculation, is described in Chapter 3. Whipsaw risk, a more complex analyses, is presented in Chapter 10. In both cases, and in other analyses, the same four phases must be considered. Although the analysis is split into four phases, all phases are closely interrelated. For example, the choice of environment will control the range of outcomes available for the analysis phase. The prepayment phase requires output from the environment phase and determines the inputs for the cash-flow-generation phase.

Environment	Prepayment	Cash Flow	Analysis

Environment

The environment phase of the analysis is the most important phase and often the most overlooked. The goal of the environment phase is to specify the range of influences on the securities' performance that will be included in the analysis. The environment phase is important because it sets the boundaries of the analysis. Factors which are left out in this phase will not be considered in the analysis.

Due to the complexity of mortgages, many more factors need to be included when analyzing MBS. However, too often methods that work for other instruments are blindly applied to MBS without due consideration of other factors. For example, the performance of an MBS might be related to activity in the housing market. Failure to assess the impact of changing economic conditions might result in overlooking a potential risk of an MBS investment.

The primary component of the environment that affects MBS, as well as other fixed-income investors, is interest rates. For non-callable securities, the interest-rate environment determines the value and risk of the investment. For MBS and other callable securities, interest rates affect MBS through the valuation process as well as through their impact of mortgage cash flows. A wide range of interest-rate assumptions is possible.

Interest-rate assumptions can vary from the simple, where interest rates are expected to remain constant at their current levels; to the more complex, where interest rates are expected to change linearly over the next twelve months, each move having a probability given by the current volatility of interest rates; to the sophisticated, where interest rates are generated by a two-factor log normal mean reverting process, which satisfies a no-arbitrage condition and whose variances and covariances are consistent with historical observation.

The choice of interest-rate assumption determines the type of analysis. Chapter 3 describes an analysis using a simple interest-rate assumption. Chapter 7 uses more complex interest-rate scenarios. Chapter 8 addresses the use of sophisticated interest-rate models. In Chapter 9, we analyze the relationship between interest rates and cash flows in depth.

Interest rates are not the only factors that affect the performance of MBS. As warm-blooded securities, the value and performance of MBS are influenced by whatever factors affect the borrowers. Changes in an individual's family (marriage, divorce, children, death) will affect his or her home-ownership decisions. Changes in income and employment will also affect borrower behavior. As MBS represent many different individual borrowers, the decisions of any one borrower will not have a significant impact on investors. Taken together, the behavior of the individuals will determine the performance of the securities. For this reason, mortgage analysts look to economic data on employment and housing markets, as well as other demographic data, in analyzing MBS.

One of the major complexities of analyzing MBS is that these "soft" features of MBS performance must be viewed in the context of the interest-rate assumptions. It is not enough to determine that rising unemployment tends to slow prepayment levels. It is also necessary to determine how much unemployment will rise or fall as interest rates change. Additional environmental factors will be considered in Chapter 4.

| Environment | Prepayment | Cash Flow | Analysis |

Prepayment

The prepayment phase provides the link between the environment and the performance of the security. Prepayments are what differentiate MBS from all other securities. Prepayments represent the additional payments above scheduled amounts made by borrowers. There are basically four reasons for prepayments: moving, refinancing, debt retirement, and default. While default is not actually a prepayment, for most MBS investors, a default on a loan usually results in a prepayment to the investor, with the guarantor bearing the risk of default.

The job of the analyst is to relate prepayment levels to the environmental factors described above. There are many methods of providing this linkage. The two most common are prepayment forecasts and prepayment models. Prepayment forecasts are specific numerical statements of what prepayment levels are expected, assuming specific environmental outcomes. The most common is a stable rate forecast. The forecast could be a single prepayment speed for the entire life of a security or could be a series of monthly prepayment rates. Prepayment models, on the other hand, are mathematical equations that relate environmental factors to prepayment rates. These prepayment models are typically econometric models. They are developed through regression and other statistical methods based on historical prepayment data.

Prepayment forecasts can be produced from prepayment models by plugging in values for the appropriate environmental variables. However, not all forecasts are based on models. Often, analysts and other market participants develop forecasts based on their own intuition and experience.

For nonagency MBS, it is necessary to also forecast or model default and delinquency levels and determine the impact of these factors on security performance. Default modeling is much less developed than prepayment modeling because the amount of publicly available default data is limited.

| Environment | Prepayment | **Cash Flow** | Analysis |

Cash Flow

The cash-flow generation phase is the core of the analytical process. The goal in this phase is to calculate the cash flows of the security based on the environment and prepayment assumptions. The value and performance of the MBS is a result of the characteristics of the cash flows. All of the analytical methods are attempts to summarize the characteristics of the cash flow. Calculation of the cash flow is analytically the most straight-forward phase, but for many applications becomes the most time consuming.

The calculation procedure starts with the most basic component first, the underlying mortgages, and then derives the cash flows of the securities backed by those loans. Thus, MBS cash flows are calculated based on the mortgage cash flows. CMO cash flows are calculated using MBS cash flows Portfolio cash flows are calculated based on MBS and CMO cash flows.

The greatest complexity in this phase is in gathering the appropriate indicative data that describe the securities. Each mortgage pool has unique characteristics that determines its cash flow. Another important consideration is determining the appropriate level of detail for the analysis. Rarely is loan-by-loan information available; so most analysis is based on weighted average characteristics of the mortgage pools. In some cases, more information may be available. The analyst must determine the trade-off between additional accuracy and computational efficiency.

Environment	Prepayment	Cash Flow	Analysis

Analysis

The final phase is analysis. Based on the calculated cash flows, summary measures are produced in the analysis phase. The purpose of these measures is to aid the investment process. These analytical results generally provide insight into valuation, risk, and income.

Valuation measures provide guidance in identifying rich and cheap securities. While better measures provide more reliable indicators of future performance, all existing measures have both strengths and weaknesses. Risk measures provide guidance in assessing the range of outcomes for an investment as well as how that investment will perform relative to other securities. Finally, income measures provide insight into the pattern of future cash flows from the MBS.

The accuracy and effectiveness of these measures stems from the full analysis process. The analysis tools capture only those factors contemplated in the environmental phase, impounded in the prepayment phase, transmitted in the cash-flow phase, and summarized in the analysis phase.

■ CONCLUSION

The varying complexity of mortgage-backed securities and MBS investment strategies creates the need for a variety of analytical tools. Different problems require different types and scopes of analysis. While analysis tools differ greatly in ease of computation, data requirements, and technical complexity, most MBS analytical tools require the same four phases of analysis: environment, pre-payment, cash flow, and analysis.

The choices made in each phase will determine the effectiveness of the tool for addressing a specific problem. Each phase is closely related to the others. A good tool maintains comparable levels of complexity across the four phases. Complex measures based on simple assumptions would provide unrealistic appearance of accuracy, while simplistic measures based on complex assumptions are a waste of effort.

Good MBS analysis requires matching the solution to the problem and designing the solution method effectively. In the following chapters we will describe a wide range of tools for analyzing MBS. Each tool will be presented in the four-phase framework. We will show situations where these tools are effective and where they fall short. Through this process, we hope that the reader will gain greater insight into the methodology for choosing the right tools and will learn the skills to develop tools for his or her own unique requirements.

CHAPTER THREE

■

Applying the Framework:
Static Analysis

■

The salesperson tells you, "I've just spoken to the trader. He said he'll sell you the Fannie 8s for Sep at 90 to the 10 year at a 190 speed. He's got a good ax for October and will offer the bonds there at 93. Do these levels work for you?" So goes the typical banter of an MBS trade. Stepping into the market can be a little like entering a foreign country. At first, the language and customs seem a bit new, but over time they become familiar. Still, the best way to get started on your tour in MBS land is to have a handy phrase book. In this chapter we lay out the critical terms and conventions to the MBS market.

The static environment is a little fantasy used by traders and investors to deal with the uncertainty of the real world. In the static environment, the future is seen with certainty as our crystal ball foresees the correct path of interest rates, prepayment rates, and mortgage cash flows. The static environment holds all factors constant when analyzing value between securities. This may not be the most advanced way to look at the securities, but it proves to be a useful starting point.

Static analysis provides the basis for the more complex analytical tools we will develop later in the book. It is also the most common language used to communicate pricing in the mortgage market. In this chapter, we will apply the four-phase approach described in

Chapter Two. While the tools developed in this chapter do not fully exploit the four-phase analysis, viewing even simple tools within this framework may provide additional insight.

Table 3-1 Chapter Overview

Environment	Prepayment	Cash Flow	Analysis
• Static environment	• SMM	• Mortgage math	• Yield
• Current yields	• CPR	• Accrued Interest	• Average Life
	• PSA	• Delay days	• Yield Spread

Table 3-1 shows the phases of the approach and the topics we will consider in each phase. To understand the static environment and more advanced topics related to MBS, we must cover some ground regarding unique aspects of mortgage securities. These aspects include characteristics unique only to MBS and other fixed-income market conventions, which have special meaning when applied to mortgages. The tour of the static environment commences with the measurement and reporting of mortgage prepayments followed by the calculation of MBS cash flows; we then review conventions related to trading and investing in MBS. In the last section of the chapter we show yield and yield-spread calculations.

Environment	Prepayment	Cash Flow	Analysis

■ ENVIRONMENT

The basis for comparison in the static world is the treasury yield curve. The treasury yield curve represents the yields of actively traded treasury bonds and notes. Figure 3-1 shows the yield curve. For static analysis, we assume that yields on treasuries with similar maturities will remain at current levels. That is, if the five-year treasury currently has a yield of 5.14%, that next year and the year after and so on the yield of the then five-year treasury will be 5.14%. What that implies is that in two years the five-year treasury will be a three-year treasury and will yield 4.52% based on current yield levels.

Figure 3-1

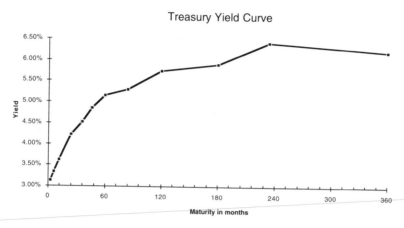

Treasury Yield Curve

For static analysis, we also assume that all other interest rates remain constant, in particular we assume that mortgage rates remain constant. Prepayment projects are developed based on these interest-rate assumptions.

| Environment | **Prepayment** | Cash Flow | Analysis |

■ PREPAYMENT CONVENTIONS

The typical home buyer with a fixed-rate loan makes equal monthly mortgage payments. In the event that the person moves, refinances into another loan, or makes additional payments on the mortgage, we would record a prepayment. The prepayment rate would be determined at the pool level, that is, at the aggregation of numerous mortgage loans.

Prepayments reflect the difference in the actual balance of the MBS pool compared with the balance expected by normal amortization. Because MBS pools contain different dollar balances, simply reporting the prepaid dollars would make it hard to understand the relative prepayment rates across pools. To put the prepayment comparisons on a more uniform basis, the market uses three general ways of expressing MBS prepayments. These conventions have been summarized in Table 3-2.

Table 3-2 Definition of Prepayment Conventions

Single Monthly Mortality (SMM): The SMM measures the percentage of dollars prepaid in any month, expressed as a percentage of the expected mortgage balance.

Conditional Prepayment Rate (CPR): A percentage prepayment rate determined by putting the SMM on an annualized basis. CPR relates the percentage of the nonamortized balance prepaid on an annual basis.

Public Securities Association Prepayment Model (PSA): A market convention adopted by the Public Securities Association in which prepayment rates, expressed in CPR, are assumed to follow a standard path over time. A 100% PSA curve implies that the prepayment rate starts at 0.2% in the first month then rises by 0.2% in each month until month 30 when the prepayment rate levels out at 6% CPR. More about PSA later.

Actually, the market has also used other ways to express prepayment rates. For example, back in the early 1980s, most MBS investors used an assumption that the securities prepaid at the end of 12 years. This assumption was presumably based on some demographic information about home ownership. During this time period, interest rates were generally high and most MBS traded near par or at a discount, so the prepayment rate assumption, while important, was not critical.

This all changed in the mid-1980s. As interest rates began to fall, prices for MBS began to rise above par. However, the lower interest rates led many borrowers to refinance their loans. Because prepayments come back to the investor at par, MBS holders became acutely aware of the call risk embedded in the securities.

In the corporate bond world, we sometimes use the yield to call as a measure of relative value. The MBS market began to adopt this type of price/yield approach by using a prepayment rate to project the future cash flows. Most firms used either the SMM or CPR projections. Generally, the CPR measure became the most widely reported measure of prepayment rates. Working with an annualized number seems to have more of an intuitive feel.

Analysis of prepayments also began to be more closely examined in the mid-1980s. One of the first outcomes of the prepayment

Prepayment Conventions

analysis was a recognition that newly originated loans were not that likely to prepay. Borrowers who had just taken out new loans did not show a great propensity to either move or refinance immediately. Over time, the likelihood of prepayment increased. This notion of rising prepayment rates over time has come to be termed aging. Pools of loans past this aging period are generally called seasoned.

In order to normalize the reporting of prepayment rates across MBS with different ages, the PSA research committee adopted a prepayment-rate-reporting convention. Under the standard PSA prepayment curve, a mortgage was assumed to age over the first thirty months of the loan life. After thirty months the prepayment rate was assumed to level out and remain constant over the remaining term of the mortgage.

The choice of thirty months roughly corresponded to the prepayment pattern of mortgages selling at par or below. At the time the PSA decided to propose the standard prepayment curve, most of the prepayment data related to GNMA securities. Typical 30-year GNMA prepayment rates for par priced seasoned MBS were around 6% CPR, leading to the correspondence of 100% of the PSA curve with 6% CPR.

To illustrate the PSA prepayment curve, consider Figure 3-2 below. This graph shows the relationship between CPR and PSA for two different cases, 100% and 400% of the PSA curve. Note that in both cases, the prepayments start at 0% CPR then rise gradually for 30 months. In the 100% PSA, the long term CPR is 6%, while the long term CPR for 400% PSA equals 24% CPR.

One of the advantages of the PSA curve is that it allows us to compare the prepayment rates of pools, which may have the same coupon but have different ages. Thus a two-month-old loan paying at 1.6% CPR and a 31-month-old loan paying at 24% CPR would both be paying at 400% PSA. This type of comparison is very useful when comparing prepayment rates across different origination years for MBS.

Figure 3-2

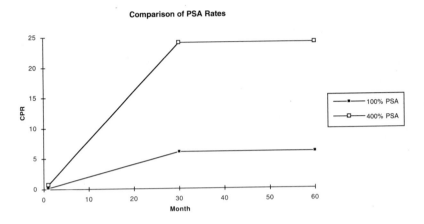

Comparison of PSA Rates

■ TIME SERIES OF PREPAYMENTS

The use of a constant CPR or PSA presumes that prepayment rates will occur based upon a nice, standard pattern. In reality, prepayments are no more likely to be constant than the weather. During periods of volatile interest rates, MBS analysts may look to use a time series of prepayments. This time series may embed various assumptions about the prepayment experience of the pool.

One typical way the time-series approach is used is during times when interest rates have been volatile. For instance, in the early and middle parts of 1992, interest rates had fallen. As a result, record numbers of borrowers refinanced their mortgages, leading to severe surges in prepayment rates. While Wall Street dealers made long-term forecasts for prepayments, these were considerably different than the short-term outlook for prepayments.

In situations when interest rates have been volatile, MBS investors may not be best served by using a constant prepayment assumption. A more realistic approach may be to use a time series of prepayments. The time-series approach may recognize that prepayment rates may in the short term follow a recent rate movement, but over the longer term may trend to an average level.

An illustration of using the time-series approach can be seen in Figure 3-3. This figure projects prepayments assuming that interest rates have recently fallen. The prepayment rates slowly begin to accelerate, then reach a peak within four months. Over the longer term the prepayments decline, reflecting the fact that the pool has some borrowers who do not wish to exercise their prepayment options.

Figure 3-3

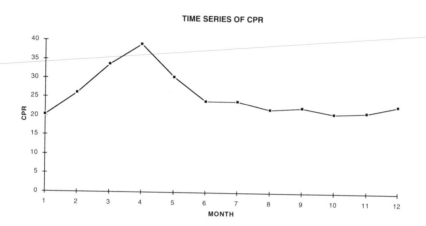

TIME SERIES OF CPR

■ CALCULATING PREPAYMENT RATES

Each month the agencies provide updates to the pools, which they have issued. Among the data supplied is the updated factor for the pool. Factors are reported to an accuracy of seven decimal places (for example 0.7654321). The factor (sometimes called the paydown or paydown factor) reflects the percentage of the original pool balance still outstanding. Factors start at the level of one and then drop to zero over the life of the security.

Getting the factor information provides enough data to calculate the prepayment rate. In general, we look at the difference between the actual reported factor and the expected factor to determine the level of prepayments. The expected factor derives from the amortization schedule of the mortgage. That is, we can apply standard mortgage math to amortize the pool from one month to the next. This amortization assumes no prepayments. When prepayments occur, we can determine the size of the prepayment from the actual reported balance of the pool. Formula 3-1 shows how SMM is determined.

Formula 3-1 Single Monthly Mortality (SMM)

$$SMM = 100 \times \frac{(\text{Scheduled Balance - Actual Balance})}{\text{Scheduled Balance}}$$

Once we know the SMM, it can be annualized to put the prepayment rate on an annualized basis as in Formula 3-2.

Formula 3-2 Conditional Prepayment Rate (CPR)

$$CPR = 100 \times (1 - (1 - \frac{SMM}{100})^{12})$$

With knowledge of the SMM/CPR and age of the loans in the pool we can then put the levels into a PSA basis. Formula 3-3 can be used to turn CPR into PSA.

Formula 3-3 Public Securities Association Prepayment Model (PSA)

$$PSA = 100 \times \frac{CPR}{\min(\text{age}, 30) \times 0.2}$$

In the formula, we use the current CPR and the age of the pool to find the proper point on the PSA curve.

■ CALCULATING CASH FLOWS

One of the primary considerations when determining the cash flows for a mortgage is the prepayment rate. However, there are also other key data points about an MBS, which play a role in the determination of cash flows. In this section, we review some of the critical data points about the MBS pools and then go into further depth regarding the relationship between these factors and the actual MBS cash flows.

Mortgage Math: Indicatives

The mortgage pool represents a collection of loans made to individual borrowers. The basic characteristics of these loans have generally been standardized depending upon the agency and program. That is, 30-year fixed-rate loans are grouped together in pools, 15-year loans are grouped together in other pools, and so on.

While the loans may share broad similarities, differences do exist. For example, not all the borrowers may be paying the same coupon. The loans may not be the same age when grouped. In recognition of these differences, aggregate pool indicatives are calculated. The values of these indicatives are important inputs to the cash flow calculations.

Fixed-rate MBS have similar indicatives, which have been summarized in Table 3-3.

Table 3-3 Indicatives for Fixed-Rate MBS

Weighted Average Remaining Maturity (WAM, sometimes called WART or WARM): The average remaining term of the loans in the pool, averaged based on current balances.

Weighed Average Mortgage Coupon (WAC): The WAC represents the gross coupon (the coupon paid by the borrower) weighted by current balance. For GNMA fixed-rate loans the WAC will be 50 basis points above the net coupon paid to the investor. FHLMC and FNMA will permit a range for the gross coupons in their fixed-rate pools.

Loan Age: The number of months since the origination date of the mortgage note. For FHLMC and GNMA fixed-rate MBS this term is actually computed each month and goes by the name Weighted Average Loan Age (WALA). In the case of FNMA securities, the age is inferred based on the original loan term and the number of months since the creation of the pool. FNMA calls this term Calculated Age (CAGE).

Net Coupon: The coupon paid to the investor. All loans in a FNMA and FHLMC fixed-rate pool must have a gross coupon higher than the net coupon.

Servicing and Guarantee Fee: The difference between the gross coupon and the net coupon equals the servicing and guarantee fee paid to the agency. Servicing is the fee paid to the party who collects the monthly cash flows from borrowers and passes them along to the investors. The guarantee fee reflects the "insurance" premium paid to the agency. In the event of borrower delinquency or default, cash is paid to the investor from the guarantee fund.

The indicatives in Table 3-3 have direct bearing on the determination of cash flows for an MBS. The WAM and WAC are used to amortize the mortgage pool. For instance, loan age will be used to calculate the point on the PSA curve for securities less than 30 months old. For any given principal amount, a higher WAC increases the borrower's monthly payment.

MBS Cash flows

Up to now, we have been spending a great deal of time talking about prepayments, indicatives, and their influence on MBS cash flows. It now seems appropriate to actually give some formulas for how the cash flows are calculated. For a fixed-rate mortgage with a 30-year term, the monthly cash flow can be determined from a standard annuity formula, as seen in Formula 3-4.

Formula 3-4

$$\text{Monthly Payment} = \frac{\text{Balance} \times \text{Borrower's Monthly Coupon}}{1 - (1 + \text{Borrower's Monthly Coupon})^{-\text{Remaining Term}}}$$

The formula gives the monthly payment needed to amortize a fixed-rate loan. Each monthly payment will be equal. However, the amount allocated to the principal and interest will vary. An illustration of this can be seen in Figure 3-4. The figure contains the monthly cash flows for the mortgage, divided between interest and principal. The example used is a 30-year mortgage with an 8% net coupon, an 8.6% gross coupon, and a $100,000 balance.

Figure 3-4

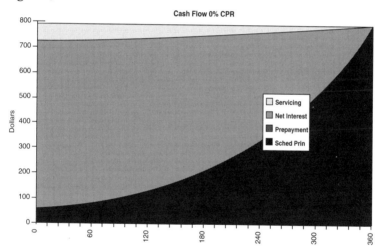

Related to the cash-flow calculation, we can determine the outstanding balance at any point in time, as given in the formula below. In order to know the balance, we use information about the borrower's coupon, the age of the loan, and the number of months of original maturity. This is shown in Formula 3-5.

Formula 3-5 The Balance at Month t

$$\text{Balance}_t = 1 - \frac{(1 + \text{Borrower's Coupon})^{\text{Age}} - 1}{(1 + \text{Borrower's Coupon})^{\text{OWAM}} - 1}$$

where OWAM = original weighted average maturity.

The charts and formulae above represent the behavior for a single loan. When loans are aggregated together into a mortgage pool, it is likely that some of the loans will prepay. In the case of level prepayments, we can use our knowledge of the outstanding balances to determine that amount of prepayments in any given month. Formula 3-6 gives the cash flow in the case of level prepayments.

Formula 3-6 Cash Flow for Level Prepayments

$$\text{Revised Cash flow}_t = (1 - \text{SMM})^{t-1} \times (\text{Cash flow}_t + \text{SMM} \times \text{Balance}_t)$$

The updated cash flow uses information about the prepayment rate, expressed in SMM. It also requires calculations for the cash flow assuming no prepayments, and the outstanding balance assuming no prepayments. Both of these terms are in the right side of the equation. The revised cash flow equation presents a big shortcut in computing cashflows for level-paying mortgages. It does not require us to recalculate the payment level necessary to amortize the loans.

The cash-flow graph looks somewhat different in the presence of prepayments. Figure 3-5 contains the monthly cash flows, broken down between interest, amortized principal, and prepaid principal.

Figure 3-5

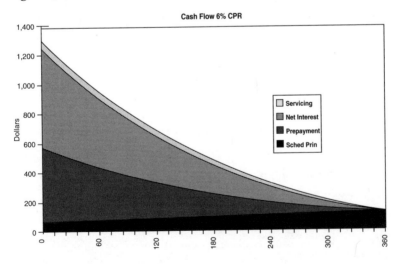

MBS Cash Flows

As seen in the chart, the cash flows for the pool decline over time. With the prepayments, less of the pool remains outstanding, which reduces the coupon flow to the investor. The investors still receive all of their principal, albeit sooner than expected.

The cash flow chart related to a PSA prepayment assumption is slightly different than the cash-flow graph above. To illustrate, we have taken the same mortgage as before and determined the cash flows based on 100% of the PSA prepayment curve. The cash flows can be seen in Figure 3-6.

Figure 3-6

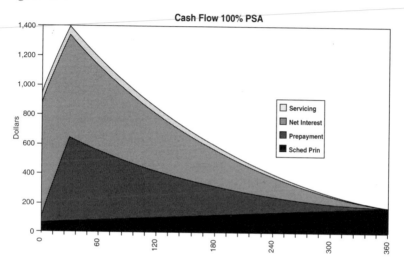

As before, the cash flows have been divided between interest, scheduled principal, and prepaid principal. During the first 30 months, the amount allocated to prepaid principal is rising, reflecting the upward slope of the PSA curve. After the third year, the cash-flow graph looks roughly the same as the level CPR chart.

MBS Cash-flow Calculations for Balloon MBS

In early 1991 and 1992, the yield curve in the U.S. markets began to steepen dramatically as short-term interest rates began to decline. This steepening of the yield curve had numerous implications for the MBS markets, especially regarding the innovation of new products and prepayments on existing products. Some of the more successful products during this time period were the five- and seven-year balloon mortgages. Borrowers found this product attractive because of the lower monthly payments it offered relative to the 30-year loan.

The typical balloon mortgage amortizes like a 30-year level-pay mortgage until the balloon date, when all the remaining principal comes due. At this time, the borrower must refinance the loan. The type of loan that is refinanced into is the prerogative of the borrower, although the programs sponsored by FNMA and FHLMC allow the balloon borrower to automatically refinance at an above-market rate. Although the borrower would essentially refinance the loan, the investor receives all of the remaining principal at the balloon date. The calculations for the cash flows for a balloon loan do not differ from the normal 30-year MBS, other than the termination at either 60 or 84 months.

■ CONSIDERATIONS FOR ADJUSTABLE-RATE MORTGAGES

Up to now, the discussion of the static environment has covered only the fixed-rate segment of the MBS market. Adjustable-rate mortgages (ARMs) constitute a noticeable amount of the mortgage markets. ARMs have many additional factors that influence their cash flows.

Until the late 1980s, the traditional fixed-rate 30- and 15-year mortgage was the instrument of choice for the mortgage borrower. However, as Figure 3-7 illustrates, the ARM market began to comprise a significant segment of the newly originated MBS by the middle 1980s, actually capturing over 70% of all new originations.[1]

---

[1] Market-share information based on *The Mortgage Market Statistical Annual for 1993*. Washington D.C.: Inside Mortgage Finance Publications, Inc., 1993.

Figure 3-7

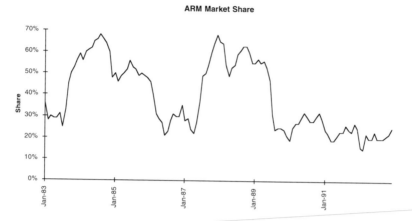

ARM Market Share

Several factors led to the growth in the ARM market. ARMs were popular with borrowers who were living in strong real estate markets, which characterized much of the United States in the mid-1980s. A positively sloped yield curve led to a large differential between the interest rates on the adjustable mortgage compared to the fixed rate loan. Borrowers who expected the strong real estate market to give them an opportunity to trade up, purchased as valuable a home as they could afford.

In addition to the strong housing markets, many originators aggressively offered an adjustable loan at initial below market "teaser" rates. For example, a lender may have offered a borrower a loan at 5% for 12 months, when the actual coupon rate should have been 7%. The aggressive pricing only spurred the strong real estate markets, causing some borrowers to refinance out of their teaser-rate loans into another teaser-rate loan when the loan was reset to market rates.

ARMs share some characteristics with fixed-rate mortgages. They work off of similar descriptions about remaining term, age, delay, and settlement. However, ARMs have some unique characteristics, which are related to the manner in which the coupon is set and restrictions that may be placed on the coupon.

Table 3-4 ARM Characteristics

Index Value: The ARM coupon will be based on some index. The most prevalent indices are the 1-year Treasury, LIBOR, CD, or the 11th District Cost of Funds.

Initial Net Coupon: Because of competitive market pressures ARMs are sometimes originated with a below-market "teaser rate." The initial net coupon reflects the rate paid to the investor until the first reset.

Gross Margin: The spread to the index paid by the borrower. This spread includes servicing and guarantee fees.

Net Margin: The spread paid to the investor after servicing and guarantee fees.

Reset Frequency: Standard amount of time between coupon resets. Some ARMs have a monthly reset; most Treasury ARMs reset on an annual basis.

Periodic Rate Cap: The maximum amount at which the coupon paid by the borrower is allowed to change. Typical conventional 1-Year Treasury ARMs have a 2% periodic rate cap, GNMAs have a 1% periodic rate cap.

Net Life Cap: The top potential coupon paid to the investor. In many cases, this may be between 500 and 600 basis points of the initial coupon (a side benefit to the borrower of having teaser rates is a low-life cap).

Net Life Floor: The lowest potential coupon paid to the investor.

■ MARKET CONVENTIONS

Our description of the static environment has considered only the characteristics of the securities. Participants in the MBS market now not only care about how their cash flows are calculated, but also about such matters as when they take delivery of their securities and when the cash flows are actually supposed to be received. In this section we review some of the major market considerations related to settlement and timing of cash flows.

Settlement Timing

Like with most other financial transactions, settlement for MBS is the process by which the buyers and sellers exchange cash and securities. For our purposes, we would like to examine the key issues related to settling MBS trades: timing and determining the amount of cash to change hands.[2]

---

[2] For detailed information on settlement refer to the PSA publication, "Uniform Practices for the Clearance and Settlement of MBS," New York.

Typically, passthrough MBS trade on a forward basis, where settlement occurs once per month. Each type of mortgage is assigned a particular day during the month for trade settlement. During any particular calendar month, the active month for which most trades will settle will be the next monthly settlement for that security. For example, during the month of June the active trading month will be for July settlement. By the middle of July, traders will generally shift the active settlement month to August. Secondary CMO securities trade mostly on a corporate (five business day) settlement basis.

Active trading in the one-month-forward market stems from the settlement procedures for MBS coupled with the increased importance of the CMO market. Among most Wall Street dealers, the biggest trading counter party of the MBS passthrough trader is the dealer's primary CMO desk. The passthrough trader will be responsible for purchasing the CMO collateral needed for any deal. As most CMO deals settle one (or more) calendar month from the pricing date, trading for collateral is most active in the one-month-forward market. This does not preclude other settlement possibilities for investors. Up until two days before the settlement within any particular month, it is still possible for investors to purchase bonds for current-month settlement. Dealers will still make markets for current-month settlement, but not always with the same liquidity as the most actively traded month.

However, there are times when attractive opportunities arise for investors as current settlement approaches. In cases when a dealer still needs collateral to settle a CMO, he or she may have an aggressive bid for current settlement collateral or be willing to create an attractive drop in the role market.

There are also times when buyers and sellers arrange for immediate settlement. These trades occur more in unusual situations, subject to arrangements made between dealers and institutional investors.

Settlement Cash Flows and Security Delivery

At the time of the trade, the two counter parties agree to the date, price, and quantity of securities. At the time of settlement, the purchaser will pay to the seller the price times the quantity of securities, plus any accrued interest. The interest-accrual period will cover time from the first of the month until the settlement date.

Most trades occur on a to-be-announced (TBA) basis, where the purchaser does not know the actual pools being delivered until just prior to settlement. All they know is that the pools meet PSA good delivery guidelines.

Trades also occur on a specified pool basis. These trades may reflect special inventory that a dealer holds or that a client needs. Trades on specific pools usually occur at prices above the current TBA quotes. In addition to specific pools, buyers and sellers may negotiate other types of characteristics such as year of origination or number of pools to be delivered.

Specified pool trading occurs frequently for seasoned or WAM bonds. These are mortgage pools that have older or seasoned loans. Due to their prepayment characteristics relative to the average pools (faster for low-coupon mortgages and slower for high-coupon mortgages), WAM bonds tend to have greater value than the generic pool and, therefore, sell at higher prices than the TBA price. Specified pool trading is also used by Wall Street traders to obtain pools for structured transactions or to reduce back office costs by restricting the number of pools to be delivered.

Delay of Cash Flows

Nearly all borrowers make their mortgage payments in arrears on a monthly basis. Likewise, investors receive their cash just once a month. The time between the expected cash payment from the borrower and the ultimate cash flow received by the investor has been termed the delay. The effect of this delay must be treated by the yield calculations performed on MBS because it represents a true loss of economic opportunity.[3] Actual delay numbers for standard MBS products can be seen in the Table 3-5.

Table 3-5

MBS Type	Payment from Borrower	Payment Received by Investor	Actual Delay
GNMA I	June 1	June 15	14
FNMA	June 1	June 25	24
FHLMC Gold	June 1	June 15	14
FHLMC NonGold	June 1	July 15	44

While the delay factor is meant to cover many of the exigencies that occur when borrowers are late with their payments and the mechanical complications of processing the cash flows, it also provides an important source of income to the financial intermediaries. Both FNMA and FHLMC derive significant income from the float earned between the time they collect cash flows and disperse them to investors.

Accrued Interest

The MBS begins to accrue interest on the first calendar day of the month. This corresponds to the same accrual period of the borrower. At the time of settlement, the investor must pay the previous holder the interest through the settlement date. After settlement, the investor is entitled to the entire month's interest.

MBS accrue interest on a 30/360 day basis. That is, accrued interest calculations assume that each month has thirty days and that each year has 360 days. Practically speaking, this means that each month the investor receives 1/12 of the annual coupon. Also for calculating accrued interest, the investor receives 1/30 of the monthly interest payment for each day up until settlement. No additional interest is

[3] In addition to the actual delay, some market participants use a term known as stated delay. The stated delay accounts for the fact that mortgage loans are in arrears. It therefore includes the time during which the interest accrues, making the measure more of a time-to-payment calculation. The stated delay equals the actual delay plus 30, under the assumption that we do not consider the starting accrual date.

paid for settlement on the 31st of the month. Typically most settlement occurs in the middle of the month, so the extra day is not an issue.

Delivery Standards: Variance and Pools Per Million

In the nuts and bolts of trading MBS, some accommodations are made to smooth the settlement process.[4] Many MBS pools are not originated in round dollars. However, trades between dealers and institutional investors usually take place in even lot sizes of one million dollars or more. To accommodate the anomalies of pool size, the seller has some leeway regarding the number of pools that could be delivered and the actual amount of principal to settle.

In settling a trade, the seller can modify the amount of principal delivered. This deviation from the original trade amount is called variance. Current trading practices stipulate that variance must be between plus or minus two percent of the dollar amount of the transaction agreed to by the parties. This variance is applicable to TBA trades. In the case of specified pool trades, no allowance for variance is permitted. If the variance is not within the two percent limits, the pools are not considered good delivery.

When the market may be declining, sellers of MBS will probably deliver as much as possible into the trade, taking full advantage of the upper end of the variance limit. The opposite will occur in a rising market.

In order to keep someone from delivering a large number of low principal dollar pools, the PSA also puts some limits on the number of pools for a trade. The limits on pools can be seen in Table 3-6.[5]

---

[4]Information in this section is based upon *Uniform Practices for the Clearance and Settlement of Mortgage-Backed Securities*, Public Securities Association, 1993.
[5]Table taken from the Uniform Guide, Public Securities Association, page 10-2.

Table 3-6

Coupon	Less than or equal to $500,000	Greater than $500,000 but less than $1,000,000	$1,000,000
Below 11%	1 pool	2 pools	3 pools
11% and above	3 pools	4 pools	5 pools

Keeping the number of pools to a small amount has some operational benefits for the MBS purchaser. Tracking the monthly principal and interest payments requires allocation of administrative support and cost. Left unchecked, sellers would try and dump all of their small pools on someone else.

Over time, the delivery requirements have been modified somewhat, allowing for more pools per trade for the higher coupon MBS. The increased number of pools reflects the high paydowns and the resulting low balances.

Environment	Prepayment	Cash Flow	**Analysis**

■ ANALYSIS

Once we have established the environment, estimated prepayments, and calculated the security cash flows, we are ready for the analysis phase. In the analysis phase, we try to quantify the relative value of the MBS. Virtually all measures of value are relative. We are not attempting to say that A or B is a good or bad investment, we are merely saying that A is a better investment than B, given some set of objectives.

Yield is the standard measure of value for fixed-income securities. Yield represents the internal rate of return of the security cash flows as an investment assuming that the purchase of the security is the initial cash outflow. The purchase price of the security is stated as a percentage of the face amount. For example, at a price of 105, the purchase price of a $1,000,000.00 MBS pool would be $1,050,000, plus accrued interest. Fractions of 1 percent are expressed in thirty-seconds. A price of 102-16, equals 102.5, where the 16 represents 16 thirty-seconds (16/32) or one-half (1/2). 64ths are expressed by adding a plus (+) to the price. For example, a price of 97-5+, would represent 97.171875% of face value.

If a security is priced at par and has no delay days, the yield is calculated in such a way so that the yield is equal to the coupon. Delay days reduce the yield because it extends the time until you get your money back. Accrued interest generally serves to offset the impact of the settlement day not being the first day of interest accrual. The combined effect on yield of settlement day and accrued interest together is generally fairly small.

The mathematical definition of yield[6] is that

$$\text{Price} = \sum_{i=1}^{I} \frac{\text{cash flow}_i}{(1 + \text{yield}/12)^{t_i}}$$

where yield is stated as a percentage, cash flow i is the cash flow of the security in period i, and t is the time of the cash flow i in months. Note that the yield is divided by 12 in computing the price. This is because mortgage cash flows occur monthly. Yield calculated in this way is called a mortgage-equivalent yield, or MEY.

Most other fixed-income securities have semiannual cash flows. When calculating yields on these securities, the period of analysis is six months. Because of the predominance of these securities and the fact that treasuries, which pay interest semiannually are typically the benchmark securities, mortgage yields are almost always converted to bond-equivalent basis. To convert MEY to BEY, it is necessary to determine what coupon would give the same annual return.

---

[6]Yield and other calculation standards for MBS can be found in *Standard Formulas for the Analysis of Mortgaged Backed Securities and Other Related Securities*, Public Securities Association (PSA), New York.

$$(1 + MEY/12)^{12} = (1 + BEY/2)^2$$

Since mortgage yields assume more frequent reinvestment, converting mortgage-equivalent yield to bond increases the yield. For example an 8.0% MEY is equivalent to an 8.13% BEY.

If two bonds have similar characteristics, but differ in price and coupon, yield spread, or the difference between the two yields, can be used as a measure of value. Typically yield spreads are calculated by subtracting the yield of an "on-the-run" (actively traded) treasury from the yield of the MBS. Yield spreads are quoted in basis points. A basis point is one-hundredth of a percent. In Table 3-7, the FNMA 6 has a bond-equivalent yield of 6.58% and the 10-year treasury has a yield of 5.73%. The yield spread is 0.85% or 85 basis points. The choice of which treasury to use requires a risk measure. When calculating yield spreads, we want to compare instruments with similar levels of risk.

Table 3-7

FNMA 30yr Coupon	WAM	Price	PSA	MEY	BEY	Avg Life (years)	Spread (bp)
6.0	358	96-15	121	6.49%	6.58%	10.3	85
6.5	358	99-6	171	6.59%	6.68%	8.5	140
7.0	356	101-13	276	6.62%	6.71%	5.9	157
7.5	354	103-3	414	6.49%	6.58%	4.1	174
8.0	352	104-15	550	6.20%	6.28%	3.1	176
8.5	348	105-4	653	5.98%	6.05%	2.4	184
9.0	324	106-9	585	5.73%	5.80%	2.3	159
9.5	300	108-1	568	5.50%	5.56%	2.4	135

Risk

The standard measure of risk for MBS under static analysis is weighted average life (WAL). For most other fixed-income securities, maturity is the primary indicator of risk. Securities with longer maturities tend to fluctuate in price more than securities with shorter maturities as interest rates change. Maturity is not a good measure of risk for MBS. All newly issued 30-year MBS have thirty-year maturities, however most of the cash flow will be received substantially earlier. Moreover, the risk characteristics of the security will change as prepayment rates change, but the maturity will remain constant. Weighted average life provides a better measure of the cash-flow timing for MBS. Weighted average life is calculated by weighting the principal cash flows (scheduled and prepayments) by the time of receipt. Interest cash flows are not included in the calculation.

Figure 3-8 shows an example of the average life calculation. The graph shows the annual principal cash flows of the security. Note that the last cash flow occurs in year five, so the maturity of the security is five years. However, more than half the cash flow occurs in the first two years. In this case, the weighed average life (WAL) is 2.33 years. MBS are typically compared to the treasury with maturity just less than the average life of the mortgage. The FNMA 6, with an average life of 10.3 years will be spread off the ten-year treasury, while the FNMA 8.5 with average life of 2.4 years will be spread off the two year.

Figure 3-8

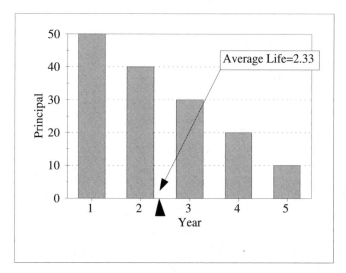

Table 3-8

Coupon	Price				
6.0	96-15	CPR:	3	6	9
		Yield:	6.46	6.55	6.65
		Avg Life:	14.3	10.8	8.4
8.0	104-15	CPR:	20	30	40
		Yield:	6.66	6.06	5.38
		Avg Life:	4.3	2.8	2.0

Table 3-8, shown above. summarizes the static analysis. In order to calculate these measures, it is necessary to have a description of the security, including type of mortgage, maturity, WAC, WAM, and age. Based on this information, a yield can be calculated given a price and a prepayment speed. Without a prepayment speed, it is impossible to calculate a yield and average life. The table shows the MBS to have high-yield spreads to Treasuries. Does this mean that MBS are the superior investment? Maybe, maybe not. Static-yield spreads are limited in their usefulness. In later chapters, we will explore the risk and return characteristics of MBS in more depth and learn some of the limitations of static-yield spreads.

Another commonly used measure of risk is duration. For noncallable fixed-income securities, duration provides a measure of price risk. For MBS, typical duration calculations may not provide a meaningful risk measure. In the next chapter we will discuss, MBS risk and duration in more detail.

■ CONCLUSION

In the static environment we take a simple view of the MBS, relying on the characteristics of the MBS pools and forecasts of future prepayment rates. The MBS market relies on standard indicatives regarding the coupon, remaining term, age, and prepayment forecast to create the MBS cash flows. Over time, the MBS market has developed standards to describe these indicatives of underlying mortgage pools and to report ongoing prepayment information. Mortgage prepayments will typically be reported and forecasted on the basis of a characteristic function called the Public Securities Association (PSA) curve.

In addition, the market has adopted a uniform set of rules to govern the settlement of securities trades and the payment of principal and interest. MBS securities settle on a monthly basis with dates specified by the Public Securities Association. In order to meet the needs of mortgage bankers, an active forward market exists for MBS. Most trades occur on a TBA basis, meaning that the investor does not know exactly which pools will be delivered. However, the PSA stipulates the number of pools that can be delivered into a trade. The number of pools depends upon a transaction's size and underlying coupon.

Using the standard definitions of the static environment, we can begin to analyze MBS in greater depth. Static measures of value and risk are, however, quite limited in value. They are truly meaningful only if the world is truly static. If the yield curve was flat and rates never changed, then these measures would be sufficient. In the next chapter we consider alternatives for analyzing the static environment, including the choice of interest-rate scenarios, prepayment forecast, and uncertainty.

CHAPTER FOUR

Environmental Alternatives

What sells mortgages? In some cases, the combination of solid analysis and a good story. The story needs some basis in reality and usually it covers one of the various factors that affect the MBS market. These factors range from the standard macroeconomic issues to the way that regulators will develop investment guidelines for Japanese farming cooperatives. With the advent of CMOs, the sell side has had to get much better at telling stories, given the increased number of securities to sell. Some of the stories make sense; others don't even qualify as good entertainment.

■ UNDERSTANDING THE ENVIRONMENTAL ALTERNATIVES

MBS valuation and cash flows rely on many factors. Some factors involve fundamental issues related to interest rates and the valuation of cash flows. Other factors involve technical issues related to regulatory standards for some particular sector of the MBS investing community.

Before moving onto more sophisticated analysis, we must delve into the various things that influence the behavior of MBS. For our purposes, we will call these things the environmental alternatives. The use of the term alternatives suggests that, while there may be several classes of things that affect value, there may also be ways of looking within a single class of issues for a different understanding of what makes MBS change.

This chapter has two main parts: (1) an identification of the issues that must be considered when analyzing MBS; (2) the types of quantitative approaches that address these issues. To borrow a medical analogy, we identify both the cause of the ailments and the treatments. Understanding the causes of the ailments is not always straightforward, not unlike medical specialists who do not agree on the causes of particular maladies.

Still, we try to lay out the ways that the environmental alternatives may be considered. There may never be an entire list of the alternatives, nor is it particularly important that there should be. As we continue to emphasize throughout the book, any analysis of MBS must fit the problem. No analysis can completely explain all the factors in the real world. Rather, the factors must be sufficiently identified given the scope of the challenge facing the MBS investor.

■ VARIABLES

When we bring up the term variables, we are suggesting the quantitative factors, which have an effect on MBS valuation. Quantitative factors cover those economic variables that will drive both the prepayments of MBS and the discounting of cash flows.

In addition, the variables will have effects on larger market issues related to the supply and demand for MBS. The factors related to the supply and demand for products are out of the scope of our chapter. We will instead focus on more "micro" issues that drive the fundamentals of mortgage securities. Our critical variables will include interest rates and the macroeconomic factors that influence the housing markets.

■ INTEREST RATES

The study of fixed-income securities revolves around the role of interest rates. When we say interest rates, we imply the rates of interest that will occur in the future. Our analysis of interest-rate environments will consider how to form opinions regarding the ways that interest rates can vary in the future. This will include how to develop an expectation and how to form opinions about how much rates can vary from this expectation.

In the most simple of worlds, that is noncallable U.S. Treasury securities, interest rates directly influence valuation through the discounting of cash flows. As we move into more complicated securities, interest rates play a dual role. They again serve as the rates by which we discount cash flows. However, many classes of securities have cash flows that are uncertain and depend to some degree on the level of interest rates. In the jargon of finance, many of these securities are also known as contingent claims.

Callable securities have uncertain cash flows. In the case of corporate or Treasury securities, call rules have clear specifications regarding the prices and dates at which the issuer can redeem the bonds. With respect to MBS, the call procedures are murkier. Each borrower can decide when they wish to call their loans. Not only that, they can call their loan in part or in full. This uncertainty presents a mixed blessing to the investment community, yet provides a continued source of steady income to research analysts.

In our analysis of interest rates, we have to make some assumptions regarding the future. Looking out into the future and making predictions leads to all sorts of problems, including the extreme likelihood that any prediction will be wrong. Still, we must make some assumptions about the path of interest rates, even if all we can say is that they will not change.

In the real world of modeling callable securities like MBS, we do not make the bold assumption of only one potential scenario for future interest rates. Rather, some allowance is made for uncertainty. The range of interest rates will be allowed to vary, giving us some room to examine the behavior of MBS over a range of rates, and then to employ some sort of statistical/mathematical procedures to measure expected performance and risk.

The Base Case Assumption: Forward Rates

In the environment of interest rates, we will generally consider two aspects: the expectation for future rates and the probability distribution around these expected rates. Typically, fixed-income pricing models use an assumption that the expected course of interest rates can be derived from looking at actual rates today. That is, the market implicitly gives its best estimate of the course of interest rates. This best estimate relates to the implied forward interest rates.

Forward interest rates are a fascinating topic.[1] For many years, numerous people have remarked that they do not "believe" in forward rates. To this, one can only say that forward rates do not require any measure of belief. They simply present the market's valuation of future cash flows.

Many investors make (and lose) lots of money by betting against forward rates. The best example of this occurred in 1992—the year of the inverse floater. Based upon the steepness of the yield curve, the implied forward rates indicated that short-term rates were expected to rise sharply. Investors wanted to be against this, reasoning that outside influences, from such parties as the Federal Reserve, would want to keep short-term rates down in order to stimulate the economy out of a recession. This turned out to be the best bet for those who went against forward rates.

Betting against forward rates doesn't always turn out so well. In the late 1970s and early 1980s, savings and loans borrowed short term through savings accounts and lent long term through mortgages. It seemed that they were earning a profitable spread when they entered into the transactions. However, as interest rates rose, their spread vanished as they had to pay higher rates on their savings accounts and CDs. Forward-rate analysis would have indicated that the spread they were earning was far more vulnerable than they expected.

A Quick Excursion into Forward Rates

Like a poor poker player, the fixed-income markets continually tip their hand regarding the future expectations for interest rates. This information is made available to the investing community at the price of a few calculations.

---

[1]For more information about forward rates and the term structure of interest rates, refer to Thomas S.Y. Ho, *Strategic Fixed-Income Research,* Dow Jones Irwin, 1990, Chapter 3.

Suppose that the current interest rate quoted for a one-year zero-coupon Treasury STRIP was four percent and five percent for a two-year STRIP (assume quotes are stated as an annual equivalent rate). Using this information, we can determine what the market currently expects for one year rates, one-year hence.

According to the standard no-arbitrage argument, we should be indifferent today about a series of two investments, each lasting for one year, or a single investment that would last for two years. In order to make this argument work, we need to calculate that special rate, which makes us indifferent. This special rate is the forward rate. Our forward rate would be calculated as shown in Figure 4-1.

Figure 4-1

Calculation of One Period Forward Rate Occurring in One Year ($_1f_1$)

$$(1 + r)^2 = (1 + r_1) \times (1 + {_1f_1})$$

$$((1 + .05)^2 = (1 + .04) \times (1 + {_1f_1})$$

$$\frac{(1 + .05)^2}{(1 + .04)} = 1 + {_1f_1}$$

$$_1f_1 = .06$$

As shown in Figure 4-1, the market would be calling for 6 percent rates one year hence.

Financial market participants always seem a bit skeptical about forward rates. Let's push the point a bit further. Suppose you don't "believe" in forward rates. Under the assumptions above, would you be willing to lend us two-year money in a series of two loans? That is a one-year loan starting today for four percent and then another four percent loan starting in one year? If you say yes, reading any more of the book would not be a good idea; contact the authors directly to arrange terms. Should your answer be no, then you have got the idea.

Forward Rates: Why Such a Big Deal?

Forward rates matter. They serve as the assumed expected rates at the center of most option-pricing models. Probably any MBS, callable corporate, or swap you have ever purchased was priced off of a model that makes forward-rate assumptions. Dealers will price their options using forward-rate assumptions, because they can lay off their forward rate risk through either the exchange-traded futures or options markets.

Swap dealers set up their hedges in the Eurodollar futures market. This market simply represents the forward expectations for LIBOR rates. MBS market makers will always be ready to quote prices several months forward. These forward drops represent the costs of financing a position using short-term money. The costs of financing may not be arbitrage free—that is, the implied rates applied to forward MBS price calculations may often reflect technical factors, which make certain collateral rich or cheap to own.

Another implication of the forward curves is their effect on total return analysis. While we will discuss this at greater length further on in the book, the choice of the base case curve has a substantial impact on the calculation of total rates of return. When properly calculated, use of the forward-rate assumption will make an investor indifferent about owning any particular Treasury security (assuming it is one of the current coupon securities used to generate the yield curve). That is, if we were looking at a twelve month horizon analysis that used forward rates, the analysis would tell us that the expected return on the ten year Treasury equaled the two year, which in turn equaled the current one-year rate.

In an unchanged yield-curve environment, the forward rates would suggest indifference about any particular security. On the other hand, if one were to assume that the stable case curve equaled the current yield curve, total-return analysis would give a strong preference to the longest term Treasury being analyzed (assuming an upward sloping yield curve). Ignoring the forward rates neglects the implied forward drop for future prices.

Even with all this talk about forward rates, it is important to review certain truisms. First, forward rates serve as an unreliable forecasting tool for interest-rate movements. They do give some indication about the direction of rates, but they do not always give infallible information about the timing or exact magnitude of rate movements.

Implied Yield Curves and Paths of Interest Rates

Not only can we calculate any sample forward interest rate, but we can also determine other expected interest rates, including the entire yield curve at some future date and the path of yields for some constant maturity target, such as the ten year treasury. These types of calculations give us insight into the behavior of MBS, both the valuation of the cash flows and the expected impacts on the prepayment rates.

As an illustration of the information derived from forward rates, consider the two yield-to-maturity curves in Figure 4-2. The two curves correspond to the current yield-to-maturity curve of the U.S. Treasury market and the expected yield-to-maturity curve one year forward. The current yield curve has an extremely positive slope, implying that the market expects short-term rates to rise markedly over the next year. Rates are based off the closing market quotes of 12/31/92.

Figure 4-2

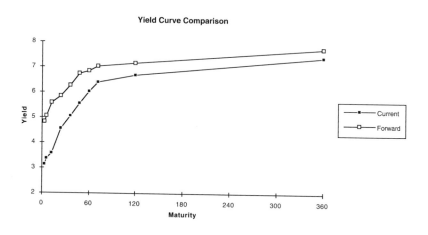

Yield Curve Comparison

The flatter curve will be built into the various pricing models used to evaluate MBS. Both the flattening and rising rates on the long end of the curve will have material impacts on the level of prepayment rates. Using the forward curve as the stable or base case curve for total-return analysis will give very different results than using the current yield curve as the stable-rate assumption. It would not be too shocking to learn that analysts choose their base case curve depending upon the security being examined (although our experience shows that using the current curve as the base case curve usually results from ignorance rather than any ulterior motives).

Volatility of Interest Rates

The discussion of forward rates gives us an anchor for future interest-rate expectations. Still, the critical part of pricing mortgages is the uncertainty of future cash flows. Because we do not know exactly when the principal of an MBS will be paid, we rely upon building some expectations for performance over various scenarios.

As a standard way to develop the interest-rate scenarios, an assumption will be made regarding the way in which interest rates change. The pricing fixed-income securities with embedded options utilizes a statistical concept to describe the interest-rate changes. This concept relates to the volatility of interest rates.

Now used as an adjective, the term volatility conjures up images of instability, sudden flares of activity, and unpredictability. For our purposes, volatility is a much more controlled phenomenon. In the parlance of fixed-income securities, volatility applies to the standard deviation of yield movements. When someone says the volatility of interest rates is rising, they generally mean that the standard deviation of yield movements has been increasing.

A Brief Excursion into Statistics

Statistics provides a large number of ways to analyze and categorize information. When we collect data, for example, daily yields, we can calculate certain measurements, which describe the information, like the average and standard deviation. In an intuitive sense, the standard deviation tells us how much the yields have spread out or dispersed across our observations.

When pricing financial options and bonds containing options (such as the call option embedded in MBS), we often state the uncertainty of future interest rates in terms of the standard deviation of interest rate fluctuations. In common statistical intuition, we would expect to be within one standard deviation of the mean approximately 67 percent of the time and within two standard deviations 95 percent of the time.

The standard deviation of interest-rate movements, which is usually termed the volatility of interest rates, will usually be stated in terms of an annualized percentage. So, if the interest-rate volatility was quoted at 15 percent and the rate was 10 percent, then we would implicitly be saying that over a one-year period the standard deviation of interest rates would equal 150 basis points. Besides giving a range to understand reasonable ranges for interest-rate fluctuations, we could use this information when developing probabilities for potential interest-rate scenarios.

Calculating the volatility of interest rates is a straight-forward exercise and will be demonstrated in Table 4-1, which contains data related to yields on the 10-year Treasury rate.[2] As part of the measurement, we will be taking a daily time series and then transforming it into a relative return measurement. We use this relative return measurement in order to state the volatility as a percentage basis.

---

[2] This description of the volatility measurement is based upon an example given for stock prices in *Options, Futures and Other Derivative Securities*, Second Edition, John Hall, 1993, pp. 214-217.

Table 4-1

Day	Yield	Relative Yield Change Y_i / Y_{i-1}	Daily Relative Change $Ln(Y_i / Y_{i-1})$
1	5.43		
2	5.46	1.0055	0.0055
3	5.39	0.9872	-0.0129
4	5.35	0.9926	-0.0074
5	5.37	1.0037	0.0037
6	5.33	0.9926	-0.0075
7	5.33	1.0000	0.0000
8	5.36	1.0056	0.0056
9	5.39	1.0056	0.0056
10	5.4	1.0019	0.0019

In order to calculate the daily volatility, we take the standard deviation of the daily relative change series. In the example above, the standard deviation is 0.006936. This number represents the daily percentage volatility. To place this on an annual basis we must scale the measure by the number of trading days in the year. Generally, this is approximated to be 250 (365 minus weekends and a few holidays). Since we are looking to develop a standard deviation, as opposed to a variance measure, we multiply the daily standard deviation by the square root of 250.

$$\text{Annual Standard Deviation} = \text{Daily Standard Deviation} \times \sqrt{250}$$

$$= 0.006936 \times \sqrt{250}$$

$$= 0.1097$$

From our example of the 10-day yield series, we would calculate an annual yield volatility of 10.97%.

The pricing models for MBS make some assumptions regarding volatility. Before we discuss these assumptions, let's try to get an understanding

A Brief Excursion into Statistics

of what interest-rate volatility means. First, we will look at some measures of volatility. Then, we will examine how these volatility numbers translate into interest-rate fluctuations.

Historically, volatility, when measured as a percent, declines as maturity increases. To illustrate this, consider Table 4-2, which contains yield-volatility measures for selected Treasury instruments.

Table 4-2

Maturity (Years)	Yield Volatility (%)
1	24.46
2	21.26
5	16.41
7	14.52
10	12.56
30	9.63

When considering volatility based off of actual basis-point movements, we may see less divergence between the changes in short and long rates. That is, if we were to multiply the yield volatility by the actual level of the yield, we would obtain a standard deviation measure stated in basis points. An example of this can be seen in Table 4-3.

Table 4-3

Maturity (Years)	Yield	Yield Volatility (%)	Yield Volatility (Basis Points)
1	3.37	24.46	82.4
2	3.86	21.26	82.1
5	4.82	16.41	79.1
7	5.08	14.52	73.8
10	5.48	12.56	68.8
30	6.12	9.63	58.9

This information about the volatility can be used to give some ranges for the potential fluctuations of interest rates. Consider the calculation of a two standard deviation range of interest rates. Loosely speaking, this represents a 95 percent confidence interval for interest rates. Now, following our development of forward interest rates from above, we can combine the measures of volatility along with forward rates to give some scenarios about future yield curves. Figure 4-3 compares the implied forward curve based one year, based on the 12/31/92 closing yields, with two standard deviation ranges from this interest-rate expectation. These standard deviation ranges give approximately a 95 percent confidence interval for the future rates.

Figure 4-3

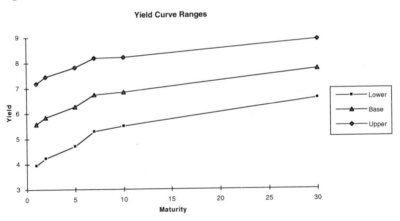

The graphs indicate a rather wide range for the future yield curve. This reflects two factors, the large statistical band and the relatively high rate of volatility. When considering security risk and performance, the yield-curve bands may prove useful to examine the outer extremes of potential interest rate movements.

The bottom line of our volatility discussion centers on the correct level of volatility to use for future interest-rate movements. Choosing the "right" volatility level to use when pricing options and securities containing options remains somewhat of an art. Option dealers often make their bid/ask markets in volatility terms, making it hard to treat volatility as some benign input to an option-pricing model. In terms of pricing MBS, choosing a volatility measure may be difficult because we must make a 30-year projection of future interest-rate fluctuations. This 30-year assumption sometimes can be strongly influenced by very current events, effectively making the option too susceptible to transitory fluctuations in the market.

Mean Reversion

Up to now we have stressed two major themes in the understanding of the interest-rate environment: the use of forward rates and the effect of volatility. In valuing a series of complicated options embedded in MBS, we must sometimes account for the valuation of intermediate options contained in the security structure.

These intermediate options can be found prevalently in the adjustable rate mortgage (ARM) market. ARM securities contain a series of periodic caps on the coupon as well as a lifetime cap on interest rates. Properly valuing the intermediate caps means we must make some assumptions about the intermediate fluctuations of interest rates.

In theory, interest rates can range from zero percent to infinity. In the absence of a runaway hyperinflation, political reality may put some artificial constraints on the upper and lower bounds for rates. To the extent that rates reach the extremes of historical experience, we may expect them to tend (revert) back toward more "normal" (average or mean) levels.

Within the context of the various option pricing approaches, one may adopt a form of mean reversion. As rates begin to diverge from the expected levels based upon the forward interest rates, an artificial force is introduced. This artificial force looks at the difference between the rate suggested by the model and the expected forward rate. If the modeled rate is higher, the process assigns some factor that lowers the rate. Similarly, when the rate falls below the expected forward, it is increased.

The net effect of adding mean reversion is to dampen the effect of volatility over time. For many types of MBS, this additional complication may not be a useful adjustment. However, for certain securities, particularly adjustable-rate MBS, the application of mean reversion may be a required feature of an option-adjusted pricing model.

When dealing with the adjustable product, we must value the periodic and lifetime caps. Actual experience with the cap market indicates that traders assign differing volatilities to cap options of differing lives. This structure of volatility usually declines, suggesting that our model contains some element of mean reversion (which decreases the volatility over time). Without applying some element of mean reversion to our pricing method, we may wind up seriously overstating the value of the various cap options.

Multifactor Models

When examining the relative value or risk of securities with interest rate dependent cash flows, we often allow one or more factors to fluctuate. These factors often go under a more technical term called state variables in the financial literature. The term state variable connotes some element that provides crucial information about the performance of a security.

In the analysis of MBS, these state variables often relate to interest rates. A model that contains one state variable, such as the short-term interest rate usually allows for only parallel interest rate movements. In some cases, this assumption may be adequate to describe the behavior of an MBS. At other times, we may have to increase the number of factors. For instance, to explain both parallel and nonparallel changes in the yield curve, a two-factor interest rate model may be developed. One of these factors would be related to the parallel curve movements, while the other would explain the degree to which the curve twisted.

There are other times when additional factors may be added to address other types of environmental factors that vary. This may lead to a generalized multifactor options-pricing model. While the additional factors may relate to more subtle influences on behavior, they may create complications in the specification and implementation of the model. Understanding the interrelationships between the factors may be difficult to anticipate and may make the model behave in unexpected ways as the factors change. In addition, more factors may add significantly to the computation time of the model.

■ MACROECONOMIC ELEMENTS

Until now, we have dwelt with interest rates as our primary variable of uncertainty affecting the cash flows of MBS. While interest rates play a critical role in the determination of MBS cash flows, other variables must be considered. These variables come under the general term of macroeconomic elements.

It cannot be denied that most macroeconomic factors correlate very closely with interest rates. While the correlations may be strongly positive or negative, we may not know if some macroeconomic factor is being influenced by interest rates or if interest rates are being influenced by some macroeconomic factor. For example, do lower interest rates stimulate economic activity or does economic activity stimulate a demand for capital, which then drives interest rates?

In developing a framework for analyzing MBS, there are several macro-economic factors that affect the cash flow of the securities. These factors have some relationship to interest rates but are not exclusively driven by rates. To the degree necessary, these variables can be added to the valuation and risk analysis. The elements to consider include: overall economic growth, housing market activity, and performance of financial assets.

Economic Growth

Gross domestic product (GDP) represents the measure of overall strength in the economy. This variable will influence the degree to which all segments of the economy are performing. To the extent that the overall economy grows, income, demand, and mobility increase. Increases in these levels lead to more individuals and families who are able to afford an increase in their housing accommodations. Adding more demand to the housing markets may lead to increased turnover and, thus, the potential for higher rates of MBS prepayments. On the other hand, as the economy performs poorly, the incentive or ability to trade up in house may be less, leading to a slowing in MBS repayments and, perhaps, to an increase in delinquencies and defaults.

Housing Market Activity

While the GDP may give some indication about the economy as a whole, the analysis of MBS may require an additional focus on the specifics of the housing markets. Typical housing market indicators may include sales of both new and existing homes. Housing activity, particularly sales, translate directly in MBS prepayments. To the degree these sales cannot be explained solely by interest rate levels, they must be treated as an additional factor affecting cash flows.

The need to control for housing market activity away from general economic conditions may be best suited to periods when the housing sector may be leading or lagging the overall economy. In other cases, we may be examining a specific region of the country where local housing conditions may play a paramount role in the understanding of refinancing and prepayment experience.

Financial Market Performance

Mortgage cash flows exhibit some relationship to the overall performance of financial assets. Perhaps the most relevant financial asset is the rate of growth in home prices. If home-price appreciation is strong, homeowners may have a strong incentive, as well as the financial ability, to increase their housing quality. In cases of deteriorating housing markets, borrowers may not be willing or able to refinance their mortgages, putting a drag on prepayment activity.

With regard to the role of performance in other financial markets and their relationship to MBS, the links are somewhat tenuous. It seems reasonable to assume that sudden swings (particularly downward) in the stock market may give borrowers some second thoughts about any plans to move or relocate to another section of the country. Likewise, borrowers who hold financial assets may consider liquidating assets in order to pay down mortgage debt when the expected return from holding the financial instruments significantly underperforms the potential savings from lowering mortgage payments.

■ TYPES OF TERM STRUCTURE MODELS

The type of model chosen to simulate the future yields, needs to follow two principles: (1) It must be consistent with observed prices and yields in the current marketplace, and (2) It should represent the factors that influence the security under analysis. Some consideration must also be made for the time frame in which the results are needed and the resources that are available. An approach that comes close to approximating reality has little value if the computation time is excessively long.

When considering the term structure, we look at a factor, which we call the state variable (or variables). This variable can represent an interest rate, a set of rates, or some other correlated variables (like interest rates and inflation). The general approaches to the creation of term structure can be seen in Table 4-4.

Table 4-4

State Variable	Implementation	Advantages	Disadvantages
Single Factor (Short-Term Interest Rate)	Binomial Tree	Accurately Prices Current Yield Curve	Does not capture yield-curve slope change
	Trinomial Tree	Straightforward implementation	Binomial/Trinomial difficult to implement for CMOs
	Monte Carlo Simulation		
Multifactor (Short- and Long-Term Rates)	Monte Carlo Simulation	Captures yield-curve twists	Long computation time
		Matches formulation of prepayment model	

Single-factor models have been primarily used for callable corporate securities. The financial literature is rich with descriptions of models and various implementation techniques. A table of references can be seen at the end of the chapter. While the single factor models are versatile, they have some limitations when applied to MBS. Most single-factor models have been implemented through binomial trees. Our experience has shown that binomial approaches are faster than the Monte Carlo simulation techniques by a factor of 10.

While the single factor approach offers easy implementation, it neglects the role of the yield-curve shape on MBS cash flows. It seems to be well accepted that the shape of the curve influences both the prepayment decision made by borrowers and the nominal spread between MBS and Treasury yields. Consequently, a single factor approach may not be consistent with the current formulation of prepayment models.

There is, however, a method to apply the single factor approach to the valuation of MBS. Along with Van Drunen, we have developed a model, called the Refinancing Threshold Pricing (RTP) model, which does not rely on an econometric prepayment model. Instead, it models the prepayment decision of the borrower. At each point in time, the borrower is faced with the decision of refinancing or continuing to pay his loan. In cases when the present value of the remaining cash flows (plus refinancing costs) exceeds the current principal value, the loan will be repaid.

One of the standard technical problems with using a binomial model for MBS, is the disregard for path dependency. When solving for the binomial tree, the solution procedure starts with the next-to-last time period and then works backwards to the present time. When using a standard economical prepayment model, this approach ignores the importance of path dependency.

We have been able to implement the RTP model using the binomial approach because we do not rely on an econometric prepayment model. By splitting the MBS pool into groups of borrowers, who share the same refinancing cost, we can capture the diversity of borrower types. The MBS pool takes on the characteristics of a callable corporate bond, but with a variety of call prices.

Multiple factor models have become more popular with many types of derivative products. The additional factors allow us to capture changes in the shape of the yield curve or in relationships between various markets. Monte Carlo simulation seems to be the common method for implementation of multifactor models. This offers a richer simulation of future yields but at the cost of increased computation time. When analyzing entire portfolios across multiple scenarios, the additional computation time may prove to be a limiting factor for analytical capabilities.

■ CONCLUSION

Many different variables have the potential to be included in an analysis of MBS. These variables become relevant depending upon the type of security being studied and the level of analytical detail required by the problem. Many of the variables have a close relationship with the specific model being used to evaluate value and risk. At times, the choice of model may relate to the degree to which the model addresses a specific concern of the investor.

Although the underlying assumptions are rarely apparent to the user of mortgage models, the choice of analysis method and the variables used in the analysis often determine the quality of the results. Therefore, when developing models or when analyzing the results of models, it is important to carefully consider this aspect of the analysis.

■ SELECTED REFERENCES

Brennen, M.J. and E.S. Schwartz, "An Equilibrium Model of Bond Pricing and a Test of Market Efficiency," *Journal of Financial and Quantitative Analysis*, 17,3, (September 1982), 301-29.

Black, F., E. Derman, and W. Toy, "A One-Factor Model of Interest Rates and its Application to Treasury Bond Options," *Financial Analysts Journal*, (January-February 1990), 33-39.

Cox, J.C., J.E. Ingersoll, and S.A. Ross, "A Theory of the Term Structure of Interest Rates," *Econometrica*, 53 (1985), 385-407.

Davidson, A.S., M.D. Herskovitz and L. D. Van Drunen, "The Refinancing Threshold Pricing Model: An Economic Approach to Valuing MBS," *Journal of Real Estate Economics and Finance*, 1,2, 117-130.

Heath, D., R. Jarrow, and A. Morton, "Bond Pricing and the Term Structure of the Interest Rates: A New Methodology," *Econometrica*, 60,1 (1992), 77-105.

Ho, T.S.Y., and S.B. Lee, "Term Structure Movements and Pricing Interest Rate Contingent Claims," *Journal of Finance*, 41 (December 1986), 1011-29.

Hull, J., and A. White, "Pricing Interest Rate Derivative Securities," *The Review of Financial Studies*, 3, 4 (1990), 573-92.

Jamshidian, F., "An Exact Bond Option Pricing Formula," *Journal of Finance*, 44 (March 1989), 205-9.

Longstaff, F.A, and E.S. Schwartz, "Implementation of the Longstaff-Schwartz Interest Rate Model," *The Journal of Fixed Income*, 3,2 (September 1993), 7-14.

Luytjes, J., "Estimating a Yield Curve/Inflation Process," *Federal Home Loan Mortgage Corporation Working Paper*.

Vasicek, O.A., "An Equilibrium Characterization of the Term Structure," *Journal of Financial Economics*, 5 (1977), 177-88.

CHAPTER FIVE

Prepayments

The phone rings. It's Jim from Bears & Bulls. You told him last night at the game that you were looking for some intermediate bonds without much risk. Based on what you've heard, you told him PAC bonds sounded like the right idea even though you've never looked at them before. He shows you two bonds. Both PAC bonds are new issues with five-year average lives and PAC bands from 100 to 300 PSA. The second bond has a 10-basis-point higher yield. Jim says that it's because of the collateral. But both bonds have agency collateral, there's no difference in credit risk. Jim points out that the second bond is backed by higher coupon mortgages. Higher coupon mortgages may have less stable prepayments and are more likely to break out of the PAC bands, producing greater risk. How much extra risk? Is ten basis points enough compensation? Since the bonds are similar in all other ways, the only difference is the how they will prepay. If you are going to make a good decision, you need to analyze prepayment risk.

Prepayments are the primary distinguishing feature of mortgage-backed securities. Without prepayments, mortgages would be extremely easy to analyze. In fact, there would be no need for this book. On the other hand, if MBS were so simple, the number of investment opportunities would be severely limited. Prepayments are the double-edged sword of the mortgage-backed securities market. They create opportunity, but also create risk.

Changing prepayment patterns can drastically alter the cash flows of a mortgage-backed security. Figure 1-8, in Chapter One, shows a comparison of the cash flows of a mortgage-backed security with no prepayments, at 150% PSA assumption, and at 50 percent CPR. The cash-flow pattern of the security is determined almost entirely by the prepayment rate. Even at the relatively slow prepayment rate of 150% (a typical prepayment rate for discount mortgages), the prepaid principal cash flow is the majority of the monthly cash flow.

In order to value mortgage-backed securities, it is crucial to properly forecast prepayment rates. Proper forecasting requires understanding the causes of prepayments historically, and then utilizes judgment to determine whether those same forces or new factors will produce prepayments in the future. Because prepayments represent the combined actions of millions of individual borrowers, statistical techniques are used to measure and forecast prepayments.

■ SOURCES OF PREPAYMENTS

Prepayments arise from moving, default, and refinancing. Prepayments from moving establish a base prepayment rate for most securities. Most conventional (nongovernment) mortgages contain a due-on-sale clause. When a house is sold, the mortgage must be paid in full. Government mortgages (those insured by the FHA and VA), are generally assumable. Assumable loans can be passed to the next borrower provided that the borrower meets certain requirements. Factors that increase household relocation, such as job changes, marriage, divorce, and children, will increase prepayments.

Technically, defaults are not prepayments, but for security holders the effects are the same as a prepayment. When a loan defaults, the principal balance of the loan is paid to the investor. In this way, the investor is protected from the credit risk of the borrowers and need only look to the guarantor, generally GNMA, Fannie Mae or Freddie Mac, for assurance that the principal is secure. Prepayments due to default for mortgage-backed securities only represent a small fraction of the monthly prepayments and do not need to be forecast separately. For nonagency passthroughs, it is more important to forecast defaults to determine if the credit support is sufficient and to assess the impact of defaults on security cash flows.

Refinancing represents the largest and most variable component of prepayments. Refinancing reflects the borrower's right to prepay the loan at any time without penalty. In periods of falling rates, borrowers may seek to reduce their mortgage costs by paying off their higher coupon loans and taking out new lower coupon loans. In addition, some borrowers may seek to accelerate their loan payments. Additional principal payments reduce the principal outstanding but do not reduce the required monthly payment. Loans with additional principal payments will be retired before their original term and the additional payments are called curtailments, since they curtail or shorten the term of the loan.

A borrower's decision to refinance is driven by a wide number of factors. Each borrower faces a unique set of conditions, so borrowers tend to exercise their options differently. Some borrowers require only a slight economic incentive to prepay, while others require a greater incentive. Forecasting prepayments involves estimating how these various borrowers will react to changing economic conditions.

■ PREPAYMENT DATA

The key to understanding prepayments is prepayment data. Since each borrower faces a different prepayment decision, and since borrowers exercise their options differently, it is impossible to predict prepayments on purely economic grounds without understanding the borrowers' characteristics. Early attempts to value mortgage-backed securities relied on economic models, which valued the borrower's option. These models tended to severely overestimate prepayments. The modelers then concluded that borrowers exercised their options inefficiently and tried to measure the degree of inefficiency for different types of loans. Rather than assume that the model is right and people are wrong, we attempt to find a model that describes people's actions. People face costs and other situations that reduce their incentives to refinance. Only through examining actual prepayment patterns can be estimate the impact of these factors on prepayment patterns.

Prepayment data is perhaps the most extensive source of data on an individual's financial decision making. Most prepayment data is available at the pool level, but more and more loan-level data is becoming available. Prepayment data is available for a variety of loan types and across a variety of interest-rate environments. While the amount of prepayment data available is extensive, there are still limitations. Figure 5-1 shows the amount of GNMA 30-year mortgages originated each year at varying coupon levels. This is the raw material we have to work with. Note that in 1986 and 1987 there was substantial issuance of mortgages. These loans were concentrated around the 9% coupon. The pattern of origination reflects the continuing drop in rates over the past seven years.

Figure 5-1

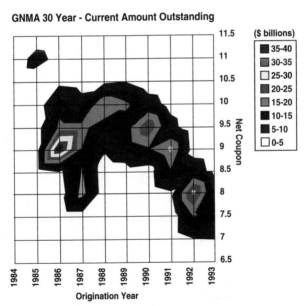

When forecasting prepayments, we attempt to understand how similarly situated loans prepaid in the past. Two of the most important determinants of prepayments are the age of the loan and the coupon of the loan relative to current refinancing opportunities. Many mortgage modelers use the difference between the mortgage rate and the current coupon yield (the yield on the MBS trading closest to par) as a measure of the refinancing incentive. We have chosen to use the ratio of the gross coupon on the loans (WAC of the pool) to the current coupon yield. We feel that the ratio provides a more consistent measure of the refinancing incentive across a wide range of interest rate levels.

Figure 5-2 shows combinations of loan age and coupon ratio for which data is available. Outside of these ranges, it is necessary to extrapolate to forecast prepayment rates. For example, over the past few years, rising rates have limited the amount of loans with a ratio less than one. Estimates of prepayments on low ratio mortgages must be made using older data. However, as economic conditions change, past prepayment data becomes less valuable for forecasting future prepayments. For example, prior to the early 1980s, there were no adjustable-rate mortgages, so prepayments that result from borrowers switching to ARMs cannot be forecast from the earlier data. The economy and the shape of the yield curve can also have a significant impact on prepayments, especially on low-ratio loans. When current economic conditions and yield-curve shapes differ markedly from recent experience, prepayment history becomes a less reliable source for predicting future prepayments. Therefore almost all prepayment forecasts must be tempered with some degree of judgment.

Figure 5-2

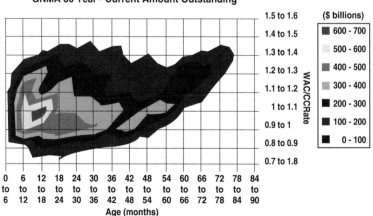

GNMA 30 Year - Current Amount Outstanding

The primary source of prepayment data is the factor tapes for agency mortgage pools. To buy or sell mortgage-backed securities, it is necessary to know the current balance of the pools in the transaction. The balance is expressed by the pool factor. These pool factors are produced monthly and can be used to calculate prepayments. See Chapter 3 for more detail. Analysis of prepayments involves linking pool prepayments to pool characteristics. While it might be helpful to link prepayments to a variety of details about the borrower, such as income or number of children, that information is generally not available at the pool level. The data that is available includes type of loans, average maturity, average loan age, average loan coupon, and geographic distribution of the pool by state. Prepayments must be forecast based on these factors. Over the past few years, the amount of information about mortgage pools has increased and improved in quality, facilitating better prepayment forecasts.

In addition to the information provided by the agencies in conjunction with the factor tapes, other market participants have sought out more detailed loan and pool data to facilitate prepayment forecasts. Financial institutions, which originated or service the loans they hold on the books, frequently have substantially more information about the borrowers and their homes. They can capitalize on this data to refine their understanding of prepayments within their portfolios.

■ ANALYZING PREPAYMENTS

Prepayments can be understood through graphic analysis. Prepayment patterns can be viewed by slicing the prepayment data into various cuts, which expose different aspects of prepayment patterns. Prepayments can also be analyzed through statistical analysis and the development of econometric models, which describe and forecast prepayments. A wide variety of factors could be considered in forecasting prepayments.

Interest-rate levels are the most important influence on prepayment rates. As interest rates fall, borrowers refinance their loans leading to higher prepayments. Figure 5-3 demonstrates this effect. The graph shows the average prepayment rates for all loans with a given ratio.

Ratios greater than one, indicate that the coupon on the loan is now higher than current interest rate levels. Ratios less than one indicate that the coupon on the loan is now below current market rates. As the ratio increases above one, the prepayment rates accelerate, reaching a peak at a ratio of about 1.5. Prepayment rates on discounts, that is loans with ratios less than one, are relatively constant, showing some decline at the lowest ratios. Remember that our data in this range is fairly limited.

Figure 5-3

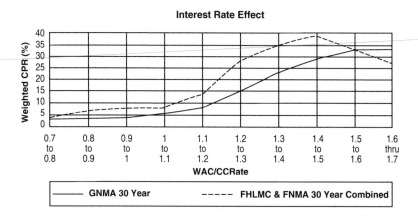

Two other features of prepayments can be seen in this graph. First, GNMA prepayments tend to be slower than comparable conventional loans. Conventional loans, those guaranteed by Fannie Mae and Freddie Mac, tend to have large loan sizes and attract more affluent and mobile borrowers. They tend to be more sensitive to changing interest-rate levels. In addition, many GNMA loans are assumable, so that low-ratio loans do not have to be prepaid if the borrower sells his home, the loan can pass to the next owner. Conventional loans are generally "due-on-sale."

Second, prepayment rates seem to decline at very high ratios. Does this mean that borrowers with very high-coupon loans have less incentive to prepay than borrowers with lower coupons? No, it doesn't. This is evidence of a phenomenon called "burnout." Generally, prepayments start to fall after being at high rates for a while. These very high-ratio loans have probably experienced high prepayments for awhile and are now beginning to decline. More about burnout in a little while.

Aging is the second major influence on prepayments. Aging reflects that new loans tend to prepay slower than older loans. Aging is the reason for the development of the PSA curve, which describes a particular aging pattern. Figure 5-4 shows the aging pattern of GNMA 15 year loans. The graph clearly shows that newer loans tend to prepay slower. Prepayments rise at a steady rate and then level off at a peak CPR. An important feature of aging, however, is that not all pools age at the same rate. In this graph, one line represents loans with coupon ratios less than one and the other line represents coupon ratios greater than one. Not surprisingly, the higher-ratio pools tend to exhibit higher prepayment rates. More surprising is that these loans tend to reach their peak CPR much sooner than the lower-ratio loans. The loans with ratios less than one reach their peak after about 50 months while the above-one-ratio loans reach their peak in about 22 months. Different types of loans may also have very different aging periods. For this reason, the PSA model must be used with caution, since it assumes the same aging periods for all types of loans and all coupons.

Figure 5-4

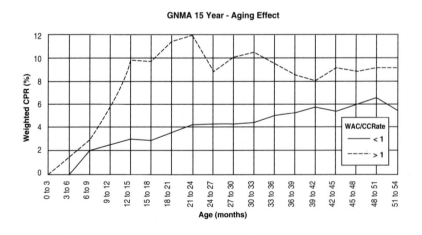

GNMA 15 Year - Aging Effect

Burnout is the next most important, and probably the most controversial influence on prepayments. Burnout reflects that as interest rates fall, prepayment rates increase and then decrease, even if interest rates remain constant. Even if rates then fall further, the prepayment rates never reach their initial peaks. Once again, graphic analysis can demonstrate this. As the sportscaster says, "Let's go to the videotape." Figure 5-5 shows the prepayment pattern of high-coupon conventional loans originated prior to 1985. The solid line shows the current coupon yield. As interest rates fell, the prepayment rate on these loans skyrocketed to 70% CPR in mid-1986. However, even as rates remained low and continued to fall, the prepayment rate began to decline. When rates rose at the end of 1987, prepayment rates declined back to the teens. Further declines in rates in 1991 and 1992 did not push prepayment rates back up to their 1986 levels. Of all the influences on prepayments, burnout is the hardest to measure and predict. Since burnout is a function of past levels of interest rates and prepayment rates, it also makes prepayment modeling and forecasting more difficult.

Figure 5-5

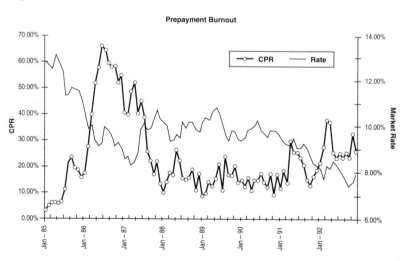

Prepayment Burnout

Seasonality is the last major influence on prepayments. Seasonality reflects the close interaction of prepayments with housing-market activity. As shown in Figure 5-6, prepayments tend to be faster during the summer months and slower during the winter months. This reflects increased home turnover during the summer months. This increased housing activity in the summer is a result of better weather, which facilitates home search and moving, and more importantly the school year. Parents prefer to move during the summer so their children's school year is not disrupted. Seasonality is more pronounced on low-ratio loans, where the refinancing effects are not as pronounced. Refinancing does not seem to have as large a seasonal component. While this is a limited data sample, it reflects some commonly observed features. Prepayments tend to be the highest in May and July and there is usually a slight uptick in December, perhaps reflecting year-end tax strategies and moving during the holidays. Seasonality tends to have little effect on valuation of most MBS. However, seasonality is important when evaluating reported prepayments. Faster prepayments in the summer may not reflect any shift in prepayments and will probably be followed by slower prepayments in the fall and winter.

Figure 5-6

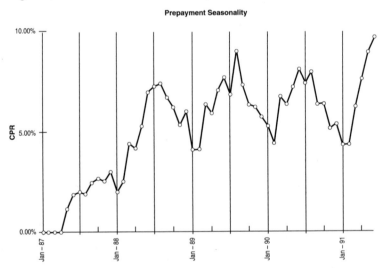

Housing markets and **yield-curve shape** also influence prepayments. Weaker economic activity, declining house prices, and unemployment all tend to depress prepayments. These factors tend to be regional in nature and can lead to large differences between prepayments from different states. The shape of the yield curve can also impact prepayments. With the development of a variety of mortgage products, such as ARMs and balloon loans, borrowers can choose products that price off of different parts of the yield curve. When the curve is steep, borrowers may refinance into shorter maturity loans to reduce their borrowing costs.

■ DEVELOPMENT OF PREPAYMENT MODELS

Prepayment models are at the core of mortgage valuation. A poor evaluation approach utilizing a good prepayment model might still provide some insight into security valuation and performance, while a sophisticated evaluation tool with an inaccurate prepayment model will only provide misleading results. Thus, in any mortgage valuation, it is necessary to understand the source of the prepayment numbers used in the analysis.

Analysts have been developing and refining prepayment models continuously through the history of the mortgage market. The quality and sophistication of these models has increased as analysts have developed a better understanding of borrower behavior and as computing power has enabled them to develop and apply more and more complex models. Mortgage analysts realized early on that, due to prepayments, it would not be correct to analyze MBS based on the full thirty year term of the mortgage contract. Early analysts used a twelve year life assumption. That is, they assumed zero prepayments for the first 11 years and then complete pay-off of the security at the end of the twelfth year of the pool. The next step was the use of historical prepayment patterns on FHA loans to estimate mortgage cash flows. These prepayment patterns were estimated across all loans and did not distinguish between loans with different coupons. These FHA experience curves formed the basis for the PSA curve, which was adopted to facilitate trading in the CMO market.

Prepayment models can be roughly broken into four generations of models. The first generation of prepayment models grew out of the experience of the early 1980s. Falling interest rates made it clear that the FHA experience curves were inadequate to address the impact of refinancing on prepayment rates. These early models expressed prepayments as simple functions of the spread between the coupon on the mortgage and the current yield on new mortgages. Researchers realized that prepayments began to increase when interest rates fell 150 to 200 basis points and continued to increase until prepayments reached a plateau. A variety of functional forms were used to express this relationship. The most frequently used form was an arctangent function. Figure 5-7 shows a graph of the arctangent function. The function has a minimum and a maximum and slopes gradually from the minimum to the maximum and provides a good approximation of pattern of prepayments shown in Figure 5-3.

Figure 5-7

Arctangent Function

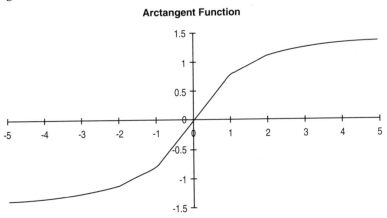

At the time of the arctangent models, analysts were seeking closed-form solutions to mortgage-valuation problems. Many of the analysts working on mortgage valuation at the time had come from scientific or engineering backgrounds. They were the so-called "rocket scientists" who were seeking to "solve" the mortgage problem. They attempted to use mathematical functions to price mortgage-backed securities in the same way as Black and Scholes priced options. While the arctangent function provided a good starting point, it was not sufficient to fully describe the complex patterns of prepayment behavior. The legacy of the arctangent function, however, continues as many prepayment models still retain the arctangent function as a part of a more complex model. In our model, we use a logarithmic function to achieve a similar effect.

The second generation of prepayment models began to take into account several different factors that affect prepayments and the interaction of those factors. This generation of model was brought on by the rapidly declining rates of the mid-1980s. As interest rates fell, most of the mortgage market became premium securities. The simple models based on interest-rate incentives and the arctangent function could not explain the complex prepayment patterns that were developing.

Two particularly troublesome effects were the aging effect and the burnout effect. The aging effect, as we have seen from the data, reflects that newer loans tend to prepay slower than older loans. The PSA curve is based on this observation. However, premium loans tend to reach their peak speed earlier than current coupon and discount loans. In a period of rapidly falling rates, the PSA curve, which was designed based on current coupon GNMA collateral, is a poor model of prepayment behavior. Even more distressing was prepayment burn-out. As we have seen, even with constant interest rates, prepayments on premium mortgages tend to rise as the loans age and then decline from their peaks.

The burnout effect can best be understood by viewing an MBS pool as the loans of a large group of heterogeneous borrowers. Each borrower faces unique conditions. Some have large families, others are single. They live in different parts of the country and have different educational and economic backgrounds. Given the diversity of the borrowers, it is not surprising that they require different incentives to refinance. As rates fall, first the borrowers with the greatest propensity to refinance do so. The borrowers left in the pool face higher refinancing costs (economic or noneconomic). These borrowers tend to prepay at a slower rate than the first group of borrowers. Eventually, the only borrowers left in the pool are those that have a very high refinancing threshold. At this point we say that the pool is burnt-out. It will continue to show some prepayments, but those prepayments will be lower than newer pools, which have not experienced prepayments in the past and the prepayment rates of burnt-out pools will be relatively insensitive to changing interest rates.[1]

As a simple example of burnout, suppose a pool of 100 loans is made up of 80 fast prepayers who prepay at 75 percent per year and 20 slow prepayers who prepay at 10 percent per year. During the first period, you would expect prepayments of 62 percent (0.80 x 75% + .2 x 10%). After one year, three-quarters of the fast prepayers are gone. Only 10 percent of the slow prepayers have prepaid. The remaining composition is 20 fast and 18 slow. The new expected prepayment rate is about 44 percent.

Figure 5-8

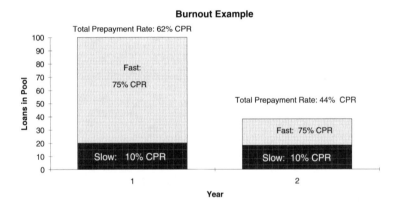

Once burnout and aging are added to the factors that must be modeled, the modeling process becomes much more complex. The arctangent model looked at the current characteristics of a loan to determine its prepayment rate. The second generation models required that the model also take into account the history of the loan in calculating a prepayment rate. Moreover, since these models incorporated several factors, it was necessary to determine the interaction of these factors.

The typical second generation model was a combination of three or four factors. The factors generally included a spread variable, an aging variable,

[1]For more on prepayments, see "Understanding Premium Mortgage-Backed Securities: Observations and Analysis" by Andrew Davidson in *Mortgage-Backed Securities: New Strategies, Applications and Research* edited by F.J. Fabozzi, Probus Publishing, Chicago, 1987.

Development of Prepayment Models

a burnout function, and, in most cases, seasonal adjustments. A simple model might be of the form:

CPR(Spread, Age, Burnout, Month) = S(Spread) x A(Age) x B(Burnout) x M(Month)

> Where: S(Spread) is something akin to the arctangent function
>
> A(age) looks something like the PSA cure
>
> B(Burnout) is a fraction that reduced prepayments based on past prepayments and
>
> M(Month) is an adjustment factor for each month of the year.

Some models used pool factor as an indication of burnout. As we showed earlier, pools with lower factors tend to exhibit lower prepayments. In other models, the burnout factor is constructed explicitly based on prior prepayments or interest-rate levels.

The example shown above shows the factors as products, however the exact combination of the factors depends on the specific formulation. In some cases, the choice of functional form is driven by the choice of statistical approach. Most analysts use some form of regression or statistical analysis to fit their models to actual prepayment data. Different statistical tools require different functional forms. For example, to fit the equation shown above using linear regression, it would be necessary to take the logarithm of both sides. A logarithmic transformation would change the products into sums.

With the development of the second generation of prepayment models, the hope of closed-form solutions to mortgage valuation declined. Since prepayments are considered to be a function of past as well as current conditions, the requirements for developing valuation tools increased substantially. Monte Carlo valuation techniques, which simulate the performance of the mortgages over hundreds of potential interest-rate paths, became the preferred valuation approach. Chapter 8 discusses this in more depth.

Over the past few years, it has become clear that these second-generation models could not fully explain prepayments. It is necessary to account for other characteristics of the loans in order to project prepayments more accurately. Recent efforts in prepayment modeling have sought to incorporate more specific attributes of the borrowers in prepayment analysis. Third-generation models attempt to incorporate macroeconomic factors into prepayment modeling. Two types of macroeconomic variables are used most frequently: variables that reflect the health of the economy and variables that reflect housing price changes.

The impact of the health of the economy on prepayments is easy to understand. With a strong economy, people are making more money and have confidence in the future. These people tend to move up in house quality. When they sell their current homes, prepayments result. In addition, a strong economy promotes mobility as people move to new places of work. These effects are most pronounced for discount and current coupon mortgages. For premium mortgages, refinancing effects usually swap these economic effects.

Housing prices, on the other hand, tend to affect prepayments in all coupon ranges. Higher home prices tend to increase prepayments. When home prices rise, some people will refinance to take additional equity out of their homes. While they may use home-equity loans first to tap their equity, as their second mortgages grow, it becomes economical to refinance the first and second loans together and take out a new first mortgage, which combines the debt of the old loans. In addition, people with a great deal of appreciation in their homes may use the proceeds of their sale to buy bigger homes. For example, suppose you bought a house for $100,000 with a $20,000 down payment and an $80,000 mortgage. If the value of the house goes up to $120,000 (a twenty percent increase in value), you have doubled your original investment. You can now sell the house, pay off the loan and have $40,000. If you use the $40,000 to make a 20% down payment on a new home, you can buy a $200,000 house and take out a $160,000 mortgage.

When home prices are falling, house sales and moving are restricted. People cannot afford to sell their homes, since the remaining equity would be insufficient to make the down payment on a new home.

Furthermore, refinancing may also be restricted as people with insufficient equity may not qualify for a new loan.

The third generation of prepayment model also takes into account the variety of choices that borrowers now have in choosing a loan type. Mortgage types have proliferated. In addition to the standard thirty year fixed-rate mortgage, borrowers have access to loans with varying maturities and interest-rate types. For example, there are balloon mortgages, which must be paid off in five or seven years, and there are adjustable-rate mortgages tied to various indices. With all of these choices, a borrower's decision to refinance reflects more than changes in the replacement cost for a thirty year loan. Borrowers may choose to refinance their thirty year mortgages and take out adjustable-rate mortgages if they see a sufficient cost advantage. Thus, it seems that variables like the steepness of the yield curve or other proxies for the range of choices offered to borrowers are relevant contributors to prepayment projections.

Prepayment models represent a fit of an equation to past data. One of the best ways to evaluate the model is to examine the fit for various mortgage coupons. Figures 5-9 and 5-10 show the fit of the model we used for this book against historical prepayment patterns. Figure 5-9 shows prepayments on a group of loans originated in 1985. The actual prepayment rates are shown with circles. The light solid line shows the current coupon rate, with the scale for the current coupon rate on the right axis. The prepayment model captures the increase in prepayments and the subsequent burnout. The slight mismatch between the model and actual prepayments in the first year reflects the dispersion of coupons. The model assumes that all loans have the same coupon, while the actual loans had a range of coupons. The higher coupons prepaid faster than the average. This error points to an important consideration in mortgage modeling. The performance of a pool of loans may be substantially different than the weighted average characteristics might imply due to the asymmetric nature of the prepayment function.

Figure 5-9

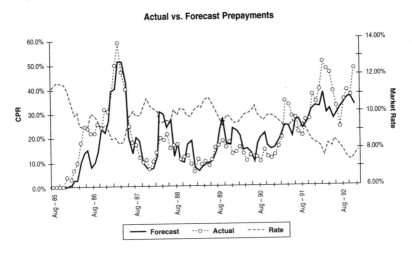

Figure 5-10 shows the prepayment rate on lower-coupon mortgages originated in 1987. The model captures the aging effect and reflects the seasonal patterns. Falling rates in late 1991 produced faster prepayments in 1992. In 1990, prepayments were slower than model predictions. This slowness is probably attributable to weakness in the economy and housing markets at the time.

Figure 5-10

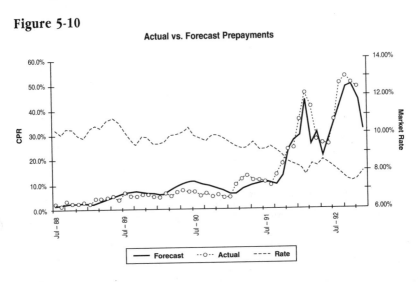

Development of Prepayment Models

While the prepayment model does a good job of capturing the major movements in prepayments, there is still some variability that the model does not explain. Many modelers seek to get an extremely good fit of the historical data. However, a good fit does not necessarily produce a good model. Developing a model that captures the essential economics of prepayments will produce a more reliable forecasting and cash-flow-generation tool, than a model that has many additional parameters, which improve historical fit without providing any additional insight into prepayment behavior.

The prepayment models described so far deal with aggregate data. The models are driven primarily by pool-level characteristics, such as the weighted average coupon, the age of the loans and perhaps the state of origination. With increasing access to mortgage data and increasing computational power to handle that data, some market participants are developing a fourth generation of prepayment models. These models address prepayments at the most fundamental level—the individual borrower. Using underwriting information and local price indices, they are seeking to more precisely predict prepayments. These types of models are also being used to assess the credit risk of mortgage pools.

In order to produce such a model it is necessary to have access to very detailed data. It is also necessary that the data be of high quality and consistency. There are currently very few such databases available. However, several of the large mortgage originators, servicers, and mortgage insurance companies have been gathering this type of data for some time now.

There is another type of prepayment model, which we haven't addressed. Telerate has developed a model called the Advanced Factor Service. Telerate's model uses title search data to estimate prepayments for the next few months. This type of information can be very valuable for trading mortgages, but is less valuable for the type of valuation that we address in this book.

It is clear from the exposition above that prepayment modeling is a dynamic field. The definitive model has not yet been developed (and may never be developed). The development of prepayment modeling reflects our changing understanding of borrower's prepayment decisions as well as changes in the economy and borrowers themselves. While history may be a good guide to prepayment projections, the future will not be an exact duplicate of the past. The developments in prepayment models have resulted from analysts recognizing that their models were wrong. Prepayment models are doomed to be somewhat inaccurate. It is only possible to test a model after it has been developed and used for a while. Then, while the model is being used, the environment will change in a way to make some of the assumptions of the model incorrect. At times, the best investment opportunities result from recognizing that the current models are no longer valid and then determining how changing conditions will produce unexpected results.

■ CONCLUSION

Given the wide variety of prepayment models and the continuing evolution of prepayment modeling, it is difficult to state precisely which models are the best. As with most issues in MBS, the best model is the model that fits the problem. For many applications, a second- or third-generation model is sufficient. For some simple analyses, even a first-generation model would be sufficient. The important idea to keep in mind when analyzing mortgages is that the quality of the analysis will be limited by the quality of the prepayment model. When evaluating model results, it is important to understand the form of the prepayment model, the variables used in the model, and its historical accuracy.

CHAPTER SIX

■

CMOs, IOs, and POs and Structuring

■

At first, it seems that learning about mortgage-backed securities isn't going to be that hard. Sure it's a large market, but everyone knows about mortgages. Prepayments seem a little complicated, but the whole thing is logical enough. Mortgages are basically GNMA, FNMA, FHLMC, or nonagency. They are usually thirty-year or fifteen-year fixed-rate loans or some adjustable-rate loans. They have a variety of coupons and ages, depending on when they were originated. Not simple, but not overwhelming. Then you take a look at the offering sheets from a Wall Street firm or the portfolio listing of an insurance company or a mutual fund. Now you are confused. Too many letters and numbers, and none seem to mean anything: FN92-35, FHLMC 1123, PAC, SEQ, INV, PO, SUP, MLT 15 E. You've entered the world of CMOs and structured mortgage products.

With the size of the securitized mortgage market exceeding the corporate bond market and approaching the size of the Treasury market, it's not surprising that the mortgage market has found a way to restructure mortgage cash flows to meet the needs and views of a variety of investors. The basic mortgage passthroughs all have very similar cash-flow structures and performance characteristics. Discounts and premiums differ to some extent, but the overall investment patterns are quite similar. While the investment characteristics of these loans are similar, the needs of the investors vary significantly. The CMO (collateralized mortgage obligation) has become the vehicle to transform mortgage cash flows into a variety of investment instruments.

The driving force behind the creation of CMOs is arbitrage. CMOs will be created when the underwriter sees the ability to buy mortgage collateral, structure a CMO, and sell the CMO bonds for more than the price of the underlying collateral plus expenses. Because of the dynamic nature of the arbitrage opportunities, the types of CMOs created will reflect current market conditions and can change significantly. If all the CMO did was rearrange cash flows, it would be difficult to create added value. CMOs are successful, nevertheless, for two main reasons. First, investors have varying needs and are willing to pay extra for a bond that meets their specific needs. Second, investors misanalyze bonds. Many investors rely on tools such as yield spread and average-life analysis. These tools are insufficient to analyze mortgage-backed securities and CMO bonds.

A CMO can be defined as a bond secured by mortgage cash flows. The mortgage cash flows are distributed to the bond based on a set of pre-specified rules. The rules determine the order of principal allocation and the coupon level. The specific choice of which CMOs and other structured mortgage products are created stems from the interaction of market demand, with credit, legal, tax, and accounting requirements. The primary ingredient in CMO creation is the availability of mortgage cash flows. The cash flows provide the raw material for the CMOs. Every CMO must address the amount and availability of cash flow.

The focus here will be on the cash-flow aspects of CMOs, however a brief discussion of the other aspects of CMO creation is warranted. An important component of the CMO is the assurance that the investor will get the promised cash flows. The market has developed several methods for achieving this goal. Generally, the mortgages or the agency-backed mortgage pools are placed in a trust, and the CMO bonds are issued out of that trust. Various legal structures can be used to create a bankruptcy-remote entity to hold the mortgages and issue the bonds. The investor looks to the trust and the cash flows of the mortgages to provide the bond's principal and interest payments. These payments are assured through either a rating agency assurance (that is a triple A rating) or though the guarantee of a Government Sponsored Enterprise (GSE), either Fannie Mae or Freddie Mac. In recent years, the GSE-guaranteed CMOs have dominated the issuance of CMOs. Some mortgages cannot be used in CMOs guaranteed by the GSEs. CMOs backed by these loans are generally issued by Wall Street firms, large mortgage originators, or mortgage conduits and are rated by the rating agencies.

The tax treatment of CMOs is generally covered under the provisions of the Real Estate Mortgage Investment Conduit (REMIC) rules. Sometimes CMOs are referred to as REMICs. In order to be a REMIC, the bonds must have a certain structure and must elect REMIC status. REMIC election drives the tax treatment of the bonds. The "Regular Interests" of the REMIC are generally taxed as ordinary bonds, while the "Residual Interest" bears the tax consequences of the CMO structure. While the original intention was that the residual would receive any cash flow not distributed to the regular interests, most residuals are now have little cash flow attached to them and are distributed primarily based on their tax consequences.

The accounting treatment for most CMOs is straight forward. However, CMO bonds sold at a premium or discount must be evaluated on a level yield basis. That is, income is determined by the yield of the bond, rather than its coupon. When prepayments change, the expected cash flows of the security changes. So, the income stream must be adjusted accordingly. This is a complex area, especially for some CMO residuals, interest only and principal only securities. The rules for treatment of these bonds are subject to change. Please consult with your tax and accounting advisors before purchasing CMOs.

Once the legal, tax, and accounting issues are resolved, the investment characteristics of a CMO will be driven by the cash flows of the underlying collateral and the structure of the CMO deal. In order to understand CMOs, it is necessary to understand the rules by which the mortgage cash flows are distributed to the bonds.

■ CMO AS RULES

The CMO can be thought of as a set of rules. The rules tell the trustee how to divide the payments that it receives on the mortgages. The rules tell the trustee in what order to pay the bond holders and how much to pay them. The rules can be generally split between principal payment rules and interest payment rules. Market participants have developed standard definitions for CMO types, these types specify the nature of the rules used to distribute cash flows. These standard types include principal pay types and interest pay types. Each bond has both a principal pay type and interest pay type. Table 6-1 shows the standard CMO definitions.[1]

Table 6-1 Standard Definitions for REMIC and CMO Bonds

Principal Pay Types:	Agency Acronym
Accretion directed—bonds that pay principal from specified accretions of accrual bonds. ADs may, in addition, receive principal from the collateral paydowns.	AD
Component—bonds comprised of nondetachable components. The principal pay type and/or sequence of principal pay of each component may vary.	COM
Capital appreciation bonds—accrual bonds similar to Z bonds issued with initial principal balances per "unit" of $1,000 or less. Most CAB accretion schedules are derived by discounting $1,000 back over the expected life of the CAB bond at its stated coupon.	PACZ, RTL
Pro rata principal strip—bonds that pay principal in some fixed proportion to the aggregate collateral paydowns.	STP
Sticky jump—bonds whose principal paydown is changed by the occurrence of one or more "triggering" events. The first time the trigger condition is met, the bond changes to its new priority for receiving principal and remains in its new priority for the life of the bond.	SJ
Non-sticky jump—bonds whose principal paydown is changed by the occurrence of one or more "triggering" event(s). The first time and each time the trigger condition is met, the bond changes to its new priority of receiving principal and reverts to its old priority for each payment date that the trigger condition is not met.	NSJ

[1]Definitions courtesy of Merrill Lynch Mortgage Capital Inc.

	Agency Acronym
Planned amortization class—bonds that pay principal based on a predetermined schedule established for a group of PAC bonds. The principal redemption schedule of the PAC group is derived by amortizing the collateral based upon two collateral prepayment speeds. These two speeds are the endpoints for the "structuring PAC range." A PAC group is therefore defined as PAC bonds having the same structuring PAC range. A "group" can be a single bond class.	PAC
Scheduled—bonds that pay principal to a set redemption schedule(s), but do not fit the definition of a PAC or TAC.	SCH
Sequential pay—bonds that start to pay principal when classes with an earlier priority have paid to a zero balance. SEQ bonds enjoy uninterrupted payment of principal until paid to a zero balance. SEQ bonds may share principal paydown on a pro rata basis with another class.	SEQ
Support—bonds that receive principal payments after scheduled payments have been paid to some or all PAC, TAC, and/or SCH bonds for each payment date.	SUP
Target amortization class—bonds that pay principal based upon a predetermined schedule, which is derived by amortizing the collateral based on a single prepayment speed.	TAC
Index allocation—bonds whose principal paydown is allocated based upon the value of some index.	XAC

Interest Pay Types:	**Agency Acronym**
Ascending rate bonds—bonds that have predetermined coupon rates which take effect one or more times on dates set forth at issuance.	ARB
Partial accrual—bonds that accrete interest (which is added to the outstanding principal balance) and receive interest distributions in the same period. These bonds have a stated coupon, which is equal to the sum of the accretion coupon and interest distribution coupon.	PZ
Excess—bonds which are entitled to collateral principal and interest paid which exceeds the amount of principal and interest obligated to all bonds in the deal.	EXE
Floater—bonds whose coupons reset periodically based on an index and may have a cap and/or floor. The coupon varies directly with changes in the index.	FLT
Fixed—bonds whose coupons are fixed throughout the life of the bond.	FIX
Inverse floater—bonds whose coupons reset periodically (like floaters) based on an index and may have a cap and/or floor. The coupon varies inversely with changes in the index.	INV

	Agency Acronym
Interest only—bonds that receive some or all of the interest portion of the underlying collateral and little or no principal. IO bonds have either a notional or nominal amount of principal. A notional amount is the amount of principal used as a reference to calculate the amount of interest due. A nominal amount is actual principal that will be paid to the bond. It is referred to as manila since it is extremely small compared to other classes.	IO
Principal only—bonds that do not receive any interest.	PO
WAC coupon—bonds whose coupons represent a blended interest rate, which may change in any period. Bonds may be comprised of non-detachable components some of which have different coupons.	W
Accrual—bonds that accrete interest which is added to the outstanding principal balance. This accretion may continue until the bond begins paying principal or until some other event has occurred.	Z

Other Types:	Agency Acronym
Liquidity—bonds intended to qualify as a "liquid asset" for savings institutions. LIQ bonds are any agency-issued bonds that have a stated maturity of 5 years (or less), or any nonagency-issued bonds that have a stated maturity of 3 years (or less), in each case from issue date.	LIQ
Residual—bond that is designated for tax purposes as the residual interest in a REMIC.	R, RS, RL
To be defined—bonds that do not fit under any of the current definitions.	TBD
Retail—bonds that are designated to be sold to retail investors.	L

Each CMO represents a combination of these bond types and, hence, of the mortgage rules. In the examples below, we will show how these rules are applied and how complex CMO structures can grow out of these simple rules. In our analysis, we will concentrate on several of the most common principal and interest rules.

The starting point for the creation of the CMO is the mortgage collateral. For the examples below, we will use newly originated agency collateral with a net coupon of 8 percent and a gross coupon of 8.6 percent. Assume a 30-year maturity and an age of five months. CMOs are generally priced as structured using the PSA model. We will use 175 PSA as our base speed and will look at the effects on the structure of prepayments at 100 PSA and at 400 PSA. Figures 6-1a and 6-1b show the principal balance outstanding and the cash flows of the mortgages. Note that the cash flows consist of principal and interest payments. The principal payments represent both the scheduled principal payments and the unscheduled payments (prepayments). The interest cash flows consist of the net interest payment to the investor and the payment to the servicer and guarantor. The change in balances and cash flows for speeds of 100 PSA and 400 PSA are shown in Figure 6-2 and 6-3. The cash flows of mortgages are the raw material for the CMO. The cash flows of the CMO bonds must come from the mortgage cash flows. As the cash flows of the underlying passthrough change, the cash flows of the CMO bonds must also change.

Figure 6-1a Balance at 175 PSA

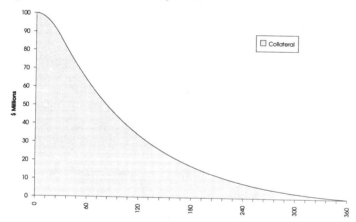

Figure 6-1b Cash Flow at 175 PSA

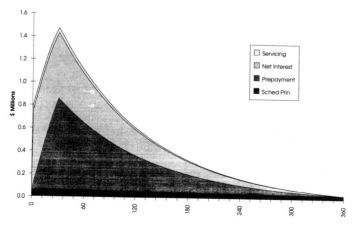

Figure 6-2a Balance at 100 PSA

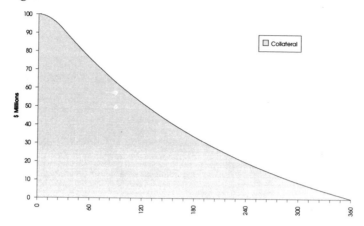

Figure 6-2b Cash Flow at 100 PSA

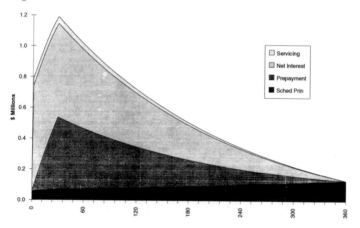

CMO as Rules

Figure 6-3a Balance at 400 PSA

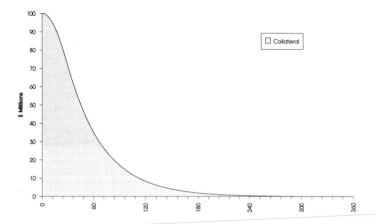

Figure 6-3b Cash Flow at 400 PSA

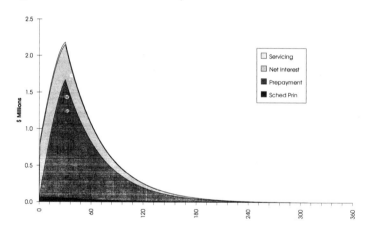

■ PRINCIPAL PAY TYPES

Principal pay rules determine how principal payments are split between the CMO tranches. These rules can be applied alone or in combination with each other. For **sequential** bonds, one bond is completely paid down before principal payment begins on the next. **Pro rata** bonds pay down simultaneously according to a fixed allocation. **PAC** or planned amortization classes are part of a group of bonds classified as scheduled bonds. These bonds receive priority within the structure for certain principal payments. **Support** bonds are created in conjunction with the scheduled bonds and absorb the remaining principal payments.

■ INTEREST PAY TYPES

Interest pay rules determine the amount of interest received by the CMO bond holders each period. Interest payment rules are linked with principal pay rules to produce a wide variety of bond types. One rule of CMO creation is that the combined interest on the CMO bonds must be less than the available interest from the collateral. **Fixed** interest payments are the most common type. The bond holder receives an interest amount, which is a constant percentage of the outstanding balance. In an **accrual** bond (or Z bond), the bond holder does not receive interest payments for some time period. During this time, the interest payments are converted to principal and the balance of the investment increases. A **floating**-rate bond's coupon changes based on an underlying index. Floating-rate bonds typically pay a margin above an index (frequently LIBOR) and have an interest-rate cap. **Inverse floating** rate bonds are usually produced in conjunction with floating-rate bonds. Their coupon moves inversely with the index, usually at some multiple of the index. They typically have a cap and a floor. **Principal only** and **interest only** payment types provide for bonds with principal payments and no interest payment or interest payments with no principal.

■ SEQUENTIAL CMOs

The first CMOs were sequential CMOs. They were created to turn mortgage-backed securities into more corporate bond-like investments. Sequential bonds tend to narrow the time over which principal payments are received, creating a more bullet-like structure. Figure 6-4 shows the cash flows of a typical sequential CMO. In this example, classes A, B, C, and Z are sequential bonds. Class A receives all of the principal payments first. Once class A is completely paid off, then class B begins to receive principal payments. Once class B is paid off, then C begins principal payments, and so on until class Z is paid off. Note that each bond receives principal payments over a relatively narrow time period.

The interest payment on each of these tranche is fixed and equal to the net coupon of the underlying MBS. Each bond receives a monthly interest payment equal to the coupon divided by twelve times the outstanding balance of that tranche. Thus tranches A, B, and C all receive interest payments beginning in month one. Class Z is an accrual bond. Rather than receiving its share of interest, its interest payment is converted to principal and is used to increase the balance of the Z tranche. The interest payment that should have gone to Z is used to make principal payments to tranches A, B, and C. This can also be seen in Figure 6-4. Figure 6-5 shows the balance outstanding of each tranche over time. Note that the balance of tranche A begins to decline immediately. The balance of tranches B and C are constant until the prior tranches are paid off. Tranche Z shows an increasing balance until all of the earlier tranches are paid off. The net effect is to shorten the average life of tranches A, B, and C. Typically shorter tranches are priced at lower yields. By increasing the amount of principal received by the shorter tranches, CMO structures are able to increase the value of the CMO arbitrage.

Figure 6-4 Cash Flows of a CMO

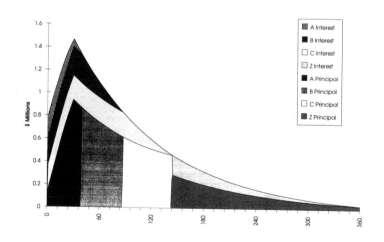

Figure 6-5 The Balance Outstanding Over Time

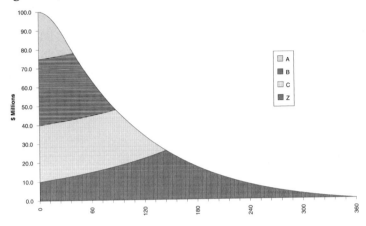

As prepayments increase, the payments on the bonds will be received earlier. While some analysts have argued that sequential bonds offer protection from prepayment risk, it is difficult to make general statements about the amount of risk in a sequential bond. Rather than rely on a general prescription of which bonds are safe and which are risky, it is better to perform an analysis of the specific tranche you are considering. Subsequent chapters describe some of these methods in more detail.

■ PRO RATA BONDS

Much of the complexity of CMO structures arises from layering different types of principal payment rules. Pro rata bonds provide one means to affect this layering. Pro rata bonds are two or more bonds that receive cash flows according to exactly the same rules. Cash flows available to these bonds are divided proportionally. Figure 6-6 shows an example of pro rata bonds. The figure shows only the principal payments of the bonds. Tranches B1 and B2 receive a pro rata share of the cash flows that went to class B in the earlier example. Here B1 receives 40 percent of the principal while B2 receives 60 percent of the principal.

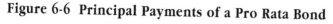
Figure 6-6 Principal Payments of a Pro Rata Bond

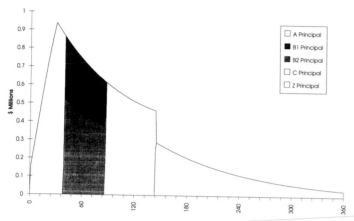

Pro rata bonds are created to allow for different interest payment rules for the same principal payment pattern. Different interest payment rules will change the risk characteristics of the bonds and make them attractive to different investors. Given this pro rata structure, there are several choices of interest pay rules possible for B1 and B2. One possibility is that they will both be fixed-rate bonds, but with different coupons. Say B1 has a coupon of 6 percent. The coupon of B2 can not exceed 9.33 percent, since the weighted average coupon cannot exceed 8 percent. Through this mechanism it is possible to create bonds that have coupons that are higher and lower than the collateral coupon.

Another example of a pro rata bond is an interest only (IO) strip. It is possible to create an IO off of any bond. For some time, REMIC rules required that all regular interests have a principal component. At that time, IOs were created with a tiny piece of principal and generally had coupons of 1,200 percent due to fed wire requirements. The limitation on principal has now been removed so that a pure interest strip can be created off of any bond. Some people call IOs, that are created off of CMO bonds, IOettes to distinguish them from IO strips created using the all the interest payments of an MBS. In a CMO, IO strips are used to lower the coupon of the CMO tranche. Due to prepayment risk, investors prefer to buy bonds at a slight discount, so their yield will be less affected by changing prepayments.

Another form of pro rata bonds are floaters and inverse floaters. Just as it is possible to create two fixed-rate bonds, where the combined coupon equals the coupon of the collateral, it is possible to create a floating-rate bond and an inverse floating-rate bond whose coupon equals the collateral coupon. Suppose bond B2 is a floating-rate bond with a coupon equal to LIBOR + 50 basis points. If LIBOR is currently 4 percent, then the coupon on B2 is 4.5 percent. The coupon on B1 would then be 13.25 percent. If LIBOR rises to 5 percent, the coupon on B2 becomes 5.5 percent, while the coupon on B1 must fall to 11.75 percent. As LIBOR rises, the coupon on B2 floats with LIBOR, while the coupon on B1 moves inversely to LIBOR. The coupon on B1 changes by 1.5 times the amount of the change in LIBOR. This inverse floater is said to have a slope of 1.5. Because the interest must come from the fixed-interest payment of the collateral, the coupon on these floaters must be capped. The floating-rate bond can not exceed 13.33 percent, while the inverse floater cannot exceed 19.25 percent. Figure 6-7 is a graph of the possible coupon combinations of B1 and B2. The coupon on the inverse floater is usually described by a formula. In this case, the formula would be 19.25 percent - 1.5 x LIBOR.

Figure 6-7 Floater and Inverse Floater Coupon

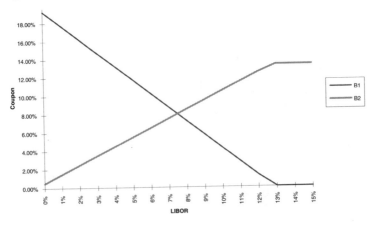

■ SCHEDULED BONDS

While sequential bonds may offer some allocation of prepayment risk, investors seeking more protection from prepayment risk have turned to scheduled bonds for greater certainty of cash flow. Several types of scheduled bonds exist. Here we concentrate on planned amortization classes (PACs). PACs are designed to produce constant cash flows within a range of prepayment rates. Unlike sequential bonds, PAC bonds provide a true allocation of risk. PAC bonds clearly have more stable cash flows than comparable non-PAC bonds. The additional stability of the PAC bonds comes at a cost. In order to create a more stable PAC bond, it is necessary to create a less stable support bond. Support bonds bear the risk of cash flow changes. Although PAC bonds are somewhat protected from prepayment risk, they are not completely risk free. If prepayments are fast enough or slow enough, the cash flows of the PAC bonds will change. Furthermore, there can be great differences in the performance of PAC bonds. As with all CMO bonds, it is better to evaluate the cash-flow characteristics of the bond you are considering as an investment, than to rely on the type of the bond to indicate its riskiness. Some PAC bonds can be very variable and some support bonds can be very stable.

PACs are created by calculating the cash flow available from the collateral using two different prepayment speeds: a fast speed, 300 PSA for example, and a slow speed, such as 100 PSA.

Figure 6-8 shows the principal cash flows of our collateral using 100 PSA and 300 PSA. The cash flow available each period under each scenario is the cash flow that can be used to construct the PAC bond. Under the 100 PSA assumption, there is less cash flow available in the early years of the CMO and more available in the later years. Under the 300 PSA assumption, there is more cash flow available during the early years of the CMO, and less available in the late years. The 100 PSA scenario determines the PAC cash flows in the early years and the 300 PSA scenario determines the PAC cash flows in the later years.

Figure 6-8 Determining PAC Bond Schedule

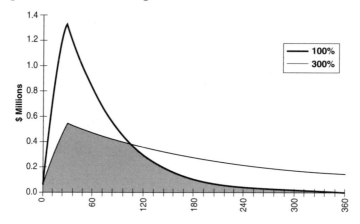

Figure 6-9 shows the cash flows of a CMO consisting of two classes, a PAC bond and a support bond, assuming a prepayment speed of 175 PSA. The PAC bond was constructed with a "PAC band" of 100 PSA to 300 PSA. The principal payment pattern of the PAC bond is exactly equal to the schedule created using the two PAC band speeds. The cash flows of the support bond flow around the PAC bond. These cash flows are neither sequential nor pro rata. The support bond pays down simultaneously with the PAC bond, but the ratio of payments is determined by the PAC schedule and varies depending on prepayment rates. Figure 6-10 shows the pay down of the balance of the two classes at 175 PSA.

Figure 6-9 Cash Flows of a CMO at 175 PSA

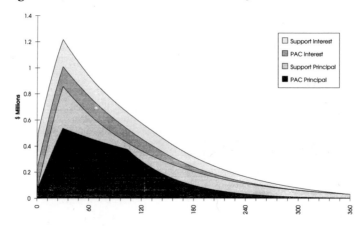

Scheduled Bonds

Figure 6-10 Principal Balance at 175 PSA

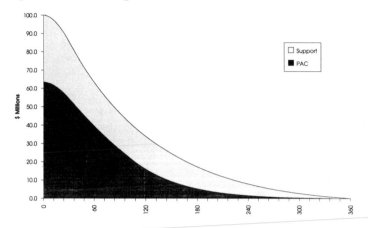

As prepayment rates change, the cash-flow characteristics shift. At a speed of 100 PSA, far less cash flow is available in the early years of the CMO. Figure 6-11 shows the cash flows at 100 PSA. In the early years, all the principal cash flows go to the PAC bond. Principal payments on the support bond are deferred. Under this scenario, the cash flows of the support bond extend. The support bond does, however, receive more interest payments. Since 100 PSA is within the PAC bands, the PAC bond still receives cash flow according to the original PAC schedule.

Figure 6-11 Cash Flows at 100 PSA

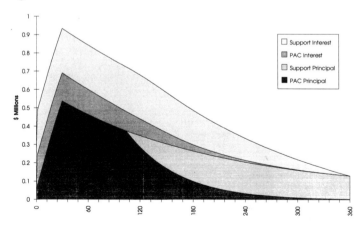

If prepayments are outside of the PAC bands, then the PAC schedule cannot be met. Figure 6-12 shows the cash flows of the CMO assuming prepayments at 400 PSA. Here the prepayment speed is outside the PAC bands. In this case, it is impossible to keep the PAC schedule. The cash flows to the support bond are accelerated. The support bond is fully paid off by month 91 and all remaining principal payments go to the PAC bond, significantly shortening its life. Even though the PAC schedule cannot be met, the PAC bond is still more stable than the support bond.

Figure 6-12 Cash Flows at 400 PSA

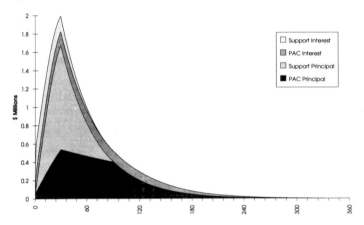

PAC bands are expressed as a range of prepayment speeds. In our example, we use 100 PSA to 300 PSA. This means that if prepayments occur at any single constant speed between 100 PSA and 300 PSA, the PAC schedule will be met. It does not mean that the PAC schedule will be met if prepayments on the collateral stay between 100 PSA and 300 PSA. Even if prepayments vary within the PAC bands it is possible that the schedule will not be met. For example, if prepayments stay near 300 PSA for several years and then fall to near 100 PSA, the PAC bond will probably extend outside the PAC band. During the years at 300 PSA, the support bond will be nearly paid off. Then when prepayments slow, there isn't any way to cushion the extension of the PAC bond. Once again, analysis of the bond's cash flows are a more useful measure of the value of the bond than can be determined from its name alone.

■ SEQUENTIAL PACs AND OTHER COMBINATIONS

Just as sequential bonds were created to allow investors to specify a maturity range for their investments, PACs can be divided sequentially to provide more narrow pay down structures. Figure 6-13 shows the cash flows of a CMO where the PAC class has been split into several different bonds. These sequential PACs narrow the range of years over which principal payments occur. Investors with short horizons choose the earlier PACs, while investors with longer horizons choose the longer PACs. While these bonds were all structured using the 100 PSA to 300 PSA PAC band, the actual range of speeds over which their schedules will be met may differ. In particular, the early bonds can withstand faster speeds than the top of the PAC band, without varying from their scheduled payments.

Figure 6-13 Cash Flows of a CMO at 175 PSA

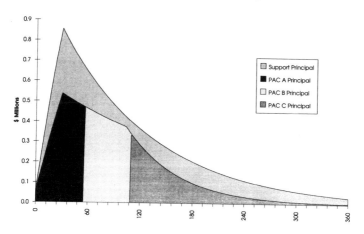

Sequential PACs are another example of how the CMO structuring rules can be combined to create more complex structures to meet a wider variety of investor requirements. It is possible to take any bond and further structure it. For example, the sequential PACs could be split using a pro rata structure to create high and low coupon PACs.

One common structure takes mortgage collateral and strips off an interest only piece to lower the coupon of all of the CMO classes and splits the collateral into a PAC and a support. Then, a PAC class within the PAC class is created. The more stable PACs are called PAC Is and the less stable ones are called PAC IIs. These bonds are divided sequentially into PACs with various average lives. These sequential PACs are divided pro rata in order to strip down their coupons so that the bonds trade at or below par. The remaining IO strips are sold individually or together as IOettes. The structuring continues with the support piece, which is divided sequentially. The sequential support pieces are split pro rata to create a variety of fixed-rate, floating-rate, and inverse floating-rate bonds. Using the few simple structures we have seen above, structures with 50 or more classes can be created.

■ INTEREST ONLY AND PRINCIPAL ONLY

Interest only (IO) and principal only (PO) bonds can be created within CMO structures as a type of pro rata bond as described above. They can also be created independently by stripping MBS. Both FNMA and FHLMC offer programs under which MBS can be split into IOs and POs. IOs and POs tend to be very volatile. By splitting principal and interest, the effects of prepayments on value are amplified.

Principal only bonds receive all of the principal payments. Therefore, the total amount of cash flow to be received by the PO investor is known from the start. On our $100 million of collateral, the PO investor will receive $100 million of cash flow. The uncertainty is over the timing of the cash flows. At faster prepayment speeds, the cash flow is received over a relatively short period. At slow speeds, the cash flow is spread out over a longer time period. The cash-flow pattern can vary greatly. Figure 6-14 shows the cash flows of the PO at various prepayment speeds.

Figure 6-14 Cash Flows of a PO at Various Prepayment Speeds

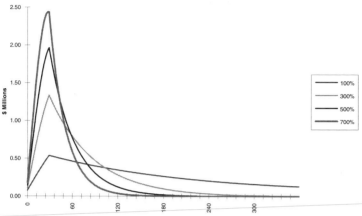

Since POs receive no interest, they are priced at a discount. Due to discounting effects, the value of the PO increases as the cash flow is received sooner. That is, other things being equal, you would rather receive your money sooner than later. The value of a PO will then be affected by the discount rate and the timing of prepayments. As interest rates fall, the discount rates fall and prepayment rates increase. Both factors serve to increase the value of the PO. POs thus become very bullish instruments, strongly benefiting from falling rates. The performance characteristics of POs, however, are very dependent upon the characteristics of the underlying collateral. POs from premium collateral have very different performance characteristics than POs from discount collateral due to their very different prepayment characteristics. Furthermore, POs are very volatile instruments because slight changes in prepayment rates can have a significant impact on value.

Interest only (IO) securities do not have any assured cash flows. The amount of interest received depends on the balance outstanding. As prepayments increase, the amount of cash flow received by the IO decreases. As prepayments decrease, the amount of cash flow increases. The change in cash flow can be significant. Figure 6-15 shows the cash flow of the IO under several prepayment assumptions. Cash flow under the 700 percent PSA assumption is just a fraction of the cash flow under the 100 percent PSA assumption. Interest only securities have a feature that is unique in the fixed-income world. IOs tend to increase in value as rates rise and decrease in value as rates fall. This is because as rates rise, prepayments tend to slow. Slower prepayments lead to greater cash flows to the IO investor. The increase in cash flow more than compensates for the higher discount rate.

Figure 6-15 Cash Flows of an IO at Various Prepayment Speeds

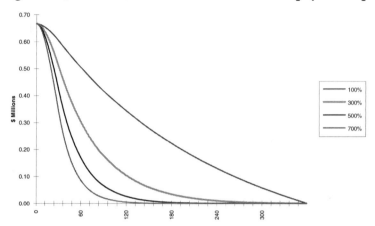

Investors should be cautious about using IOs to hedge other fixed-income instruments. Although the general direction of movement of an IO is opposite to other fixed-income instruments, it is difficult to assess precise hedge ratios. IOs are extremely sensitive to prepayment expectations and is difficult to establish precise relationships between interest rates and prepayment rates. Highly sensitive instruments like IOs and POs require sophisticated analysis tempered with a good deal of judgment. The difficulty in assessing these types of instruments is an indication of the limitation of current valuation tools.

■ SENIOR/SUBORDINATED STRUCTURES

So far we have concentrated on CMO structures where the underlying collateral or the CMO itself is guaranteed by the agencies (GNMA, FNMA, FHLMC). For collateral that does not meet the agency standards, a different type of structure is required. With agency collateral, the investor does not bear any default risk. In the case of a default, the investor receives a prepayment equal to the full principal amount of the loan. If the loan is not guaranteed by the agencies, other forms of credit enhancement are required to attract investors. Credit enhancement can either be external or internal. External credit enhancement is provided by a mortgage insurance company. The insurance operates at the pool level and provides investors with the assurance that they will not suffer from mortgage delinquencies and defaults.

Internal credit enhancement operates by relying on the overall credit quality of the mortgages to produce different classes of bonds with different exposure to credit loss. Generally, a senior class is produced, which is protected from credit losses, along with a junior piece, which absorbs the losses. Senior/subordinated structures are somewhat akin to PAC bonds. However, instead of offering protection against prepayment risk, the senior class is protected from default risk.

The construction of senior subordinated deals can become quite complex. New structures are continually being developed to make the execution more efficient. In some structures, a junior class is set up so that it is large enough to absorb worst-case losses. The guidelines for the size of the subordinated structures are set by the rating agencies (Standard & Poor's, Moody's, or Fitch). Underwriters and issuers generally seek at least a double A rating on the senior class. The junior piece generally stays outstanding until the balance of the senior piece has declined sufficiently so that the risk of loss is minimal. Additional credit protection may come from a reserve account funded with cash or with excess interest that is not going to either the senior or junior class.

These senior/subordinated structures may be further structured using any of the tools described above. These CMOs tend to have fewer classes than the agency backed CMOs. There is generally less prepayment information available on the collateral for these deals and investors tend to avoid combinations of concentrated credit risk and prepayment risk.

■ CONCLUSION

Collateralized mortgage obligations allow mortgage cash flows to be restructured to create securities with a wide variety of investment performance characteristics. Complex CMOs are generally the result of application of relatively simple cash-flow allocation rules. While the rules may be simple, the resulting securities may be quite complex. Knowing the structure of a CMO may provide some insight into the risks of the bond. However analysis of the actual cash flows under a variety of interest rate and prepayment scenarios will produce more reliable results. Very often, the performance characteristics of two same-type bonds can differ dramatically. The next few chapters describe analytical tools that can be used to assess these complex structures.

CHAPTER SEVEN

Scenario
Analysis

Many times in life one hears a person described as not being too physically attractive but possessing a wonderful personality (or vice versa). You can draw this mode of description into the world of bond analysis. As an analyst, you may be called upon to present a compelling sales story for a security. Going into the task, you must see if the bond has a "good" yield spread or should be sold based on some total-return or scenario analysis basis. The yield (much like the physical appearance of a person) can often mask the true underlying characteristics of the security, especially the embedded option risk. Scenario analysis lets you get under the surface of a security, giving you a peek at the true personality. Someone looking to develop a long-term relationship with a security, like some extended holding period, may be more concerned with the return profile than the yield.

■ MOTIVATION

Scenario analysis serves as a critical tool in understanding the dynamics of the performance of fixed-income securities, especially those with cash flows that depend upon interest rates. Unlike the static measures of yield and spread, scenario analysis gives some measure about the expected benefits from holding a security for some period less than the stated maturity. These measures of expected performance let us know about the expected price volatility as interest rates and prepayment rates change. Information such as this is critical for the growing number of institutions and fund managers that must mark their security values to the market.

The actual process of scenario analysis is not a formal valuation method; it relies upon numerous assumptions regarding how the problem will be framed. Furthermore, even within a given analytical framework, there are analytical issues, which require some subjective decision. Making poor or ill-informed assumptions undermines the integrity of using scenario analysis. Used improperly, the method turns the story of the expected behavior from one of nonfiction to that of fiction (or even science fiction).

In short, scenario analysis compares the amount of cash we have at the end of some holding period with the amount of cash we held at the beginning of some holding period. The growth rate by which the starting cash becomes the ending cash is the total return. This process will be dependent upon the cash coming from the interest and principal payments of the security and the remaining balance at the end of the holding period. Because MBS cash flows are very dependent upon interest rates, the method of scenario analysis holds particular usefulness for investors.

In this chapter, we will try and lay out some of the critical issues related to using the scenario-analysis framework for analyzing securities. Given the nature of the scenario-analysis method, we cannot cover all of the myriad ways that the process is abused, but we will try and go over some of the more egregious methods for turning sows' ears into silver purses. Table 7-1 presents an overview of the chapter.

Table 7-1 Chapter Overview

Environment	Prepayments	Cash Flow	Analysis
•Holding period	•Static forecast	•Interim flows	•Value
•Interest-rate scenario	•Vector	•Terminal pricing	•Risk
•Reinvestment	•Model	•Income	
•Scenario creation			

Using our established method for examining the aspects of MBS analysis, we will concentrate on the environment, prepayment, cash flow, and analysis components of scenario analysis. A synopsis of the application can be seen in the table. As we have pointed out, the scenario analysis method is somewhat freeform. When used properly, it gives a very insightful window into the understanding of how a security behaves. In fact, it would generally be a good recommendation that if an investor did not like the scenario profile of a security, he or she would be advised not to purchase the security even if the yield or other measurement of value seemed irresistible.

Environment	Prepayment	Cash Flow	Analysis

■ ENVIRONMENT

Understanding the environment for scenario analysis comes down to knowing how we set up the guideposts for performing the analysis. We must make decisions related to time and interest rates. These decisions should be related to some of the parameters placed on the investment manager, such as the frequency by which they will be evaluated or by which they must report their security performance.

Horizon

The scenario-analysis process requires that a horizon or ending period be chosen. This ending period will be the point at which the security will be repriced and the overall performance will be measured. In most applications, the horizon is assumed to be 12 months. Choice of the horizon depends upon the need for the information. Some investors may choose other holding periods, for instance, a holding period commensurate with the remaining months in a year.

Choosing the right holding period is somewhat of a balancing act, as shown in Figure 7-1. When the horizon is too short, the price component of total return overweighs all other components. As the holding period extends, less weight is placed on the price performance of the security and returns rely more on the assumptions regarding the reinvestment rate for the interim cash flows. Placing too much weight on the reinvestment rate may not be a good idea, because it tends to make the returns of disparate securities begin to resemble one another.

Figure 7-1

Holding Period Effect

Interest Rates: Base Case Scenario

Scenario analysis usually involves more than one interest-rate scenario. Still, most applications look at some initial curve, sometimes called the base case curve. Some models may use the most recent yield curve as this base case, while others may use the implied forward curve. Either assumption is acceptable, assuming you understand the implications.

Using the forward curve is the most consistent analytical approach. By the forward curve, we mean the yield-to-maturity curve implied to exist at the horizon. This implied curve can be determined mathematically from the current yield curve. The forward curve assumes that no arbitrage exists in the Treasury market. For any given holding period, investors would be expecting the same return from Treasury securities, regardless of the actual maturity or coupon of the Treasury security.

As mentioned, using the current yield curve as the base case scenario is acceptable. The user of the model explicitly assumes that the forward rates will not materialize. This would suggest that you would be comfortable taking a yield-curve bet. In an upward sloping yield-curve environment, longer-duration securities would consistently outperform shorter-duration securities when we assume the current curve to be the base case curve.

From the purist point of view, betting against the forward rates may appear heretical. However, there may be cases when the user of scenario analysis feels that external factors may not let market forces fully work. For instance, there may be cases when policies of the Federal Reserve may be influential in keeping the yield curve steep or in letting the yield curve flatten. Even so, creating probability weights for scenarios in the non-forward base case should not be done. When using the current yield curve as the unchanged case, interest-rate cases should be evaluated on a scenario-by-scenario basis and not probability averaged.

Interest Rates: The Reinvestment Rate

During the holding period, the security will be throwing off cash flow. For an MBS, this cash will represent the interest and principal payments. Scenario analysis assumes that this cash will be reinvested at some rate until the horizon. Choosing this interest rate will be important as the length of the holding period increases or the interim cash flow increases. The choice of reinvestment rate will depend upon the degree of aggressiveness undertaken by the portfolio manager. A sample continuum of rates has been shown in Figure7-2.

Figure 7-2

Reinvestment Rate Assumption

The choice of the investment rate will be dependent on the reinvestment policy followed by the portfolio manager. If the investor wants to follow a more aggressive reinvestment strategy, such as reinvesting in a similar security, then that is fine. However, it is easy to hide some price risk when this method is chosen, as shown in the following example.

Scenario Analysis Legerdemain: Part I

Sometimes a user of scenario analysis will make the assumption that cash flows will be reinvested into a similar security and that the reinvestment returns the yield of the security. Sometimes this leads to an understatement of the price risk of the investment because the reinvestment is treated as a money market security.

Assume that we hold $100 of a par MBS yielding 6.5% and are looking at a 12-month holding return.   For argument's sake assume that the security pays $10 of principal over the year. Taking these assumptions a bit further, let's say that the dp/dy (a measure of price sensitivity discussed later in the chapter) of the MBS is 4. Is it reasonable to assume cash flows would be reinvested in a similar security yielding 6.5%? This depends on the way that the reinvestment is treated at the horizon.

At the end of 12 months, the entire investment is subject to price risk, including all the reinvested principal and interest. For example, our $10 of principal will only be worth $9.60 (ignoring the interest paid on principal) if yield rates rose 100 basis points. This is somewhat different than a traditional implementation of scenario analysis that treats the reinvestment rate as something of a money market investment. In this case the principal would be worth $10 in all scenarios (ignoring the interest earned). Many investors would like to purchase high-yielding bonds that have zero price risk, if they existed. The moral of the story goes back to the risk/reward tradeoff: If you want to take on more yield, you must be prepared for the risk.

■ CREATING SCENARIOS

By its name, the scenario-analysis method requires that we have some interest-rate scenarios to examine. Creating these scenarios follows three general patterns: parallel interest rate movements, nonparallel shifts, and paths of interest rates. Each method of creating scenarios is acceptable, the choice really depends upon the type of analysis being considered.

Parallel Shifts

Looking at parallel interest-rate movements is the most common choice for creating scenarios. Most historical interest-rate movements have a large component of parallel shifts. So it seems that this method has naturally evolved. An advantage of the parallel interest-rate movement scenarios is the ability they present to create probability-weighted scenarios. By assuming that the interest rates have a specific standard deviation, we can attach probabilities to the scenarios. Horizon returns can be weighted for each scenario to come up with an overall expected return.

The method for attaching the probabilities to the scenarios depends upon our choice for how the interest-rate changes are distributed, usually a choice of normal or log-normal distributions. Attaching probabilities to the scenarios is a rather mechanical process and is done by matching the interest-rate movement (put into some normalized basis) with a probability distribution table.

Nonparallel Shifts

The second method for creating scenarios involves the creation of nonparallel interest-rate movements. Looking at these types of scenarios has become more prevalent over the past few years because of several factors. First, between 1991 and the middle of 1993, the yield curve has been very positively sloped. Many investors have been concerned with the effect of a flattening yield curve on their holdings. This is because of the sensitivity MBS cash flows have shown to the changing shape of the yield curve. The growth of the balloon and intermediate MBS market has been tied to the steeper yield curve. A flattening curve would affect the prepayment rates and performance for 30 year securities.

In addition, MBS value has a rather intrinsic link to the yield curve. Because MBS cash flows occur on a monthly basis, the securities have price sensitivity as rates move along the entire curve. Even though the cash flows may not change, their value will change as the curve takes on a different shape. Using the nonparallel interest-rate movements gives us some way to measure the change in the shape of the curve on the security's value.

Within the MBS market, many securities have been created with coupons that depend upon short interest rates, namely floaters and inverse floating securities. The complicated nature of the inverse floating-rate security, which has a coupon driven by short-term rates and a prepayment rate driven mostly by longer rates, makes it vulnerable to a changing yield-curve shape.

In short, the nonparallel interest rates give us an understanding of how MBS value changes along with a yield curve that can move in a variety of directions. Implementing the method may be a bit difficult as it requires an accurate pricing method given the yield-curve shape. For some securities, it may be hard to infer how the market will value the security, given some change in the yield curve. Also, determining probability weights for the scenarios created assuming nonparallel shifts may be difficult. Scenarios must be looked at on a case-by-case basis.

Interest-Rate Paths

A third way to create interest scenarios is to both choose a range of interest-rate shifts and to specify the path by which we will get to the scenario. This method is very useful for MBS because of the dependency of cash flows on the path of interest rates. Sometimes this approach is called whipsaw analysis.

Perhaps the best way to illustrate this method is to give an example. Let us consider a set of scenarios that combine the parallel and path approaches. Suppose we have a base parallel movement of up 100 basis points. Around this base case we consider five paths, representing shifts from -200 basis points to +200 basis points over a six month period. Setting up paths of rates can be seen in Figure 7-3.

Figure 7-3

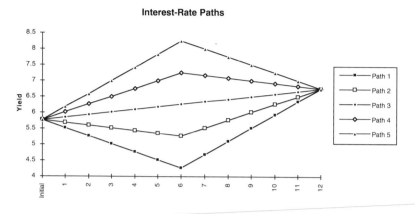

The figure shows that for any parallel shift we can attach a path of interest rates. In a sense, this method almost begins to converge on the option-adjusted spread model (as the horizon lengthens and the number of scenarios increases). Using the path approach, we can begin to understand the behavior of securities as interest rates follow different types of paths. We will explore the whipsaw analysis in greater depth in Chapter 10.

Rate Shifts: The Time Dimension

Once we establish the method to create interest-rate scenarios, we must determine the timeframe in which rates shift. Again, this part of the model lends itself to different approaches, none of which are entirely correct or incorrect. The two general ways to make interest rates move are to either have rates shift immediately or to have them move gradually.

The immediate method for shifting interest rates is simple and very easy to implement. Unfortunately, the approach deviates significantly from reality. Even in periods of unusually high volatility, we do not experience daily rate movements of several hundred basis points. Still, this approach is perhaps the most conservative because it accentuates the changes in rates.

As an alternative to the immediate rate-shift method, we can have the interest rates move gradually. This approach adds a more realistic approach to the manner in which interest rates move. The choice of timeframe is important. One well-accepted fashion is to allow the rates to move in a gradual manner over the entire holding period. That is, consider the typical 12-month scenario analysis. We would assume that the rate shifts would occur gradually over the 12-month period. So if we had a 100 total basis point shift scenario, the monthly shift would be 8.33 basis points. This is shown in Figure 7-4.

Figure 7-4

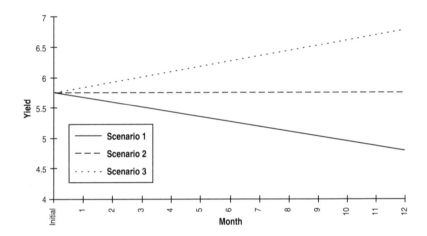

A variation on the gradual rate shift movement would be to let the rate shifts occur on a different time scale. Suppose we were looking at a five year horizon analysis. We could assume that interest rates have a general movement of 100 basis points per year. A gradual shift in the +200 basis point scenario would take two years, the +300 basis point shift scenario would take three years, and so on. This approach stretches out the length of rate shifts. Overall, this method would register the least impact on MBS as the slower gradual rate shifts lessen the changes in prepayment rates.

When comparing the immediate shifts with the gradual, we should recognize that immediate shifts put the MBS under maximum stress. If we have a 12-month scenario and interest rates shift immediately, then the full impact of the prepayment rates will be felt for the entire year.

This makes prepayment-sensitive securities look particularly bad on a total-return basis.

| Environment | **Prepayment** | **Cash Flow** | **Analysis** |

■ PREPAYMENT

Building the prepayments into scenario analysis gives some measure of the option-exposure risk. Changing prepayment rates will affect both the interim cash flows for the security and be factored into the valuation of the MBS at the end of the horizon. The two standard ways to address prepayments within scenario analysis are to use either a prepayment model or a static forecast.

Most scenario analyses use static prepayment rates. These rates will vary by scenario and will usually be expressed as some multiple of the PSA curve. The manner in which the rates are determined can range from the sophisticated (such as using a prepayment model), to the ad hoc (using prepayment rates based on a relative coupon basis). Still, the method allows one to see the prepayment rates that are used in each scenario.

The static measure ignores the time-series characteristics (such as aging and seasonality) of prepayments. In addition, the static forecast cannot properly address the prepayment dynamics of burnout. In a time period of especially high prepayment rates, the expectation would be for rates to decline from the burnout effect. Using a static rate would tend to ignore the burnout effect. On the other hand, trying to build the burnout effect into a static measure could be even more misleading. Suppose prepayment rates were expected to be at 1000 PSA for six months and then fall to 500 for the next six months. Using a static average 750 PSA would be quite inappropriate for a security like an IO. At the end of 12 months, we would have different balance amounts outstanding when comparing the vector approach with the static method.

The static forecast method can be adapted to the gradual rate shift scenario approach. Like the interest rates, prepayment rates would also move gradually. During the shifting period, rates would move from the unchanged scenario forecast to the specific scenario forecast.

A more precise manner to build prepayment assumptions into the scenario analysis method is to use prepayment rates derived from some prepayment model. This method fully builds in the dynamics of the interest-rate effect, aging, burnout, and seasonality. It also adds flexibility when considering the macroeconomic data affecting prepayments. For example, we may wish to change estimates for economic growth and the housing market strength depending upon the manner in which interest rates move. Alternatively, we could compare similar interest-rate scenarios but look at the implications of differing economic forecasts.

The disadvantage of using the prepayment model for scenario analysis is that the method becomes something of a black box. An investor may feel uncomfortable not being able to summarize the prepayment information in a single value. One way to get some understanding about the prepayment rates used in a particular scenario would be to come up with some measures for summarizing the vector of prepayment data into some comparable measure. Sometimes it may be informative to know the single PSA measure that gives the same weighted average life as the vector of prepayment rates. The weighted average life equivalent PSA measure is sometimes used as the static prepayment forecast for prepayment scenarios.

| Environment | Prepayment | Cash Flow | Analysis |

■ CASH FLOW

Interim Cash Flows

Once we get all of the preliminaries out of the way, we get to the heart of the matter: creating the cash flows for the security and the horizon value for the remaining principal. Once we have this information, nothing stands in the way of calculating the scenario total rate of return.

The total-return calculation can be summarized as follows:

$$\text{Total Return} = \frac{\text{Ending Cash}}{\text{Starting Cash}}$$

Ending Cash = Interest + Principal (amortized and prepaid)
+ Market Value of Remaining Principal
+ Reinvestment Income

We know the starting cash; it equals the market price of the security plus any accrued interest. The interim cash flows will be affected by the coupon of the underlying security and the prepayment rates. The higher the prepayment rates, the more the amount of principal returned, and the lower the interest income. These interim cash flows will thus depend upon the scenario and the associated prepayment rate.

Terminal Value: A Heuristic Approach

The terminal value equals the market value of each remaining dollar of principal. Total-return calculations will be very dependent on the terminal value because this usually represents the greatest component of the cash flows. Determining this value requires that we make some relative value assessment. Our method for coming up with the terminal value can be based upon methods that employ some heuristics or more technical option-pricing approaches.

The standard heuristic approach assumes that we can derive the terminal prices based upon some nominal spreads. To illustrate this approach, let's assume that we observe the following average life spreads[1] in the 30-year GNMA MBS market as shown in Table 7-2.

---

[1] The average life spread equals the yield of the MBS minus the yield of the Treasury with a similar average life. This average life is based upon taking the yield-to-maturity curve for the Treasury securities and interpolating the yield at different average lives.

Table 7-2

GNMA Coupon	Average Life Spread
6.5	83
7	87
7.5	90
8	99
8.5	119
9	129
9.5	147
10	143
10.5	138

At the time, the GNMA 7.5s were the current coupon. Therefore, the 6.5s were 100-basis-point discounts and 10s were 250-basis-point premiums. Knowing this, we can transform the nominal spread table into a relative spread function. This function can be seen in Figure 7-5.

Figure 7-5

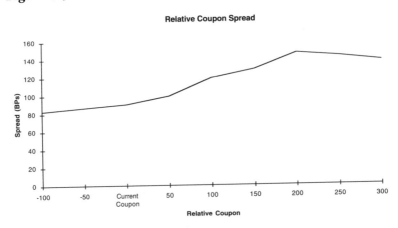

The graph of static spreads tells us how to price the security in different scenarios. Consider the case of analyzing the GNMA 7s. In an unchanged yield scenario, we would base the ending price upon a static yield of 87 basis points to the yield of a treasury with similar average life. In a scenario when interest rates fall 100 basis points, the GNMA 7s go from being a 50-basis-point discount security to being a 50-basis-point premium. In this scenario, we would price the security at a spread of 99 basis points. The additional spread is due to the increase in option risk for the security. On the other hand, as rates rise, spreads tighten, reflecting the decline in option risk.

The spread approach is a reasonable method for determining the terminal prices for investors who do not have sophisticated option models at their disposal. It represents how the market currently prices option risk into the securities. However, the method relies upon an implicit assumption that the characteristics of the relative coupon securities are somewhat similar. In the example above, the remaining term of the GNMA 9s may be significantly lower than that of the 7.5s. In an interest-rate scenario, when rates were to fall by 150 points, it may not be reasonable to use the spread on the seasoned GNMA 9s for the pricing of unseasoned 7.5s.

While shown for passthrough securities, the static spread method could also be applied to certain CMO products. Using the method in the manner described above, the implementation would require the grouping of similar securities together, such as PAC bonds. Functions could be determined based upon market prices and current spreads. The underlying collateral coupons would be noted so that we could determine what spreads to use across changing interest-rate scenarios. For example, we could use the spread on an 8 percent collateral PAC bond when determining the spread on a 7.5 percent PAC bond in a falling 50 basis point scenario.

In practice, implementing this method for CMOs may be somewhat problematic. Given the differences in deal structures may make the cross-deal comparisons somewhat difficult to apply on a consistent basis. Still, the method may form the basis for a more sophisticated matrix pricing method.

Terminal Value: An Options Approach

As an alternative to using a static-spread-based method for terminal pricing, one could employ a valuation model. Typically, the approach would be to use an option-adjusted spread (OAS) type pricing model to determine the value of the MBS in the different interest-rate scenarios. OAS modelling is described in Chapter 8. The horizon price would be based on an OAS calculated using the initial market value and yield curve. This spread would then be applied to each scenario and the model would be used in the mode where it solves for a price given a spread.

The constant OAS approach presents an analytically sound method for determining horizon prices. For various complicated derivative products, it may be the only reasonable way to determine the price. Relying on a trader's static spread for an inverse IO security may not be too reliable if the yield curve changes in some unusual manner. Despite its strengths, constant OAS has both technical and practical drawbacks.

On the technical side, the assumption of constant OAS suggests that relative value within the MBS market fixates around particular values for securities. Given the amount of time and effort expended on analyzing trading ideas and strategies, it would seem that relative value shifts around somewhat in the MBS market.

In addition, actual experience with constant OAS scenario analysis leads to cases where the numbers are analytically defensible but impractical. In certain cases of falling interest rates, the constant OAS pricing may suggest that certain CMO securities trade at prices significantly higher than traders would feel comfortable bidding for the bonds.

Instances such as this occur when examining PAC bonds during falling interest-rate scenarios. In scenarios when prepayment rates stay within the PAC band security, values would generally rise. Traders may feel very loath to start pricing PAC bonds above $105 even though the OAS model claims this to be fair value.

From the practical perspective, constant OAS pricing requires that we perform an OAS calculation for each scenario. For individual securities, this may present no problems. However, when applied to an entire portfolio, the required computer time may be too considerable compared with the benefit of the analysis.

These drawbacks are important but not sufficient to discredit the approach. Constant OAS provides a useful way to determine horizon values for all types of MBS products. Availability of resources may prove to be the limiting factor.

Environment	Prepayment	Cash Flow	Analysis

■ ANALYSIS

Scenario analysis provides a rich amount of information regarding the behavior of MBS. Our examination of the analysis section considers three areas: value, risk, and income. Each of these three areas provides some in-depth understanding of the ways that an MBS will behave in various interest-rate changes. A summary of the types of analysis we will examine is shown in Table 7-3.

Table 7-3

Value	Risk	Income
Expected Return	Return Profiles	Net Margin
Break-Even Analysis	Duration/Convexity	Cash-Flow Analysis

■ VALUE

Expected Return: Single Scenarios

First and foremost, scenario analysis provides some information regarding the economic viability of purchasing and holding some form of investment. Our basic return calculations assume that a security is purchased, held for some specific time period, and then sold at the end of the holding period.

The interest and principal received comprise the funds that flow to the investor during the holding period. Principal amounts include both the scheduled amortization and prepayments. All interim funds are assumed to be reinvested at some rate. Choosing the reinvestment rate represents a subjective decision, but a conservative approach would be to choose a short-term, low-risk money market rate.

While the total return represents the aggregate measure of value flowing through to the investor, each element of the return could be further itemized. That is, we could break the return into components by the source of funds. This would give us a return attributable to the interest, principal, and horizon pricing. Breaking the components of return down may give us some insight into the relative importance of assumptions regarding such issues as the prepayment rate or horizon price.

The horizon market value equals the ending price multiplied by the remaining balance. For MBS, this remaining balance will be less than the original balance due to amortization and prepayments. Methods for determining the price have been described above. In the examples that will follow, the OAS model has been used for our pricing source.

Reporting the return numbers will usually be stated in terms of bond-equivalent yields. The return calculations shown above would represent a simple annual return. This annual equivalent yield would be converted to the bond-equivalent yield using the following formula:

$$\text{BEY} = 200 \times \left(\sqrt{1 + \frac{\text{AEY}}{100}} - 1 \right)$$

Expected Return: Multiple Scenarios

The concept of expected return comprises the calculation of a probability weighted return across multiple interest-rate scenarios. This gives us a way to calibrate a measure of value when we are uncertain of the future course of interest rates. After calculating the expected return we could compare two securities to get some understanding of relative value.

Calculating the expected return is something of an extension of the single scenario return calculation. For the method of weighting scenarios, we must make some assumptions regarding the distribution of interest-rate changes. Standard approaches to the scenario analysis assume that interest-rate changes are either normally or log-normally distributed.[2]

Under the normal distribution, interest-rate movements of the same magnitude (in basis points) are assumed to be equally likely. That is, we would expect the probability of a downward shift of 100 *basis points* to equal the probability of an upward shift of 100 *basis points*. For the log-normal probability distribution, proportional changes are considered equally likely. That is, we would have the same probability of a 10 *percent* increase or a 10 *percent* decrease in rates.

Figure 7-6 contains probabilities for scenario shifts of up and down 150 basis points over a one-year period. A standard deviation of yield shift equaled 85 basis points, corresponding to a volatility of 15 percent.

Figure 7-6

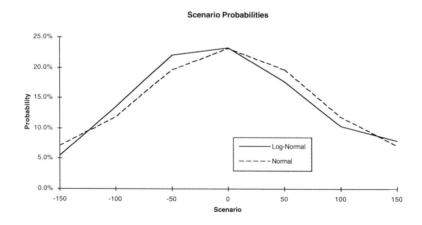

[2]Those interested in getting more information about the log-normal distribution can refer to *The Lognormal Distribution* by J. Aitchison and J.A.C. Brown, Cambridge University Press, 1966.

The normal distribution is symmetrical; for a given scenario the probability of rising and falling rates remains the same. For the log-normal distribution, the proportion of rising and falling interest rates remains the same. This leads to higher probabilities on the more extreme rising-rate scenarios.

In order to come up with the probabilities, we must make some assumptions regarding the volatility of interest-rate movements. This assumption will usually mean coming up with a measure for the standard deviation of interest-rate movements. For a normal distribution, our standard deviation will be measured in basis points, while for the log-normal distribution, the measurement will be made in percentage terms. Once we know the standard deviations, we can carve up the probability functions to get the percentages.

After we get the probabilities, the expected or averaged return is computed using the following formula:

$$\text{Expected Return} = \sum \text{Probability of i} \times \text{Total Return of i}$$

We should keep the measures in annual equivalent yield while doing the probability weighting in the expected-return calculation. After performing the calculation, the return should be converted from annual yield to bond-equivalent yield. The importance of following this procedure is illustrated in the example below.

Scenario Analysis Legerdemain: Part II

Suppose you are given $100 dollars and told that at the end of one year there was an equally likely payoff of $110 or $90. What would be your expected gain on the investment? The correct answer is $0 since the expected payoff is $100. However, misuse of the total return method could give you an errant result.

Suppose we look at our investment using the following tree:

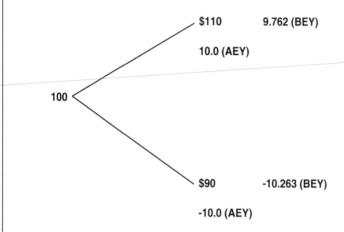

Based upon the probability weighting of the bond-equivalent returns, we expect to lose 0.24% on the investment! When looking at securities with very large negative and positive returns (such as IOs and POs), the discrepancies become even more glaring. Keeping the weighting done in terms of annual equivalent yield solves the problem of mis-calculating the expected return.

The Base Case Yield Curve

The choice of the base case scenario affects both the individual scenario returns and the expected return calculations. Standard approaches to scenario analysis would use either the implied forward curve or the current-yield curve as no change scenario at the horizon. To illustrate the implications of base case curve choice consider the yield curves in Figure 7-7:

Figure 7-7

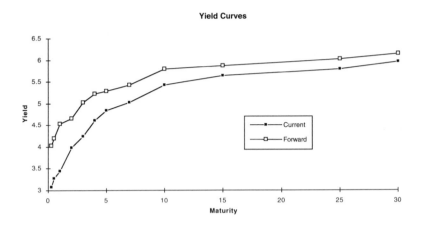

The current yield curve is steeply upward sloping, implying that the market expects rates to be higher in the future. Our forward yield curve is both higher and flatter than the current curve. The implications of the forward curve would be twofold. First, we would expect prices to be lower at the horizon than the current price given the higher yield curve. This is consistent with the drop in price seen in the forward MBS market. Secondly, during the holding period we would expect prepayments to slow as the curve drifts from its current levels to the forward rates.

For a current-coupon, conventional 30-year MBS, we would calculate the following returns under the two base case curve assumptions. These returns and horizon prices can be seen in Table 7-4.

Table 7-4a Total Returns (%): Forward Curve Base Case

Conventional Coupon	-200	-100	Base	+100	+200
6.5%	9.75	8.41	4.52	-0.69	-5.90
7.5%	7.12	6.32	4.92	1.67	-2.60
8.5%	6.70	5.84	4.87	2.74	-0.63

Table 7-4b Total Returns (%): Current Yield Curve Base Case

Conventional Coupon	-200	-100	Base	+100	+200
6.5%	10.07	9.38	6.44	1.23	-4.17
7.5%	7.48	6.73	5.83	3.24	-0.95
8.5%	6.80	5.89	5.10	4.09	2.15

The returns for the current curve are consistently higher than the forward curve, due primarily to the lower horizon prices. When coming up with an expected return, we can only legitimately use the forward case; otherwise we will be introducing arbitrage into the analysis. The effect of this arbitrage will be to make long duration securities appear very attractive on a total-return basis. It's okay to use the current curve as the base case as long as we do not try to compare the probability weighted returns.

In a no-arbitrage, unchanged world, we would expect the same one-year return across all Treasury securities. This rate would equal the current one year T-Bill yield. For a 30-year Treasury security our higher coupon income will be offset by the decline in price, with the price decline resulting from the higher horizon yield curve. If we were to assume that the yield curve would be unchanged, the 30-year security would have a return higher than other Treasuries. With the curve being very steep, the 30-year would have the highest coupon income. Its price would also increase due to the curve roll-down. (The effect of curve roll-down would be stronger for other securities with maturities occurring at steeper sections of the yield curve.) Based on a probability weighting in the current yield curve base case, the 30-year Treasury would usually appear to offer the best value in the Treasury market.

Break-Even Analysis

As a measure of relative value, we can compare the return on the MBS to the return on some benchmark security. In some cases, this benchmark may be the Treasury security with a maturity equal to the horizon.

So, in the case of a 12-month horizon, we would compare the return of the MBS to the one year T-Bill.

In most cases (unless the MBS is incredibly rich), the MBS will trade at some positive spread to the Treasury. As a measure of the relative value of the MBS, we could determine how much spreads would have to widen before the return on the MBS would equal the Treasury return. Knowledge of the implied spread widening would give some subjective understanding about how likely it would be that the security would underperform its benchmark.

Risk

The scenario-analysis method provides a wealth of information regarding the overall risk characteristics of an MBS. These measures of risk relate to either price variability or the timing of principal payments. One standard way to get some understanding about the risk characteristics would be to examine a graphical summary of key data. Depending upon the application of the information, this data could be examined using either an immediate curve-change assumption or a look at the horizon characteristics of the MBS.

The first form of risk measure is the total-return profile, as shown in Figure 7-8. This measure of risk shows how the returns vary by interest-rate scenario. We have included three securities, representing discount, slight-premium, and high-premium MBS.

The return profiles illustrate one of the key features an MBS possesses—the negative convexity. We see the returns begin to level off as interest rates continue to decline, even for the lower-coupon, 6.5 percent MBS. The effect of higher prepayments begins to put a drag on the amount of price appreciation.

Figure 7-8

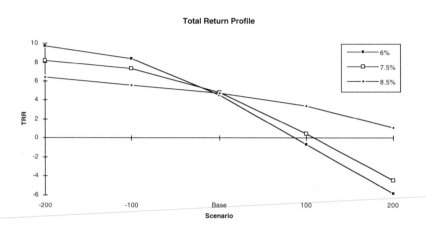

Total Return Profile

To follow this point, we can see our next measure of risk, the price profile. This profile looks at the horizon price for the security. In most applications of scenario analysis, the price return will be the largest component of the total return. Having an understanding of how the price behaves gives a lot of insight into the total return characteristics. We have plotted the price profiles in Figure 7-9 for some representative MBS.

Figure 7-9

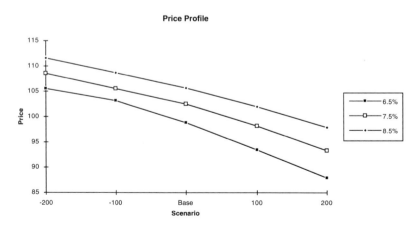

Price Profile

Again, we see the effects of the prepayment option. Price gains begin to really slow down for the 6.5 percent as interest rates decline past 100 basis points. From an investor's point of view, we can use the price profile to get an idea of how the MBS would behave in fairly large market moves. From these price profiles we can determine some summary information regarding the price sensitivity to interest-rate changes. These sensitivity measures, called effective duration and convexity, have been calculated and are displayed in Table 7-5.

Table 7-5

Bond Coupon	Effective Duration	Convexity
6.5%	4.962	-1.067
7.5%	3.597	-0.754
8.5%	3.179	-0.445

MBS Effective Duration and Convexity

From an MBS investor's perspective, duration and convexity reflect the relationship between parallel changes in the yield curve and price, recognizing that cash flows change with interest rates. The terminology in this area can be somewhat confusing; before laying out the mechanics of MBS duration we need to define some concepts. Once we review the essentials of duration we can look at convexity, which measures the change in duration.

Macaulay duration: This measure comes in two units, years and percentage price changes. When expressed in years, the Macaulay duration equals the time-weighted present value of all cash flows. Macaulay duration can also be shown to be equal to the percentage change in price for a percentage change in yield. For a security with unchanging cash flows, the two measurements will be equal. Because of this assumption, Macaulay duration has little relevance to MBS.

Modified duration: The percentage change in price for a basis point change in yield. Modified duration can be calculated with a simple adjustment to the Macaulay duration calculation. This measurement also assumes that the cash flows for a security do not change with interest rates.

Effective duration: The percentage change in price for a basis point change in yield. This sounds like modified duration, however, cash flows are allowed to change with interest rates. Sometimes this measure is called effective modified duration. Calling the duration effective implies the option component has been recognized. The **dP/dY** measure is very similar to the duration, only it examines the actual change in price for a basis point change in yield.

Using this perspective, effective duration will be the standard tool for MBS risk analysis. Calculating an effective duration requires some of the tools of scenario analysis. We have to determine how the MBS price changes in differing interest-rate scenarios. This concept of interest rate scenarios can be seen from the effective duration formula:

$$\text{Effective Duration} = \frac{\text{Price}_{-\Delta\text{Yield}} - \text{Price}_{+\Delta\text{Yield}}}{2 \times (\Delta\text{Yield}) \times \text{Price}_{\text{Base}}}$$

In the formula, we start from a base case price and then look at an interest-rate shift up and down. The size of the shift is called ΔYield and should be large enough to cause some change in the prepayment rates. Generally we consider changes of 25 basis points or greater.

For each of the scenarios, we allow prepayments to change and will reprice the securities at the new yield levels. The calculation of scenario prices can be made depending on the tools available. If you have access to an OAS model then the MBS could be analyzed by shifting the yield curve and then repricing the security using the OAS from the base case. The result of this approach is sometimes called the OAS effective duration.

For those without access to an OAS model, a simple bond calculator can be used to get a value for effective duration. For each scenario, a revised prepayment forecast and static pricing spread should be used to calculate the price. Approaches to pricing spreads could use some of the methods we have described earlier for terminal scenario prices.

To illustrate the calculation of effective duration we can use information from the price profile graph. Looking at the 7.5% MBS in the up and down 100-basis-point scenarios, we would calculate effective duration as follows:

Given

ΔYield=.01

$Price_{-\Delta Yield}$=105.58

$Price_{+\Delta Yield}$=98.21

$Price_{Base}$=102.44 ˙

$$\text{Effective Duration} = \frac{105.58 - 98.21}{2 \times (.01) \times 102.44}$$

$$= 3.597$$

The effective duration implies that we would expect prices to change by 3.597% for a 100-basis-point change in interest rates. This interpretation assumes that duration does not change, that is convexity equals zero. However, for MBS, the interest-rate sensitivity does change and so to fully understand the interest-rate sensitivity, we must also consider convexity.

Convexity measures the change in duration, making it equal to the change in the change in price. This is known as a second order term, reflecting the curvature of the price profile graph. Unlike duration, it is a bit harder to get an intuitive feel for convexity, still we can draw some conclusions based on the sign of the convexity term.

From a formula perspective, convexity can be measured as follows:

$$\frac{Price_{-\Delta Yield} + Price_{+\Delta Yield} - 2 \times Price_{Base}}{100 \times (\Delta Yield^2) \times Price_{Base}}$$

Using the same data for the 7.5% MBS, we would calculate the effective convexity as follows:

$$Effective\ Convexity = \frac{105.58 + 98.21 - 2 \times 102.44}{100 \times 0.0001 \times 102.44}$$

$$= -1.064$$

Most MBS are negatively convex. This would imply that as yields decline so does the duration. When yields rise, duration extends. These undesirable results present both an opportunity and a risk to investors. The opportunity stems from the yield premium the investor demands for holding a security with these attributes. The risk stems from the difficulty in measuring the duration drift and in determining the proper yield premium.

We can use the duration and convexity measures when calculating the approximate change in price for a change in yield. For a given change in yield ($\Delta Yield$) the price change would be given by the following formula:

Percentage Change in Price = (Duration $\times$ $\Delta Yield$) + [0.5 $\times$ (Convexity $\times$ $\Delta Yield^2$)] $\times$ 100

When applying the formula, we usually use the negative of the duration. Yield and price have inverse relations to another for nearly all MBS but by convention we report durations as positive numbers. The formula indicates that for a negative convex security, price increases will be limited in falling-rate scenarios while price declines will be exacerbated in rising-rate cases.

Returning to the 7.5% MBS, the approximate change in price for a 200-basis-point decline in rates (ΔYield = 0.02) would equal:

$$\text{Percentage Change in Price} = [3.597 \times 0.02 + 0.5 \times -1.064 \times 0.02^2] \times 100$$
$$= [0.05066] \times 100$$
$$= 5.066$$

From our price profile (Figure 7-9) we had a base price of $102.44 and a down-200 scenario price of $108.51. The calculated price equals $102.44 $\times$ 1.05066 = $107.629. Using the duration and convexity, we were able to fit the price to within 88 cents of the actual price. Our ability to fit the price depends upon the degree by which duration and convexity describe the function between price and yield.

Cash-Flow Timing

Besides information regarding the total return and pricing characteristics, we can use the scenario-analysis method to look at how changing interest rates affect the timing of MBS cash flows. No doubt, cash-flow variability is directly related to the pricing and return characteristics. By looking at how the cash flows change, we can develop some intuitions about the reasons for the pricing and return sensitivity. Continuing with our investigation of MBS, we have plotted the weighted average life profile in Figure 7-10.

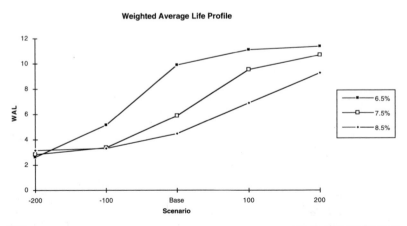

Weighted Average Life Profile

Figure 7-10

The chart of average life shows the overall shortening and extension of our investment as interest rates change. For the different coupons, we see that the average life behaves somewhat differently, reflecting some of the nuances related to burnout. As we move to the more extreme scenarios, the effects of extension and call risk lead the average lives to converge.

Another way to look at the cash-flow profile of the securities would be to examine the terminal PSA profile. The terminal PSA is determined by taking the vector of CPRs from the horizon to the remaining term and calculating the weighted average life. Then we use a numerical procedure to solve for the equivalent PSA rate, which gives the equivalent average life. A comparison of the PSA rates can be seen in Figure 7-11.

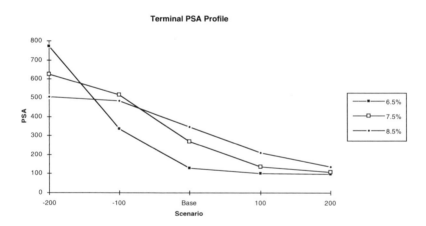

Terminal PSA Profile

Figure 7-11

Examination of the PSA graph tells us how the prepayment model directly influences the security during different interest-rate environments. While important to understanding how the security's value would be affected by an interest-rate movement, the PSA speeds also provide some insight into the sensitivity of the prepayment model. This adds to our interpretation of looking at the price sensitivity across different interest rates.

Income

Most of our measures of value have concentrated on comparing the final amount of cash to the initial amount and solving for some growth rate that equates the two. There are other ways to look at measures of income under the scenario-analysis approach. These alternative measures reflect the ways in which we may attribute income based upon capital and funding characteristics. Many financial institutions require that investments provide a defined level of income. Income may relate to cash flow, performance relative to a benchmark, or accounting-based income measures.

One way to calibrate our returns would be to move away from total return as an absolute measure and to put it upon some relative basis. That is, we could take the total return number on our investment and compare it the some benchmark, perhaps a Treasury security or some index. For depository institutions, the benchmark may reflect the over-all cost of funds. The general calculation would go as follows:

Net Return Margin = Return on MBS - Return on Benchmark

This measure gives us some idea about how much the MBS outperforms its benchmark. We could look at this measure based upon the probability-weighted total returns or through examination of individual scenario returns. Looking at the individual scenarios would give some information about the times we would expect our potential investment to out or underperform its benchmark.

Other ways of examining the total return would be to consider the return based upon some funding characteristics. For instance, particular depository institutions must place different levels of capital for various types of MBS investments. Instead of taking our net return margin based upon some benchmark, we could consider the total return relative to some cost of capital. Such measures could include the total return expressed as a return on equity. A calculation such as this may work as follows:

$$(\text{MBS Total Return} - \text{Funding Cost})/\text{Equity Employed}$$

In this type of measure, our funding cost could depend upon the MBS being examined. That is, we may match the duration of the funding to the duration of the MBS. The equity would depend upon either the regulatory guidelines or whatever firm policy may be regarding the equity levels for particular investments.

One last way of measuring the income within the scenario analysis framework would be to put the cash flows on some sort of accounting basis. Cash flows estimated across scenarios could be used to derive income statements for the investor. This type of analysis is useful when we must consider an entire portfolio of holdings. By aggregating cash flows we can come up with larger scale measures of portfolio accounting income.

■ CONCLUSION

Scenario analysis extends our range of analytical techniques to consider the performance of MBS as we vary the environment. The method provides significant flexibility to consider a variety of interest-rate movements. These range from instantaneous-parallel-rate movements to setting up paths of interest rates. When applying the model, we retain control over numerous options about the reality and complexity of the analysis.

Scenario analysis creates information regarding the expected total rate of return from holding MBS and various risk profiles. These risk profiles can help us to understand how well a particular security will perform relative to a portfolio or investment objective. Likewise, the method could be used for an entire portfolio to determine the overall risk and return profile.

Unfortunately, the scenario-analysis method is limited by the range and simplicity of scenarios we consider. The method of generating scenarios, in order to develop risk and return measures for MBS, has been extended further to the use of simulation techniques, known as the option-adjusted spread model. In the next chapter, we consider this method and its usefulness for analyzing MBS.

CHAPTER EIGHT

■

Option Adjusted Spread

■

"The client says he can only buy the PAC bond if it can give him an OAS of 65 or better," says the salesman to the trader. So the trader thinks for a moment about all of the assumptions that go into the OAS model. The bond is only giving an OAS of 63, only two more basis points and the bond is sold. "Maybe," he muses, "that volatility assumption is too high or maybe the prepayment model is too fast." Jiggering the assumptions a bit gets the OAS to 65 basis points, and the sale is made. The investor is not only purchasing a security, he is also buying into a set of assumptions. Likewise, the trader is selling the bond packaged around a set of assumptions.

Perhaps the worst thing an investor can do is buy a bond solely on the basis of its option adjusted spread (OAS). After working with these models since 1987, we can safely say that few analytical techniques are as abused as the OAS technology. This being said, OAS models provide a very useful way to understand the relative option cost and expected spread of complicated MBS.

OAS models extend from the scenario-analysis framework of the environment. Instead of confining the analysis to consider only a limited number of interest-rate scenarios, the OAS approach hopes to understand the relative value and risk of a security by considering its average performance over a wide number of future scenarios. The number of scenarios that we consider using will depend upon the degree of accuracy required by the analysis.

The critical piece of the OAS model will be the prepayment function. Most models used by Wall Street dealers will be roughly similar in their approach for simulating interest rates. However, OAS results across dealers will usually not be the same. Differences in prepayment models are the primary reason for the differences in OAS results.

In our investigation into OAS technology, we will continue to apply the general framework of examining the environment, prepayments, cash flows, and analyses. A brief overview of the matters considered in this chapter can be seen in Table 8-1. Our investigation of the OAS technology considers the manner in which the models are both developed and used.

Table 8-1

Environment	Prepayments	Cash Flow	Analysis
• Interest-rate simulation	• Information flows	• Relationship between	• Spread measures
• Volatility	• Economic data	borrowers and investors	• Value measures
• Mean reversion		• Combinations of pools	

The interest-rate environments will have a direct relationship to the prepayment models; so it is important to understand the way future interest rates will be simulated. We will also examine the analysis component of OAS models in some depth because of the abundance of information generated by the models. Usually, most of the information is discarded in the search to determine the proper spread. We have found, though, that much of this information can be organized and reported in ways that provide additional insight into the understanding of securities risk and value.

Throughout this chapter, we will be making use of a simple OAS model to illustrate the construction and application of the approach. This modeling process follows the standard approach used by most dealer models. At one time, these models could only be run on very powerful computers. With the advent of more powerful personal computers and work stations, the distribution of these models has become wider, making it easier for many investors to contemplate having their own OAS-type model. This chapter should address some of the issues that a developer of these models is likely to encounter.

■ OAS MODEL PROCESS

The approaches used in creating OAS models do not differ much from dealer to dealer, although you would not know this by comparing results. The general flow of the modeling process can be seen in Figure 8-1. In the process, the interest-rate simulation leads to the prepayment calculation, which then gives the cash flow. Calculating the OAS comes after all of the cash flows have been simulated.

Figure 8-1

OAS PROCESS

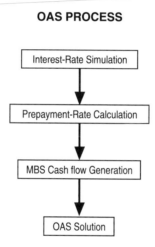

The OAS calculation represents the average spread to the Treasury curve measured across all of the simulated cash-flow trials. We discount each path of cash flows by the simulated Treasury rates to get a present value for the path. If these cash flows were discounted flat to Treasury rates, the present value would be higher than the market price. We must add some spread to the Treasury rates in order to get the MBS present value lower. The OAS model calculates what spread must be added so that the present value averaged across all of the simulation trials equals the current market price. This spread represents the additional yield an investor expects from the MBS net of the option component.

The notion of averaging has important implications for users of OAS models. An average represents some summary measure for a distribution of results. In some cases it becomes important to have additional information about the distribution. Likewise, it would be useful to know how sensitive the average is to some of the assumptions made in the modeling process. Issues such as these will be considered in greater detail in the analysis section of this chapter.

Environment	Prepayment	Cash Flow	Analysis

■ OAS: THE ENVIRONMENT

The primary insight that OAS models provide the investor is a sense of the expected behavior of a security over a wide range of potential interest-rate movements. The manner in which these scenarios are created goes by the technical term of a Monte Carlo Simulation. Rather than prespecifying a set of scenarios, we rely upon the computer to randomly select scenarios. In our investigation of the environment, we will examine the types of rates that will be simulated, the importance of the volatility assumptions, the role of mean reversion, and the use of alternatives to the traditional Monte Carlo interest-rate process.

Interest-Rate Simulation

Example Box: A Simple Simulation Model

A straight-forward OAS simulator can be built off of a single interest-rate simulation. This simulation process contains a term for mean reversion, which is described further in the chapter. The formula for simulating the short interest rates is as follows:

$$R_t = R_{t-1} + (F_t - F_{t-1}) + k * (F_{t-1} - R_{t-1}) + R_{t-1} * S * z$$

In the simple simulation model the variables are represented as follows:

R_t - the simulated variable for period t

F_t - The expected forward rate for period t based upon the initial term structure

F_{t-1} - The expected forward rate for period t-1 based upon the initial term structure

k - The speed of the mean reversion process.

S - The standard deviation of interest-rate movements, initially calibrated as a percentage of the interest rate

z - A normalized random variable generated by the computer

The random variables have a mean of 0 and a variance of 1.

The process bases the current simulation for a period on the previous rate plus the expected change in the rates due to the term structure. The difference between the previous period's simulated rate and the expected forward rate is used to push the simulated rates back to the expected forward rates. When the previous simulated rate falls below the expected forward rate, the mean reversion pushes the rate up. In the other cases when the simulated rate is above the expected forward rate, the mean reversion term pushes the rate down.

The last term of the simulation equation adds the random variable shock to the process. The size of the random shock is determined by the standard deviation of the rate movements, the size of the previous random rate, and the random number. In cases where the rates increase, the size of the random shock will also increase given the same simulated random number. This occurs because the size of the random shock is proportional to the level of interest rates.

When the volatility of the simulation model equals zero (that is S equals zero), the process follows along the expected forward rates. Because there is no random shock, the mean reversion term will have no value and the only change from period to period will be the change implied based upon the change in the forward rates.

Variables

The types of variables that we simulate in the OAS model will be determined by two factors: the rates that we need to generate MBS cash flows and the rate we need to use in discounting the cash flows. When generating the MBS cash flows, we must send some interest rate levels into the prepayment model. Within the past few years, most prepayment models have been extended to consider both the long end (usually considered to be the 10-year Treasury) and short end of the yield curve. The addition, the shorter part of the yield, reflects the growth in the origination of balloon MBS.

As with our general approach to developing analytics, we stress that the proper variables to use in the simulation process should reflect the needs of the model. There is little to gain by overspecifying the simulation process to include other variables, which have no bearing on the determinates of cash flows for the underlying securities. However, we need flexibility when creating the simulated interest rates. There may be cases, such as the application of Monte Carlo techniques to ARMs, when we need to simulate different variables than those used in the fixed-rate MBS valuation approach. In our investigation of the OAS model, we will use variables related to the very short end of the yield curve, an intermediate Treasury rate, and a long Treasury rate.

The choice of variables may also be driven by the manner in which interest calculations are done for the securities. If we are pricing some sort of floating-rate product, it would be useful to simulate a variable related to the index used to set the coupon payment. This variable may have no bearing on the actual prepayment model. For example, we may be trying to determine the OAS of a CMO floater security-which is indexed to the seven-year Treasury. Our normal OAS calculation would need to know the short, intermediate, and long rates. Now we must add another variable to the simulate process, the seven-year Treasury. This adds further complication to the model but does not make the valuation process impossible.

Volatility

The primary motivation for using OAS-type models is the multiplicity of scenarios that they create. This dispersion of interest rates throughout the scenarios can be calibrated by the volatility of interest rates. Raising our volatility assumption in the model makes us more likely to sample random numbers further from zero. This increases our likelihood of large interest-rate fluctuations.

For most option-pricing models, volatility is quoted as the standard deviation of interest-rate movements. It is usually expressed as an annualized percentage number. If the current interest-rate level was five percent and interest-rate volatility was ten percent, then the standard deviation of annual interest rate movements would be 50 basis points.

From our simple simulation example above, we can consider the volatility as the S term. Raising the volatility increases the size of the interest-rate shock; lowering the volatility decreases the size of the shock. As an analogy, think about the random sampling process as if it were based upon drawing a set of balls out of a barrel, with each ball having a value. On average, the value of the balls will be zero, as negative values cancel out the positive values. Increasing the volatility leads us to draw higher and higher value balls out of the barrel, but the average value will still be zero.

To see the effect of volatility on simulated interest rates, let's look at some that show the effect of different volatilities. Figure 8-2 contains ten sample OAS simulation trials based upon a ten percent interest-rate volatility, while Figure 8-3 contains a similar number of simulation trials but based upon 20 percent interest-rate volatility.

Figure 8-2

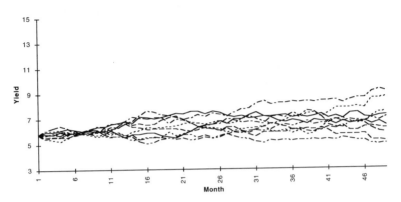

Simulation Paths At 10% Volatility

Figure 8-3

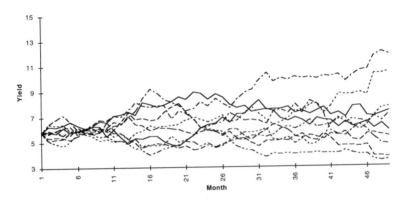

Simulation Paths At 20% Volatility

Comparing the paths in Figures 8-2 and 8-3 gives some perspective on the effect of increasing the volatility. Going back to the simulation example from before, it is useful to point out that the actual random variables (the z term) do not change between the two graphs. It is only after multiplying by the standard deviation that we get some difference between the paths.

In the context of an OAS model, increased volatility makes the prepayment option more valuable. With more volatility, we give greater likelihood to cases when interest rates fall sufficiently in order to make the refinancing option come into the money. The effect of volatility will differ across products, but will usually be greatest for securities with extreme prepayment exposure, such as IOs and POs.

Mean Reversion

Many analysts believe that in a well-defined interest-rate process, interest rates should not get "too high" or "too low." That is, although our simulation process may allow for interest rates to rise to very high levels or fall to next to nothing, experience suggests that persistent deviations of interest rates from historical ranges are not realistic. This notion of interest rates returning to long-term averages goes by the name of mean reversion in the analytic jargon.

Within the confines of most OAS models, mean reversion has the effect of pushing the simulated rates closer to the implied forward rates based upon the initial term structure. Another way to implement the mean reversion feature is to push the rates toward some long-term averages. Under both approaches the outcome is similar—the simulated interest rates show less dispersion. In effect, this decreases the volatility over time.

To illustrate the effects of mean reversion, let's compare some OAS simulation paths. In Figure 8-4, we have generated 10 sample OAS paths based upon 25 percent volatility and no mean reversion. Figure 8-5 contains similar paths at 25 percent volatility but with mean reversion. The strength of the mean reversion term in Figure 8-5 pushes rates back to the forward rates at a speed of 60 months. That is, deviations between the simulated rates and the implied forwards are expected to converge over five years. The choice of reversion speeds for this example is arbitrary.

Figure 8-4

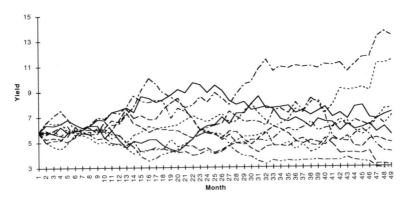

Simulation Paths at 25% Volatility

Figure 8-5

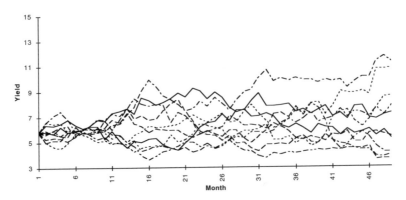

Simulation Paths At 25% Volatility With Mean Reversion

Between the two figures, we see that mean reversion essentially pushes the rates closer together. This decreases the swings in interest rates, which is the same as decreasing volatility. To further develop this notion of decreased volatility, consider a quick statistical analysis of the standard deviation of interest rates based upon three OAS simulations.

These three cases consider situations of no reversion along with two levels of reversion. In the moderate case, rates revert over a ten year period, while the strong-case rates revert over five years. The statistic we examine will be the dispersion of interest rates, which we term the

Mean Reversion

volatility shown in Table 8-2. Volatility measurements for simulations are drawn at several time periods to show the effects of mean reversion as we move farther into the future.

Table 8-2 Short Term Interest Rate Volatility

Reversion Level	2 Years	5 Years	10 Years	15 Years	20 Years	25 Years
None	21.1%	25%	24%	24.3%	16.1%	16.5%
Moderate	19.4	20.8	16.4	14.3	10.1	9.5
Strong	17.9	17.4	12	10.2	7.6	4.8

Our starting volatility measure in all the simulations was 25 percent. In the no reversion case, we see that volatility holds fairly close to our starting assumption until we move out past 15 years. We may regard the two-year measure as something of a statistical anomaly. In the past 15 years, the effects of the interest-rate ceiling and floor put something of a damper on the dispersion of rates, effectively reducing the volatility.

When we add mean reversion, our measures of volatility decline. Under a moderate case of reversion, we reduce the volatility to 16.4 percent by the end of ten years. With stronger reversion, the volatility gets cut almost in half by year 10, when we record a standard deviation of 12 percent.

As indicated by Table 8-2, mean reversion leads to a significant decline in the standard deviation of interest-rate dispersions. This makes the prepayment option significantly less valuable as we move through time. For products such as IOs, the use of mean reversion has a material effect on the OAS results. To demonstrate this, we have analyzed the change in OAS when considering the moderate and strong mean-reversion cases in Figure 8-6.

Figure 8-6

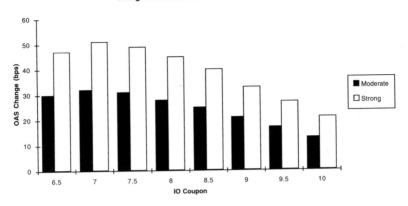

Change In OAS Due to Mean Reversion

The bar chart indicates that the addition of mean reversion has a noticeable effect on the OAS for IOs. Because the mean reversion reduces volatility, OAS increases for the IOs. IOs represent one of the more extreme cases of mean reversion effects. The effect on the underlying passthroughs would be only a few basis points.

The use of mean reversion in models is not universally accepted and to some modelers it remains an unsettled topic. Not all Wall Street dealers use mean reversion in their OAS models, adding to confusion when trying to compare results across different houses.

Mean reversion began to be used when OAS models were first developed and applied to ARMs (adjustable-rate mortgages). One of the considerations for modeling ARMs is the valuation of the periodic interest rate caps. Actual pricing in the cap market applies lower volatility to longer dated caps than shorter caps. This would imply that we should use lower volatility as we move farther out into the future. One way to get this lower volatility is through the adaptation of mean reversion. The degree or strength of the mean reversion term can sometimes be inferred by either finding the level that reproduces the current volatility structure based upon the cap market or by finding the level that accurately reprices caps (which is very similar to the other procedure).

The decision to use mean reversion in an OAS-based model really depends upon the scope of the problem being examined. If the securities

Mean Reversion

being analyzed have underlying option characteristics, which follow some process where volatility changes over time, the application of mean reversion seems appropriate, and perhaps even necessary to preserve the analytical integrity of the options-based analysis. On the other hand, using mean reversion for nontime dependent options really adds little to the analysis, and may really lead to some confusion over interpreting the results.

Simulation Framework

Within the OAS methodology, there are two general ways to create the simulated rates. The first way allows the simulated rates to be created in a somewhat unrestricted manner. This is similar to the way the simulation works in the example above. Using this method, some restrictions can still be put on the rates. These restrictions may include certain floors and ceilings, which may represent reasonable ranges. The idea of reasonableness can be relative and should be reviewed from time to time.

Controlling a Random Process

Traders can sometimes have a love/hate relationship with analytical models, especially OAS. The OAS technology gives the user many potential knobs by which they can adjust or fine tune the process. To the sophisticated user, this may present opportunities by which an unsuspecting investor could be convinced that dross is gold.

One former trading colleague became incensed with the low rates being created along certain OAS simulation trials. He felt that interest rates could never get this "low." Since we were looking at MBS, the low rates made his prepayment-sensitive products look especially unattractive. He was especially concerned in cases when the rates fell to below 3 percent and insisted on a version of the model that would never let rates go below 3 percent. In the summer of 1992, the Federal Reserve lowered short-term interest rates to below 3 percent. Confronting reality, he gave in and permitted us to restore the model to its proper condition. Although he did exclaim that rates would never go above 9 percent again!

Another way to create the simulated rates is to use a more controlled environment. In some implementations of the model, the paths of interest rates are created by sampling rates from an interest-rate tree. Interest-rate trees are used extensively in the analysis of callable corporate securities. Some interest-rate trees are binomial, that is interest rates can only fall or rise at each successive period. Other interest-rate trees can be constructed as a trinomial process. With a trinomial process, interest rates are allowed to move in one of three potential directions, usually modeled as moving up, staying the same, and moving down.

To provide some illustration about the use of interest-rate trees to create interest-rate paths, consider the trees in Figure 8-7 and 8-8. The first tree contains rates that follow a binomial process with 15 percent volatility. At each time period, rates either rise or fall, with the movement of rates equal to the volatility times the starting rate.

Figure 8-7 Binomial Tree, 15% Volatility

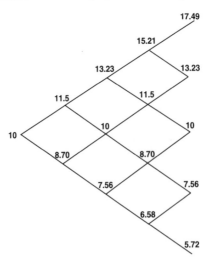

The second tree contains a general trinomial process in which the central rates stay the same. Under other implementations of the trinomial process, there can be other properties for the central path. In some cases, it could be gradually increasing, reflecting the upward drift of rates due to higher expected forward yields.

Figure 8-8 General Trinomial Tree

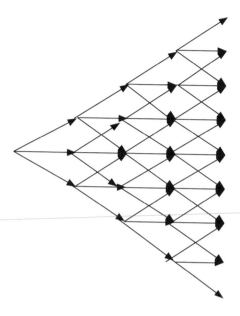

Rate paths can be sampled through the trees in an uncontrolled fashion or using more systematic approaches. One way of setting up the simulation process in an uncontrolled fashion would be to use a uniform random number generator to decide if we should move up or down at each point in the tree. A uniform random generator produces results between 0 and 1 with equal probability. For any draws above 0.5 we would move up, draws 0.5 or below would cause us to move down.

One of the drawbacks of the uncontrolled simulation may be that we need a large number of paths in order to get statistically meaningful results. Methods to reduce the number of trials while maintaining the proper level of statistical significance have been implemented in an OAS context.[1] Methods that provide a proper sampling of rates also have extensions to the application of OAS models for scenario analysis.

A primary advantage of the interest-rate-tree approach is that it provides some consistency with scenario-analysis approaches for valuation. OAS

---

[1] One method to determine a proper sampling procedure for rates is the Linear Path Space method developed by Tom Ho. The method has been developed in "Managing Illiquid Bonds and the Linear Path Space," *The Journal of Fixed Income*, 2,1 (June 1992), 80-94.

pricing methods can be set up to calculate long-term spread measures that are similar to the methods used to calculate holding period returns.

| Environment | **Prepayment** | Cash Flow | Analysis |

■ PREPAYMENT RATES

Within the context of the OAS modeling framework, the prepayment model represents the most important element and primary source of difference between OAS models. When projecting prepayment rates, the prepayment model must consider various types of information related to both the underlying information about the mortgage security and the state of the world. By state of the world, we are referring to the behavior of the overall economy and, in particular, the housing markets. The user of the model has some important decisions to make about the way the state of the world is considered. In many cases, details about this information, which can be quite material when considering very prepayment-sensitive securities, do not find their way into the hands of the investor.

Information flows into and out of the prepayment function along a process depicted in Figure 8-9. The basic MBS information includes standard data regarding the vital statistics of the MBS pool. The economic information includes data regarding the environmental factors affecting prepayments. There is some feedback within this process; the prepayment rate will be used to update the pool factor.

Our sources of input to the prepayment model can be categorized along three categories: intrinsic MBS data, information about the environment, and other data. The other data will include information about the month because MBS prepayments contain a seasonal component. We may allow additional information to flow into the model.

Figure 8-9

Flow of Information Into Prepayment Model

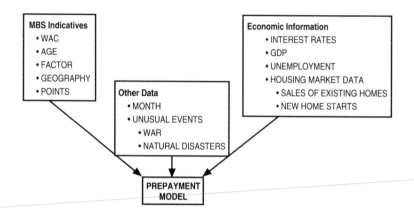

Prepayments will be affected by unpredictable events. For example, the time period between the U.S. buildup of military forces in the Persian Gulf and the resulting war lead to declines in prepayment rates—generally attributable to borrower uncertainty. In addition, natural disasters, such as Hurricane Andrew or the Great Midwestern Flood of 1993, affect prepayments. Depending upon the type of security we are analyzing, we may want to control for these effects when fitting or applying the model.

Unfortunately, data analysis shows that economic factors other than interest rates play a role in the understanding of prepayment rates. We use the term unfortunate because projecting or modeling prepayments requires that we must make some assumptions regarding various macroeconomic variables. Time and history have demonstrated that projections of the economy are invariably wrong, sometimes very much off the mark.

This leaves OAS users a choice with a limited upside. On the one hand, they could ignore the fact that macroeconomic factors play a role in prepayment rates. Ignoring the truth is likely to lead to some unfortunate results when projecting prepayments. For example, does it sound reasonable to ignore the implications of an economic boom when interest rates are rising? Or, is it sensible to ignore the implications of a housing recession in the midst of low interest rates? On the other hand, making assumptions regarding the macroeconomic levels is bound to be incorrect. Still, it may be realistic to be within the ballpark when projecting some economic information, especially over short periods of time.

Filtering the economic information into the OAS model can be done in two ways: exogenous assumptions, which flow from the user; or endogenous functions, which can be driven off the simulation. The exogenous assumptions are separate from the modeling process, they simply reflect one's outlook about the economic state of the world regardless of the interest-rate levels or cycles. On the other side, there are the endogenous functions, which can be directly tied to the simulation process. When we want to tie our simulation process with the economic variables (the endogenous method), we would follow the process in Figure 8-10.

Figure 8-10

Simulating the Economic Information

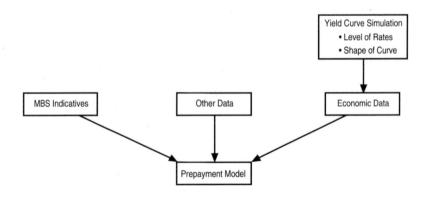

Our assumptions regarding the strength of the economy can be determined from a model that predicts GDP given a historical series of long- and short-term yields. Housing market strength can also be modeled as a function of interest rates. By developing these models, we can begin to understand some of the complex interactions between the shape of the yield curve, the path of interest rates, and prepayment rates.

Creating these functions requires some effort and expertise in the world of econometric modeling. Furthermore, there is little or no guarantee that the model will do well in the future. One of the major problems with using these types of functions for the long-term option modeling embedded in the OAS framework is the limited role that innovation and changing economic structures plays. We have no real way of knowing how the economy will change going into the future.

These macroeconomic functions could be set up as either perfect forecasting tools or combined with some stochastic elements. That is, we could add some randomness to the projections. This randomness could depend upon the overall strength of the model fit and would serve as a tacit admission of our inability to perfectly see and predict the future. The drawback of adding the stochastic element is the additional interest-rate paths, which must be run.

The advantages and disadvantages of using the two approaches for making economic projections are summarized in Table 8-3.

Table 8-3

Exogenous Economic Assumptions:
Determine Economic Levels Outside of the OAS Model

Advantages
- Simple approach, can be used when making short-term forecasts.
- User has complete control of the information, no unintended results.

Disadvantages
- Decouples the link between interest rates and economic behavior. Implies that economic performance is unrelated to interest rates.
- Can lead to situations when the consumer of OAS information receives output based upon unknown and highly subjective projections.

Endogenous Functions:
Determine Economic Variables Using Simulation and Statistical Models

Advantages
- Captures the relationship between interest rates and various economic information. Preserves the relationship between interest rates and prepayment rates.
- Allows for analyzing subtle inter-relationships between variables.

Disadvantages
- Time and effort related to data gathering and modeling.
- Modeling is somewhat imperfect, cannot capture effects exactly.
- No assurance that relationships which held in the past will persist.

Environment	Prepayment	Cash Flow	Analysis

■ GENERATING CASH FLOWS

Determining the cash flows within the OAS model requires some decisions to be made by the model user. Calculating the cash flows for a mortgage is a rather mechanical procedure; another exercise in mortgage math. However, some assumptions must be made when determining how to create the cash flows from combinations of mortgage pools, especially combinations, which contain passthroughs with different characteristics.

The cash-flow process starts with the payments made by the borrowers and then flows through to the payments received by the investors. The

OAS model will capture the payments made to the investors and the model will segregate the cash depending upon the type of security being valued. This process has been illustrated in Figure 8-11.

Figure 8-11

CASH-FLOW PROCESS

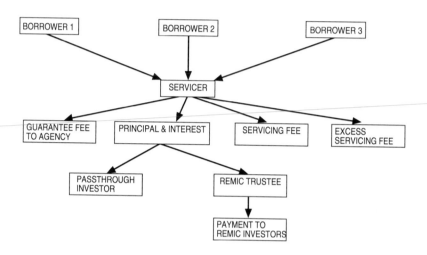

Timing of Cash Flows

The cash-flow step requires that we know the underlying information about the mortgage pool and the prepayment rate. From the discussion above, the prepayment rate will be the output of some prepayment model. Most OAS models work with a monthly time step, consistent with the timing of mortgage cash flows.

In most implementations of OAS models, cash flows are assumed to occur at some arbitrary date in the month, sometimes the last business day. This is a simplifying assumption, ignoring the actual disbursement of cash flows. For most implementations, this simplifying assumption really has little bearing. It does ignore, though, that the different agencies disperse cash on different days in the month.[2]

---

[2] The impact of differing cash-flow dispersal dates for FNMA and FHLMC securities has been examined by J. Luytjes and G. Lauher of FHLMC in an internal working paper, "A Sumptuous Feast of Crow." Their analysis shows that the 10 day difference between Gold PC and MBS payments can be decomposed into the pure delay factor and the call protection factor.

For resource-constrained modelers, there is a practice to lengthen the time step for MBS cash flows. That is, the model may be set up to run on a quarterly or semiannual basis. In some cases, this simplification may be justified, but it may not be acceptable when looking at very prepayment-sensitive securities. In cases when interest rates decline, the prepayment model will spike up, keeping prepayments high over an extended period of time. This may tend to decrease the effect of burnout on prepayments. The burnout effect would imply that even if interest rates were to remain constant, the prepayment rates would decline. A consistent bias against prepayment-sensitive securities could result.

Pool Level Indicatives

Creating the cash flows may appear to be a trivial calculation, which it is. However, there are some subtle issues that give the user of an OAS model some flexibility over the level of detail to embed in the model. One of these issues is the creation of indicatives for the pool. One approach would be to take the information regarding the WAC, age, and WAM as the single descriptors of the loans in the pools. This approach is used in most implementations of the model.

Another approach is to use additional information about the pools. The pools can be broken down into groups of loans based on the dispersion of WAC and WAM. For pools that have wide dispersions of loans, this further level of detail may be a more accurate way of anticipating the prepayment rates. To calculate an OAS, the cash flows must be simulated for each type of loan, combined, then valued as a single security. This approach increases the processing time but may be useful, or necessary, depending upon the security being analyzed or application of the model.

Considerations for Combinations of Pools

In the same way that a single pool can be valued using average characteristics or by using more detailed information, groups of pools can be analyzed at different levels of detail. REMICs are comprised of pools, each having differing characteristics about the underlying loans. When creating cash flows, some models average the characteristics of the underlying pools, creating a single set of indicatives. This method has the simplicity of running a single set of cash flows, but ignores the reality of differing underlying characteristics.

In some ways this treatment of average characteristics versus the more detailed treatment of underlying pool data may appear to be a dry exercise in semantics. But let's consider an analogy. Suppose we wanted to project the demand for some consumer item, like Lexus automobiles. Would we be more interested in information about average income or in the dispersion of income? An analysis of average income may tell us little about the ability of the general public to afford the car. However, looking at the distribution of incomes would give us some insight into the wealth of the individuals to whom the car should be marketed.

There are four things that we can do when simulating CMO cash flows within an OAS model: (1) ignore the diversity of information about the pools; (2) make some adjustment calculations; (3) run a subset of the cash flows; (4) run a full set of cash flows. As with other issues related to model building, the approach one takes depends upon the level of detail needed by the model user.

When valuing a CMO using a single set of characteristics, some approximations can be made to reduce the biases of the underlying diversity. The approach in Figure 8-12 can be employed for model users who do not wish to run large amounts of cash flows but who need a fairly accurate valuation.

The difference in the prices from steps 1 and 2 above shed some light on the potential problems from using a single set of cash flows. Depending upon the price difference, one may want to use more detailed cash-flow analysis when valuing CMOs.

Figure 8-12

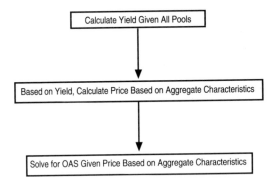

Simulating the Economic Information

For other CMO cash-flow methods, we only need to apply the same approach as described in the single-pool analysis. If we want to use information about the range of pools, then we can group the pools across various WAC, age, and WAM dimensions and then create the cash flows. The cash flows can then be combined and the security valued. Three different ways to group the information can be seen in Figure 8-13.

Figure 8-13

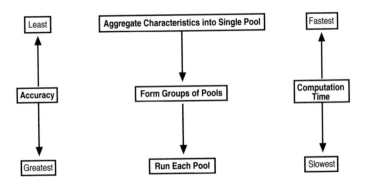

Pool Grouping Hierarchy

In most cases, information about the OAS for both passthroughs and CMOs is probably run based upon the single set of characteristics. Running the OAS at this level of detail is probably adequate. However, when undertaking more detailed risk analysis, it may be useful to use more information about the pools.

Environment	Prepayment	Cash Flow	Analysis

■ ANALYSIS
Value

The OAS represents the expected spread to the US Treasury yield curve. This expectation is determined over a large number of interest rate scenarios; the world may take many twists and turns, but the OAS is our best guess of the benefit of owning the security over the range of outcomes.

To calculate the OAS, we take all of the simulated cash flows and determine a present value along each path of interest rates. We will have the same number of present values as simulation trials. The present values are averaged and compared to the market price. If we were discounting the cash flows at no spread to Treasuries, then the average present value would probably exceed the market price for the security. When calculating the OAS, we must determine what constant spread we should add to the simulated rates so that the average present value equals the market price. The solution procedure is:

$$\text{Average Present Value} = \frac{1}{\text{NPath}} \sum_{P=1}^{\text{NPath}} \sum_{M=1}^{\text{WAM}} \frac{\text{Cash Flows}_{M, P}}{\prod_{I=1}^{M} (1 + \text{Simulated Rate}_{M,P} + \text{OAS})}$$

Our solution procedure leads us to calculate a present value across each of the simulation paths. Within each path we must determine the present value by finding the discounted cash flows of the security. Our discounting is done by taking a product of the simulated short-term interest rates for each period M and path P and adding the OAS.

Does this mean that we expect to earn the OAS no matter what? No. Our interest-rate simulation model considers numerous changes in the yield curve. An MBS will have a different value in each of the simulation trials. Consider the case when we are valuing an interest only (IO) security. The OAS represents the average spread to the curve over a range of possible interest-rate scenarios. In cases when interest rates fall, the present value will decline dramatically from the market price. The true economic value realized from the investment will be below the current market value.

Solving for the price given the OAS of the security represents a slight inversion of the above described procedure. We simulate the cash flows and then determine a present value for each path using the interest rates plus the OAS. Our value equals the average of all the present values across the simulation trials.[3]

There are a few side issues related to the calculation of OAS and value. The OAS is usually quoted in terms of semiannual bond-equivalent yield (although not all dealers may quote it using this day count). With the model working on a monthly time step the actual spread calculated is based on monthly compounding. For reporting purposes, the OAS found in the solution procedure would be converted to a semiannual yield equivalent.

The second issue is the price used in the OAS calculation. With the current standard being to use accrued interest in the calculation of yield, it would be consistent to use the full price when calculating the OAS. When solving for price given in the OAS (which includes the effect of accrued interest), we must subtract the accrued interest from the average present value calculated by the model.

Risk Measures

Besides being used as a valuation tool, the OAS model serves as a good vehicle for analyzing the risk of MBS. When we use the OAS to measure

---

[3]This may sound a bit obvious, but a good check on any OAS model is to ensure that you get back the starting price, given an OAS that you calculate.

risk, we usually follow the calculation of price given OAS approach. This process has been summarized in Figure 8-14.

Figure 8-14

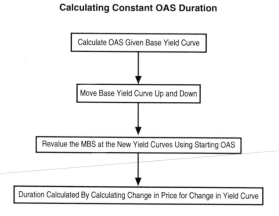

Calculating Constant OAS Duration

This procedure can be used for most standard risk calculations, such as duration and convexity in the same way as described in the previous chapter. Other procedures to measure the sensitivity nonparallel yield curve shifts can follow the same process. These risk measures will be examined more fully later in the book.

Other Considerations

There are other technical factors to consider when running OAS calculations. These relate to the overall efficiency of the model. Most users of OAS models must make some trade-offs regarding the need for timely calculations and the overall accuracy of the model.

Because of the averaging procedures, the accuracy of our results will be related to the quality of the simulation process and the number of paths. When we average the present values of the MBS along the interest-rate simulation paths, we get both an average and a standard error of the mean. From a statistical perspective, this measures whether we have truly captured the mean of the distribution.

The standard error of the mean depends upon the square root of the number of simulation trials.[4] In order to reduce the standard error substantially, we must increase the number of simulation trials dramatically. In practice, we need to balance the accuracy demanded by the application of the model with the time needed to run the analysis. To give some idea about the relationship between standard error and number of paths, consider Figure 8-15.

Figure 8-15

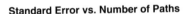

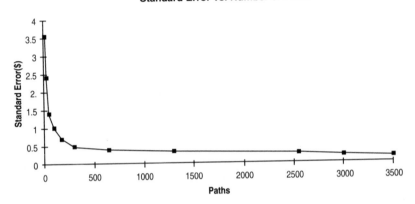

The standard error begins to drop off dramatically as we move above several hundred paths. Once we get beyond 1,000 paths, however, the declines in standard error get much smaller. This reflects the nonlinear relationship between sample size and standard error.

To put the standard error discussion into perspective, let's try to relate it to an expected range for OAS. If, for example, our average present value was $100 and the standard error of the mean was $0.03, we would consider the OAS result to have an accuracy, for two standard deviations, to within six cents of the price. To put this in basis point terms, let's assume that for our security, the value of a basis point was $0.06. If our average present value was accurate for two standard deviations, to $0.06, then our OAS would be accurate to one basis point. In

---

[4]Formally speaking, the standard error of the mean equals the standard deviation of sample divided by the square root of the number of observations.

Other Considerations

practice, we may not demand that our OAS model be more accurate than the bid/ask spread of the security.

■ CONCLUSION

The OAS model builds on the process of constructing interest-rate scenarios to measure the performance of MBS. By using simulation technology we can consider the responsiveness of MBS under a wide range of interest-rate movements. The primary objective of the model is to estimate the expected spread of the MBS to the Treasury curve net of the embedded options cost. We can also use the model for calculating various MBS risk measures, such as duration and convexity.

Unlike an option model such as the Black-Sholes pricing model, OAS results will vary from implementation to implementation. When an investor looks to get an OAS for a bond, it is highly likely that two investment firms will give differing levels. The primary source for difference between implementations is the prepayment function contained within the OAS procedure. An OAS model will only be as effective as the underlying prepayment model.

The OAS model is adaptable to a wide range of MBS, making a good general tool for use in analyzing securities. In the next chapter, we examine some of the core relationships contained within the OAS model: the relationship between MBS cash flows and the yield curve. In later chapters, we will try to exploit some of the information generated in the process of calculating an OAS. This information will look to tie the OAS method with the concepts of scenario analysis.

CHAPTER NINE

■

The Yield Curve

■

Over the years, we interviewed many MBA candidates for internships. One question was bound to stump them during the interview process. In response to the question, "What would happen to the value of the ten year Treasury if yields on the short end of the spot curve declined?" Most respondents would hesitate a moment, think it over, and say something about the value remaining the same. They would be basing valuation on the yield to maturity. Occasionally, a student would say something like, "the value would go up, because the early cash flows get discounted at lower rates." These candidates would generally get a job offer.

Understanding the interrelationship between the yield curve and MBS value adds a new dimension to the analysis of MBS. All fixed-income securities are, to some degree, affected by changes to the yield curve, generally through the discounting of cash flows. MBS are a special case because not only does the yield curve affect the value of the cash flows, but the amounts of cash paid to the investor depend upon the yield curve. Changes in the cash flow amounts come from the prepayment function, which will depend both on the level of yields and the shape of the yield curve.

Our analysis of the yield curve will follow the plan used throughout our investigation of MBS. A synopsis of the chapter can be seen in Table 9-1.

Table 9-1 Chapter Overview

Environment	Prepayment	Cash Flows	Analysis
• Curve shape	• Level of curve	• Interest payments	• Value
• Spot/zero-coupon rates	• Affect of forward rates	• Principal amortization	• Risk
• Forward rates	• Shape of curve		• Income

Within the environment section, we will be looking at our understanding of the yield curve. This will briefly review the relationship between the yield-to-maturity curve, the zero-coupon curve, and forward rates. In doing this, we will see how different shapes of the yield-to-maturity curve lead to different implications for forward yields.

Our understanding of the yield curve begins to be important for MBS when we consider the relationship between the yield curve and prepayment rates. We will discuss the implications for MBS prepayment rates. This level of understanding is very important for those investors who rely upon OAS models for assessments of relative value. After the prepayment section, we consider the implications of the yield curve on MBS cashflows. Our investigation will consider both the interest and principal paid to investors.

The last section will involve the relationship between the yield curve and analysis of MBS. Our considerations will include measuring value, which involves the calculation of a spread to the Treasury curve. Then we move on to risk measures. Our investigation will look at ways of measuring MBS risk to the entire yield curve and to selected portions of the curve. The discussion will finish with some thoughts on how the yield curve affects income measures.

Environment	Prepayment	Cash Flow	Analysis

■ ENVIRONMENT

The yield curve is a focal point of attention for fixed-income investors. The curve provides critical information about how to value cash flows received in the future. It also includes the market's expectations for the future course of interest rates. These expectations do not come from the crystal ball of any high-priced economist. Rather they are determined almost for free by using some mathematical calculations.[1] You may wind up paying the economist to tell you why the actual future yields will diverge from the forward rates.

The expectations for future interest rates are commonly known as forward rates. These are the rates that the market today expects to occur in the future. Does this mean that rates in the future will actually behave according to the current implied forward rates? No, but the rates do contain information about how we would price cash flows today. For example, if we know the two-year spot rate and one-year spot rate, we can determine what the implied one-year rate would be in one year. This rate would be determined so that an investor would be indifferent between making a single two-year investment or a series of two one-year investments.

Before going directly into the forward rates, we need to build a foundation about the yield curve. To do so, we will explain the types of yield-curve shapes an investor is likely to encounter. From this, we will see the relationship between the yield-to-maturity curve and the zero-coupon/spot curve.

Curve Shape and Zero-Coupon Rates

The yield curve traditionally comes in three shapes: positively sloped, flat, and inverted. Throughout the 1980s and 1990s, investors have had to deal with all of these types of curves. The differing shapes have very different impacts on MBS. Just so there is a common understanding of the yield-curve shapes, they are graphed in Figure 9-1.

---

[1] Some of the more detailed information about the yield curve can be found in Chapter 4.

Figure 9-1

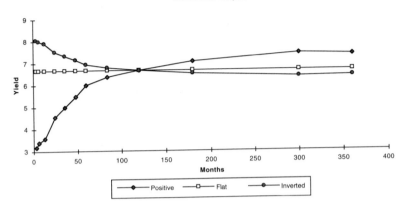

Yield Curve Shapes

The typical determination of the yield-curve shape is to look at the relationship between short-term rates and long-term rates. In the inverted or negatively sloped curve, short-term rates are actually higher than longer-term rates. This type of yield curve shape is unusual and is one of the worst yield-curve environments for banks and Wall Street dealers. These types of institutions usually find themselves with long positions in securities financed by short-term borrowings.

The yield curves we saw in Figure 9-1 were taken from the yields to maturity quoted for the bonds. This is the standard way in which yields will be communicated to the market. For valuation purposes we need to know about the spot or zero-coupon curve.[2] To value a security based upon the spot rates, we would use the Formula 9-1:[3]

Formula 9-1 Valuing Cash Flows Using Spot Rates:

$$\text{Present Value} = \sum_{t=1}^{T} \frac{\text{Cash Flows}^t}{(1 + S)^t}$$

---

[2] We use the terms spot, strip, and zero-coupon rates interchangeably.
[3] It is essential that the time step be on the same frequency as the compounding interval for the interest rates.

Curve Shape and Zero-Coupon Rates

In the formula, we discount each cash flow by the spot rate associated with that period. In other words, the cash flow we receive in year 10 is discounted by the 10-year spot rate. This method of valuation is quite different than the typical method of discounting the cash flows by the yield to maturity. In Formula 9-2, we use a single yield to find the present value of all the cash flows. In other words, we assume that all cash received will be invested at the same rate.

Formula 9-2 Valuing Cash Flows Using Yield to Maturity:

$$\text{Present Value} = \sum_{t=1}^{T} \frac{\text{Cash Flows}^t}{(1 + \text{yield})^t}$$

Assuming that all cash flows are reinvested at the same yield is a rather unrealistic expectation. The only time this occurs is when the yield curve is flat. The yield to maturity method also provides no insight regarding the change in value as the yield curve changes shape. On the other hand, using the spot rates to value fixed-income securities gives us a very convenient way to know how changes in the yield curve affect the price of securities.

Using some mathematical manipulations, we can calculate spot rates from the yield-to-maturity curve for Treasuries. One method to derive the spot curve is to take the yield-to-maturity curve for the on-the-run Treasuries. Prices of the Treasuries would be set to par and the bonds would have coupons equal to the current yield. Using a series of linear equations, we can solve for the vector of discount rates, which correctly prices the bonds with their cash flows. This method is sometimes called bootstrapping.

Regardless of the method we use, we will get the same present value for the cash flows. That is, the bond prices we determine using the spot-rate discount equals the prices derived from the yield-to-maturity basis. The Treasury strips trading desks of Wall Street dealers ensure efficiency between the coupon-bearing Treasury bond/note markets and the strip markets.

Other methods to solve for the spot curve involve opening the data sample up to more Treasuries. For example, prices and yields could be collected for all Treasury notes, including the callable issues (assuming you had access to a reasonable callable bond model) and then some nonlinear function could be fitted through the points. This nonlinear curve goes by the technical term of a spline function. This spline function represents the best fit of yields to maturities. Using this yield-to-maturity curve, we could follow the bootstrapping method to derive the spot curve.

In order to see the relationship between the yield-to-maturity curve and the spot curve, we have computed the corresponding spot curve for our positively sloped and inverted yield curves. The yield to maturity and spot curves for the positively sloped case can be seen in Figure 9-2.

Figure 9-2

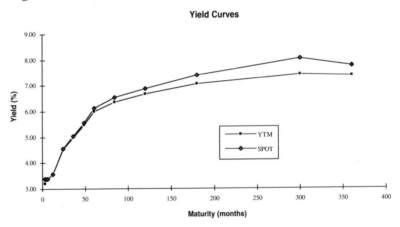

For the early maturities, the yield-to-maturity rates and zero-coupon rates lie nearly on top of each other. This is true by definition for the three-, six-, and twelve-month sections of the curve. As we move past the five-year section of the figure, the spot curve begins to exceed the yield-to-maturity curve. By the last section of the curve, we see that yields for the 30-year-zero-coupon Treasury are noticeably higher than the yield of the 30-year-coupon-bearing bond.

This theoretical information is in line with actual market data as shown in Table 9-2. To see this, let's look at some representative yields to maturities for on-the-run Treasuries and some Treasury Strips. The data is taken from quotes as of June 17,1993.[4]

Table 9-2

Maturity (years)	Yield to Maturity (%)	Yield of Coupon Strip (%)
2	4.02	3.98
5	5.14	5.20
7	5.53	5.86
10	5.95	6.33
30	6.80	6.92

To understand why the zero-coupon yields fall above the yield-to-maturity curve for the longer-maturity Treasuries, we need to go back to our pricing equation for finding the present value of a bond based on the zero-coupon rates. For the longer Treasuries, we will be discounting each coupon payment by the spot rate corresponding to the payment date of the cash. For our early cash flows, we will be discounting the coupon payments by rates significantly lower than the yield-to-maturity of the bond. To compensate for the lower initial discount rates, our longer maturity, zero-coupon yields must exceed the yield-to-maturity rates.

Taking this explanation a bit further, consider the data in Table 9-2. For the 30-year Treasury, we will be discounting the coupon payment that we receive in two years by the zero-coupon yield of approximately 3.98 percent, the coupon rate we get in month 60 will be discounted by 5.20 percent. In order to get the same present value as discounting the cash flows by the yield to maturity, our zero-coupon rates must start to exceed the yield-to-maturities. For the inverted yield curve case shown in Figure 9-3, we see a slightly different relationship between the yield to maturity and zero-coupon curve.

---

[4]The yields were taken from the *Wall Street Journal* June 17, 1993, which used Bear, Stearns & Co. for its closing Treasury information.

Figure 9-3

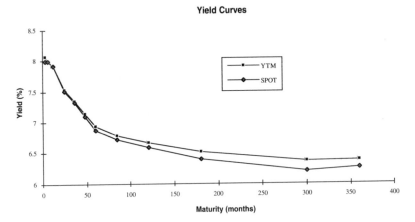

Yield Curves

In the case of the inverted yield curve, the longer-term spot rates fall below the yield-to-maturity rates. The rationale for this is the opposite of our previous case. Now we discount earlier coupon payments by zero-coupon rates well in excess of the yield to maturities. In order to compensate for the longer cash flows, the zero-coupon rates must fall below the yields to maturity.

Does our comparison of yield-to-maturity curves and spot curves suggest that strips look cheap in case of a positively sloped curve and rich in the case of an inverted yield curve ? Not really. Even though the yields of similar maturity strips and coupon-bearing Treasury curves may differ, we are not really comparing securities of the same riskiness. For comparable maturities, the strips have duration and convexity characteristics that differ from the coupon bearing securities. We would expect the market to trade these duration and convexity differences at dissimilar yields. As a result, we cannot make a definitive relative value statement simply by comparing the yields of Treasury instruments with similar maturities.[5]

---

[5]An interesting discussion of the relationship between yield, duration, and convexity can be found in "The Yield Surface," by Stanley Diller as published in *Fixed Income Analytics*, Ravi Dattatreya, editor, Probus Publishing, 1991.

Curve Shape and Zero-Coupon Rates

Forward Rates

Using the information embedded in the spot rates, we can make some determinations about the market's implied course of future interest rates. We use the term forward rates to refer to the mathematically implied rates that the current yield curve suggests. As we have mentioned in many cases before, the forward rate will not be the actual rate that prevails in the future, these rates will be determined by the multitude of factors affecting supply and demand for fixed-income securities across different maturities.

Forward rates refer to future market interest rates implied by the current term structure. For example, if we wanted to know the ten year rate that the market expects to prevail in one year, we need to know two rates: the current one-year zero-coupon rate and the current 11-year zero-coupon rate. The implied forward 10 year (which we will denote by $_1F_{10}$, corresponding to the 10-year rate 1 year forward) would be one rate that satisfies Formula 9-3.

Formula 9-3

$$(1+R_1) \times (1+ {_1F_{10}})^{10} = (1+R_{11})^{11}$$

In Formula 9-3, we find the rate that ensures that we could price a forward interest-rate commitment, which does not create the opportunity for riskless profits (arbitrage). As evidenced by such markets as the eurodollar futures and the over-the-counter market for forward rate agreements, the market does actually use forward rates to price financial contracts.

Moving back to our consideration of MBS, we need to concern ourselves with two perspectives on forward rates. First, we will need to develop some forward yield curves when looking at the scenario analysis approach to risk and valuation. Secondly, forward rate assumptions will form a critical basis when applying OAS-type models.

Nearly all prepayment models consider a long-term Treasury rate to forecast MBS prepayment rates and many models also use a shorter-term

Treasury rate. In the framework of an OAS model, the simulations will be centered around the implied forward paths of the short- and long-term Treasury rates. In cases when the yield curve is not flat, we should look at the implied forward rates to understand the valuation process.

To give some idea of how we can use the yield curve in scenario analysis, we just extend the forward rate example from above. Instead of only calculating a 10-year rate one year forward, we calculate forward rates for all of our key points of the yield curve. Figure 9-4 contains the implied forward yield curves for 12 and 24 month horizons.

Figure 9-4

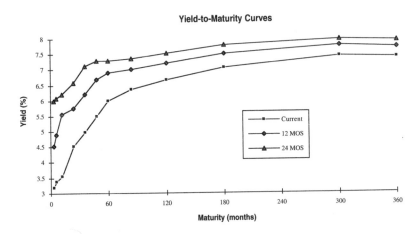

One additional consideration must be made. In determining the forward rates in the manner described above, we are calculating forward zero-coupon rates. For scenario analysis pricing approaches, which rely upon some static spread to the yield-to-maturity curve, we must convert the zero-coupon yields back into yield to maturities. This mathematical manipulation reverses the bootstrapping method we had discussed previously.

From our graph we see that the upward-sloping curve implies future yield curves that are both higher in terms of absolute yield and flatter in terms of slope. This may lead to slower prepayment rates, extending the average lives of the securities. The flatter slope would also have an effect on prepayment rates, to the degree that any model is tied to the slope of the curve.

In the context of the OAS model, we really do not care so much for the entire curve as we do for the points on the curve we use for simulation purposes. The usual simulators will consider a short-term rate for discounting as well as a short-term Treasury and a long-term Treasury. Based upon our upward sloping curve from above, we would get the following implied two- and 10-year rates as seen in Figure 9-5.

Figure 9-5

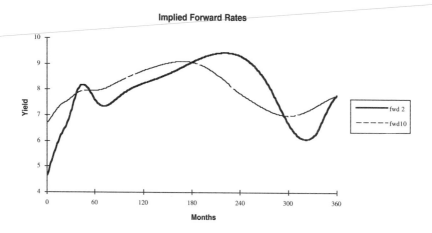

As with our previous case, our yields are expressed in terms of the yield-to-maturity rates and not the zero-coupon rates. From the figure, we see that the 10-year rate is expected to rise for approximately 15 years and then will fall gradually. This effect is due to the current shape of the yield curve between 20 and 30 years (as seen from the previous figure).

The two-year rate is expected to rise more sharply than the 10-year. Before year five, we would expect the yield curve to become inverted, the two-year rate would be higher than the ten-year rate. Past month 60, the curve would become positively sloped again, until we get to the period between years 15 and 25. Again, this is a byproduct of the inversion in our starting yield curve.

▣ PREPAYMENT

Our analysis of prepayments consistently indicates that the most influential component remains the level of rates. When using advanced pricing models such as OAS models, we rely upon the implied forward rates to set up the underlying prepayment characteristics—this would encompass both the level of rates and the shape of the curve.

Does our dependence on forward rates mean that we become slaves to the theory ? Not at all. Throughout the early 1990s, many MBS investors consistently made money by betting against the forward rates through the purchase of inverse floating-rate bonds. When priced to the implied forward rates, many of these securities would have had expected yields significantly less than the double-digit figures often reported. However, the curve did not flatten as called for by the forward rates and investors were handsomely rewarded.

On the other hand, some investors lost money, relying too much on the forward-rate expectations. In particular, holders of interest only securities suffered very large losses during the bond-market rallies of 1992. Many investors maintained their positions, while others moved into the market because of the high reported OAS levels for the securities. Much of the OAS level was being determined by the higher forward rates and the implications for a slow down in prepayment rates. The higher forward rates did not materialize, neither did the prepayment rates slow down commence.[6]

To get some idea about the effect of forward rates on prepayment expectations, let's consider the upward sloping yield curve previously presented. Using this curve, we can project the prepayment rates for some 30-year MBS. Our prepayment model projects the prepayment rates on a monthly basis. Trying to scrutinize this monthly series is a somewhat difficult task. To make the interpretation easier, we can convert

---

[6]This market was also fundamentally altered by the increased use of low and no point loans for refinancing.

the monthly time series information into a single summary measure, an equivalent PSA.

Using the equivalent PSA method, we solve for a single prepayment speed, which gives us the same value of some descriptive statistic as the vector of speeds. By descriptive statistic, we refer to measures such as the average life or yield. Our analysis looks at the single PSA, which gives us the same average life as the vector of prepayment speeds. Some analysts look at the single PSA, which gives the same yield as the time series of speeds. This equivalent measure is acceptable, but it is not always reliable. For bonds trading near par, it may be hard to find an equivalent PSA, because the yield becomes almost insensitive to prepayment assumptions.

Taking this notion of equivalent PSA, we have projected the prepayment forecasts for the reference collateral, as seen in Table 9-3. In addition to the prepayment speeds, information about the average life is also shown.

Table 9-3

Relative Coupon	PSA (%)		Average Life (Yrs)	
	Current Curve	Forward Curve	Current Curve	Forward Curve
-150	92	88	11.5	11.7
-100	101	91	11.1	11.7
-50	125	97	10.1	11.5
0	182	109	8.1	11.0
+50	296	134	5.6	9.8
+100	437	194	3.9	7.6
+150	573	313	3.0	5.2

Our information in the table is indexed relative to the current coupon security. Discounts are denoted by the minus sign and premiums by the plus. From the table, we see that the implications for the forward curve are strongest for the current coupon and premium securities. The premiums exhibit extreme slowdowns in PSA speeds using an assumption of forward rates. This stems from our higher two- and ten-year rates implied by the upward sloping yield curve (refer to Figure 9-5 to see the baseline assumption for the two and ten year).

Another way of seeing the impact of our yield curve assumption on pre-payment speeds is to look at the average life for the securities. For the premiums, we see that the average lives extend dramatically when using the forward rate assumption. The discounts show little change in average life. Their prepayment expectations are already low, rising rates only decrease the prepayment expectations marginally.

Is this discussion of forward rates just an academic exercise? Not really, if you use information about the OAS in determining the relative value for a security. When you consider the implications of the forward rate assumption, certain MBS may be analyzed based on much lower pre-payment expectations than you would expect if you felt that the current yield curve were to persist in the future.

| Environment | Prepayment | Cash Flow | Analysis |

■ CASH FLOW

The relationship between the yield curve and cash flows is pretty straightforward for most fixed-rate MBS. Our cash flows will be derived by the prepayment-rate assumptions being made. Thus, depending upon whether we project out our cash flows at the current yield curve or some other curve assumption, the cash flows will vary.

For MBS, which do not have a fixed coupon, the choice of yield-curve assumption will play a large role in the projection of future cash flows. For CMO floaters, inverse floaters, and ARMs, we will get very different results depending upon our expectations for the yield curve. In an upward sloping yield curve, we would expect short-term rates to rise, leading to increases in coupon income (as well as an extension in the average life from the prepayment slowdown).

When dealing with ARMs, the higher-forward rates could make the periodic caps restrictive on the overall coupon flow. Likewise, for ARMs, which have coupons set off the Cost of Funds Index (COFI), the projection model would be driven by whatever assumptions we plan to make about the yield curve. Again, using the forward rates would lead to very different cash flow expectations than using another yield-curve assumption.

In some applications, the choice of the yield curve to use does not have to be a restrictive choice between the current rates or the forward implied rates. At times, you may want to see how sensitive the cash flows are to some medium between the two. That is, for someone looking at a floater or inverse floater, cash flows could be projected based upon current rates, forward rates, and some multiple of forward rates.

Looking at some multiple of forward rates, for example 50 percent, would let us see the impact on value if the yield curve only went to half way between the current curve and the forward rates. This type of approach is useful when an investor may be willing to bet against the forward rates and wants to see how much of a bet she or he is willing to wager. Purchasers of inverse floating securities may find this approach to be very useful. Since they are making some implied bet against the yield curve converging to the forward rates, they may find it very informative to know at what multiple their investment begins to show poor results.

| Environment | Prepayment | Cash Flow | Analysis |

■ ANALYSIS

Up until now, the considerations for the yield curve have focused on some of the building blocks: prepayments and cash flows. Now we are going to put those tools to work in looking at how the yield curve affects our understanding of the value, risk, and income of MBS. Our examination of value will be related to value using the OAS model. The risk aspect will introduce the measurement of risk exposure to the entire yield curve.

Value

Spread to the Curve

The decision to purchase an MBS is often made based upon a yield-spread assumption related to comparing the MBS to some alternative investment. This spread assumption provides the medium of exchange by which an investor can make a trade-off between risk and return. Models such as the OAS try to make the spread comparison net of some of the risk characteristics. However, comparison of OAS across different product groups, such as corporates to MBS, is not readily done. In these cases, investors may still rely upon various spread measures to compare value.

The typical measure of spread, subtracting the yield of a Treasury security from the yield of the MBS, is an inadequate way to look at value. The comparable Treasury is usually taken to be a security with the similar average life or duration as the MBS. This measure may be useful as a basis for communication, but not as a means to determine if a security looks rich or cheap.

By comparing two yields, we ignore an important feature of MBS, namely the monthly cash flows. The cash-flow pattern of an MBS is quite different than that of other fixed-income securities. Most MBS have much more of their flow toward the front of the payment schedule, which is very different from a nonamortizing security. The shape of the yield curve is, thus, more important in valuing MBS.

Furthermore, we can use a measurement of value that reflects the relative spread of an MBS to the entire yield curve. By spread to the curve, we mean the constant spread we earn at each point in time. This spread can be determined using the following Formula 9-4:

Formula 9-4 Valuing Cash Flows Using Spread to the Curve:

$$\text{MBS Present Value} = \sum_{t=1}^{T} \frac{\text{Cash Flow}_t}{(1 + r_i + s)^t}$$

In Formula 9-4, we discount each cash flow by the zero-coupon rate plus a constant spread. The spread reflects the advantage to the MBS relative to the Treasury. Another way to look at the spread is to think of it as a break-even constant reinvestment over Treasury rates.

Besides being a measure of relative value, this spread to the curve can be used to estimate the change in the shape of the curve on value. To estimate the change in price due to a shifting Treasury curve we would move the curve and then recalculate the present value. This assumes that the spread to the curve remains constant.

Our cash-flow model in Formula 9-4 can be varied in another way. That is, our expectations for the cash flows could be driven by differing prepayment assumptions. In keeping with our discussion of yield curves and forward rates, we could base our cash flows off an assumption of rates remaining constant or rates following along the path suggested by the implied forward rates.

Comparing Spread to the Curve with Point on the Curve

Because the yield curve is not always flat, we can get different impressions of the MBS spread to Treasuries depending on the way we measure the relative value. The common measure of value quoted among most investors is the yield spread between the MBS and some benchmark Treasury. This spread is watched very closely by market participants as a barometer for the overall direction of the MBS market. As a barometer, this measure of spread serves its purpose, but it is not the end-all of MBS analytics.

Even when considering the yield-difference approach, there are a couple of ways to measure the spread. These differences have to do with the benchmark Treasury used for the comparison. Benchmarks are selected with the idea of finding a security with some comparable characteristics, such as average life or duration. Unlike a corporate bond, which will be compared to a Treasury of similar maturity, the amortizing nature of MBS makes the comparison a bit more complicated. In practice, there are three general choices for the benchmark:

1. Specific Treasury Security—For ease and simplicity, the spread for MBS is sometimes taken as the MBS yield minus the yield of a particular Treasury security. For newly issued current coupon MBS, the benchmark will generally be the on-the-run 10-year Treasury note. Other MBS will be assigned a benchmark depending on their average life. It is not uncommon to see premium MBS being compared with Treasury securities in the three- to five-year section of the curve. CMOs will generally be compared to a benchmark Treasury depending upon the average life of the CMO class.

2. Interpolated Weighted Average Treasury—Rather than choosing a benchmark that has characteristics similar to the MBS, we may try to be a bit more specific. That is, if the current coupon MBS had an average life of 11.2 years we may want to compare its yield to a Treasury of 11.2 years and not the ten year Treasury. In order to get this Treasury yield, we would form a curve of Treasury yields and average life (which is the maturity) and then interpolate to get the yield. This method gives us a benchmark with principal prepayment much closer to the MBS. In the cases when the curve is not flat, we may find this to be a more reliable indicator of MBS value. For CMO investors, the interpolated weighted average life spread may be a better gauge. Dealers will often "round down" the average life of the class when making the relative value comparison, i.e., comparing a 2.4-year CMO to the two-year Treasury. This type of behavior usually makes the bonds appear cheaper than they may really be. Interpolation can take out some of the biases that stem from a steep yield curve.

3. Interpolated Duration Treasury—Using the weighted average life provides a way to match up the principal payment of the MBS with the Treasury. Still, the characteristics of the MBS cash flow are not very similar to the Treasury. A more comparable Treasury may be the security with the same duration as the MBS. Duration reflects the payment of both principal and interest. Matching this characteristic gives a benchmark that is as comparable as one could hope for a benchmark. In practice, this benchmark is not used as much as the specific Treasury or weighted average life Treasury.

To get a comparison of the various spread measures, let's compare the results from some benchmark Treasuries in Table 9-4. Our comparison uses the relative-coupon 30-year conventional securities.

Table 9-4

Relative Coupon	Yield	WAL	Spread/ Benchmark	Spread/WAL
-100	7.85	11.7	118/10 yr	105
-50	7.85	11.3	118/10 yr	109
CC	7.83	10.3	116/10 yr	114
50	7.72	8.8	105/10 yr	117
100	7.49	7.1	112/7 yr	110

On a yield-spread basis, we compared the securities to a representative Treasury, either the ten year or the seven year. Relative to this benchmark, the current coupon security had a spread of 116 basis points. When we make the comparison to the interpolated average life security, the spread decreases to 114 basis points. The spread is lower to the interpolated average life security because the yield curve is positively sloped between 10 and 30 years. The difference in spread for the discount securities is even more pronounced. While the 10 year makes for an easy comparison, it can lead to somewhat overstated value interpretations. Investors should be cautious of this type of yield spread measure when the average life of the security diverges from the benchmark and the yield curve is sloped.

Forward Rates and Spreads: Zero Volatility Spread

The spread to the curve based on forward rates has a special application in OAS analysis. This spread is often called the zero-volatility spread, and measures our expected spread to the curve before the introduction of uncertainty. After running the OAS model, we can use the zero-volatility spread to put a measurement on the implied option cost for a security. This option cost would equal the zero volatility spread minus the OAS.

Depending upon the product, our measurement of value could lead to very different conclusions regarding the method we use to estimate the cash flows. To illustrate this idea, let's look at spreads to the curve for MBS, IOs, and POs in Table 9-5. All the securities were valued at 100 basis points OAS and were based upon newly originated conventional collateral.

Table 9-5

	MBS		PO		IO	
Relative Coupon	**Current Curve**	**Forward Curve**	**Current Curve**	**Forward Curve**	**Current Curve**	**Forward Curve**
-100	112	102	98	38	132	195
-50	123	105	138	5	103	245
Current	141	111	246	-34	-7	312
+50	160	119	456	-75	-281	397
+100	163	131	696	-103		487

In Table 9-5 we see a comparison of spreads based upon the two curve assumptions: rates remaining constant and rates traveling along the path suggested by the forward rates. Our initial yield curve was the positively sloped curve seen earlier in the chapter. As we know from this curve, the implied forward rates call for an overall rise in rates combined with a flattening of the yield curve.

For the passthrough securities, the spreads to the current curve are consistently higher than the forward curve spreads. This result is interesting, especially for the premium securities. We might presume that the forward curve, with its implied slower prepayments would prove to benefit to the spreads. However, the slowdown in prepayments is related to a steeper yield curve and the decreased value of discounting cash flows at higher discount rates. Even though prepayments are slower, the extension to the more positively sloped section of the curve offsets any benefits.

The results are most dramatic for the IO and PO securities. The effect of implied slower prepayments lead the IO spreads to be significantly higher for the forward case while the POs are much lower. The effect of the positively sloped curve leads to spreads that vary by several hundred basis points. Forward-curve effects can lead to very extreme effects on our assumptions about relative value.

What should we make of this discussion of forward curves and spreads? Does this topic simply become an exercise in analytical uselessness? From a conceptual point of view, the forward-rate expectation is our no-arbitrage perspective on the market. It serves as the pricing mechanism for fixed-income securities and derivatives. In this role it plays a large determinant in our OAS calculations. Investors who wish to make a bet about the forward rates could look at strategies, which involve purchasing of the underlying security, and then using combinations of swaps, caps, futures, and options to hedge the duration and convexity risk.

Risk

Analyzing the Entire Curve: Key Rate Duration

When we are discussing risk, our conception will not be the aspect of credit or default risk but the price risk associated with changing interest rates. Many investors have become very comfortable with the concepts of duration and convexity as parameters that calibrate the risk of fixed-income securities. While these measures are very useful, they suffer from an unfortunate limitation. Duration and convexity rely upon an assumption of parallel-yield curve shifts. These measures give us a number for price sensitivity, assuming that all yields move together. In truth, there is no strong reason to think that the yield curve must move in parallel directions. Over time, the curve changes its shape, short rates may rise or fall much more than longer interest rates. To take a more detailed look at interest-rate risk, we can use a method that examines risk along the entire curve. The generally accepted term for this approach is called key rate duration, which was originally pioneered by Thomas Ho.[7]

---

[7] The method of key rate duration can be seen in *Strategic Fixed Income Investment*, Thomas S.Y. Ho, Dow Jones Irwin, 1990.

The method of key rate duration breaks down our traditional measure of duration into a series of partial durations. That is, we look at the effect of the change in each section of the yield curve on the price of an MBS. When we add up each of the partial durations, we get back to the overall duration of the security. Key rate duration lets us see what sections of the curve play the largest role in the price sensitivity of the security. This may be particularly useful when we are trying to measure relative value, establish hedges, or set up some total-return allocation methods.

To understand the method of key rate durations, we must find a way to divide up the yield curve into pieces. The size of these pieces is somewhat arbitrary. For our purposes, our pieces will correspond to the points we use to form the yield-to-maturity yield curve. An illustration of our curve portions can be seen in Figure 9-6.

Figure 9-6

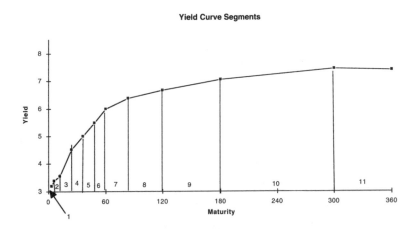

Our key rate duration measure will be determined by taking each segment and adjusting all the spot yields within a segment.[8] The securities would be valued using a constant OAS approach. The change in value attributable to moving the yields within a particular segment would be called the key rate duration.

---

[8]This approach is somewhat different than Ho's. Under his approach he looks at overlapping changes that accumulate to the 100 basis points along the curve.

For MBS, the method of key rate duration is especially useful. Because of the cash-flow pattern and amortizing nature of MBS, we are better advised to look at spreads to the entire curve. Furthermore, MBS cash flows will change depending upon the level and slope of the curve. By examining the key rate duration, we can get some idea about how much the change in curve shape affects both the timing and valuation of MBS cash flows.

We have computed key rate durations for a current coupon MBS along with its underlying IO/PO components. The key rate durations can be seen in Table 9-6.

Table 9-6

AGENCY	CPN	WAM	TYPE	0M 3M	3M 6M	6M 1Y	1Y 2Y	2Y 3Y	3Y 4Y	4Y 5Y	5Y 7Y	7Y 10Y	10Y 15Y	15Y 25Y	25Y 30Y	TOTAL
CONVTL	7.50	359	MBS	.33	.24	.46	.84	.74	.64	.54	.87	.88	.78	.40	.02	6.64
CONVTL	7.50	359	IO	.32	.21	.34	.37	.02	-.19	-.37	-1.31	-3.17	-2.39	-.30	-.13	-3.39
CONVTL	7.50	359	PO	.34	.27	.59	1.36	1.52	1.54	1.54	3.26	5.30	4.24	1.17	.18	10.03

Overall, the security has a total duration of 6.64, with most of the risk coming from the 5-15 year segments of the yield curve. The IO and PO show somewhat differing risk characteristics. The IO looks like a combination security. Because of the prepayment function, it will show some positive response to the very short end of the yield curve. As yields from the two-year and below section decline, the price of the IO increases. As we move further out the curve the prepayment function becomes more dominant and the price declines. The IO shows maximum sensitivity to the 9-10 year section of the curve. This area accounts for nearly all the price risk of the security. Similarly the PO also shows its maximum price sensitivity to this section of the curve, as this is the area that most affects the prepayment function.

The key rate duration approach is a very powerful way to isolate the risks of an MBS, including standard passthroughs and derivatives. It is very useful when understanding what sections of the curve most affect value. When used for hedging purposes, the key rate duration approach can be applied to Treasuries or other hedges. By looking at the partial durations, we can come up with the best combination of hedge products for complicated derivatives.

The key rate duration approach has a more subtle use in its ability to isolate the yield-curve effects on the prepayment function. For models that are very yield curve dependent, we may start to see sharp changes as we move into the 2-3 year section of the curve. This may suggest a model that weights the yield-curve shape very strongly.

Also, many OAS models try to find a way to translate simulated Treasury rates into something related to MBS. The common translation maps the Treasury rates to an MBS current coupon yield. This current coupon yield will be the primary driver for the prepayment function. In our implementation of the key rate duration, we have held the current coupon spread constant over the simulated Treasuries. Another approach would be to apply some model that predicts the current coupon yield given the level and shape of the yield curve. This type of model will also be very sensitive to the yield curve and its effect on MBS value would be seen in the key rate duration approach.

Other Multifactor Approaches

The analysis of the yield curve has been examined through other approaches besides the key rate duration method. One systematic way in which the yield-curve risk has been parametized is through the statistical technique of factor analysis. In this method, the yield-curve movements have been conceptualized into mathematical statements of how the yield curve moves. The three most influential factors have often been thought of as the parallel, twist, and flex movements of the yield curve.[9] An example of these types of yield curve effects can be seen in Figure 9-7.

---

[9]For more information on yield-curve movements, see "Bond performance analysis: A multi-factor approach" by R. Kahn, *Journal of Portfolio Management,* Fall 1991, Vol 18. No. 1, pp 40-47.

Figure 9-7a

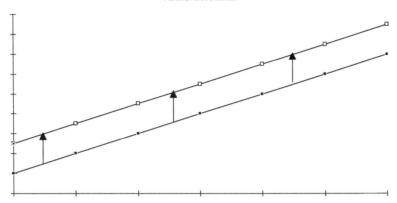

Parallel Movements

Figure 9-7b

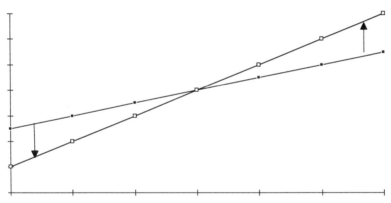

Curve Twist

Figure 9-7c

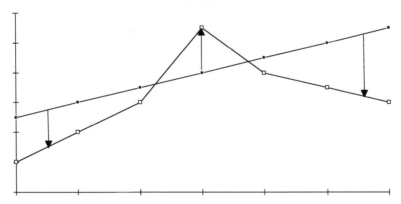

Curve Flex

We could use these yield-curve movements to come up with alternative risk measures for the MBS. That is, we could decide on a standard yield curve shift for each type of factor and then determine the corresponding price change on the security. This would give us a summarized measure of MBS price sensitivity to each type of yield-curve movement. For analytical purposes, this method could be used to compare alternative investments, looking for those that offer superior performance depending upon the yield-curve change envisioned by the investor. Likewise, the approach could be used to attribute returns for the securities.

Yield-Curve Twist Duration

One of the difficulties in measuring twist exposure is determining a method to measure and report the relationship between the change in slope and value. To consider MBS exposure let's simplify the yield-curve movements into two types: parallel shift and slope twist. Figure 9-8 shows our representative twist along with the combination of a shift and twist.

Figure 9-8a

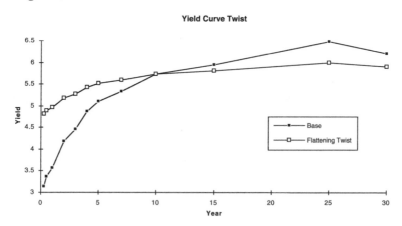

Figure 9-8b

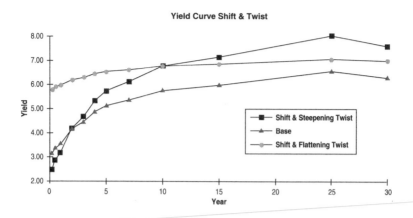

Our yield-curve twist look is based upon changing the slope between the 2- and 10-year Treasury and then pivoting the other rates around the 10 year. In the second figure, our base shift between 2 and 10 years is 100 basis points. The other rates on the yield curve will then be scaled by the relationship between the point on the curve and its relative relationship to the 2- to 10-year slope. Putting this into an equation, our shifted rate (Y'_i) is shown in Formula 9-5.

Formula 9-5

$$Y'_i = Y_i + \text{Twist Amount} \times \frac{Y_i - Y_{10}}{Y_{10} - Y_2}$$

This method allows us to preserve the relative shape of the curve. In our current positively sloped curve, rates below the 2-year point move by more than the base-twist amount. Between 2 and 10 years, the twist gradually gets smaller and then beyond 10 years, the shift changes direction, long rates move in the opposite direction of short rates. This twist method is attractive because it does not scale the change in slope based on the time but rather the relative shape of the curve. In the combined figure we see the effect of a 100-basis-point shift with two types of twists: flattening and steepening.

We can look at the effect of a yield-curve twist and the change in value in much the same manner as the relationship between shifts and price changes. For a parallel change in the yield curve, the change in value should be approximately equal to:

$$\text{Shift Effect} = \frac{100}{\text{Price}} \times (\text{Shift Duration} \times \text{Yield Change} + \frac{1}{2} \times \text{Shift Convexity} \times \text{Yield Change}^2)$$

We can apply this same type of relationship to the yield-curve twist:

$$\text{Twist Effect} = \frac{100}{\text{Price}} \times (\text{Twist Duration} \times \text{Yield Change} + \frac{1}{2} \times \text{Shift Convexity} \times \text{Yield Change}^2)$$

When we combine a twist with a shift the overall change in price will be:

Price Change = Shift Effect + Twist Effect + Interaction Between Shift and Twist

The interaction is the relative convexity of combining the two effects. It's relative size will be dependent upon the amount of the twist and shift. For small changes in yield we would expect (and hope) it to have a very small value.

In order to show the relationship between our two yield-curve factors and value we have estimated the change in price based upon constant OAS pricing. By shifting and twisting the curve 10 basis points we have determined a relative duration and convexity for each type of movement, as seen in Table 9-7.

To interpret the twist components, we consider the price effect to be based upon a steepening of the yield curve (short rates down with long rates up). Judging from the table, we see some interesting relationships. The yield-curve twist has less of an effect for the lower coupon passthroughs. As we move up, the twist duration takes on increased significance, especially for coupons 8% and above. The importance of twist convexity is rather small in both relative and absolute terms. For our twists and shifts of 10 basis points, we found the interaction effect to be very small (1 to 2 cents at most).

Table 9-7

Coupon	Shift Duration	Shift Convexity	Twist Duration	Twist Convexity
6.0	6.69	-0.25	0.26	-0.50
6.5	6.06	-0.75	0.61	-0.25
7.0	5.09	-1.50	1.04	-0.50
7.5	3.83	-2.25	1.31	0.30
8.0	2.64	-2.25	1.39	-0.25
8.5	1.76	-1.00	1.29	0.00
9.0	1.55	-0.25	1.27	0.00
9.5	1.67	0.00	1.39	0.00
10.0	1.73	0.50	1.41	0.25

Yield-Curve Twists and Inverse Floaters

For some time, the inverse floater type of security has played an important role in the ability of dealers to bring CMOs. The inverse floater offers a very attractive initial yield to the investor, making it a very enticing security for those who need current yield and are willing to bet against the yield-curve flattening.

The attractive yield of the inverse floater represents the existence of a steep yield curve. In actuality, the security really equates to a levered position in a support bond. From this perspective, the inverse offers risk in two directions. First is the risk of the coupon portion, this will be associated with changes in the index rate. Second are the changes in prepayment rates. The prepayment rates will be driven by numerous factors, with long-term interest rates being the most dominant.

One way to evaluate the riskiness of the inverse floater is to simultaneously look at both of these risks. To do so, we can create a matrix of yields for a security, allowing both the coupon and prepayment rates to change. To illustrate this measure of risk and return, we have computed a matrix of yields for FHLMC 1530 Q, an inverse floater indexed to move inversely with the prime rate shown in Table 9-8.

Table 9-8

PRIME	PSA 800	PSA 500	PSA 325	PSA 200	PSA 135
3.5	6.67	13.98	19.63	26.76	27.71
4	4.41	11.60	17.15	24.27	25.21
4.5	2.18	9.24	14.69	21.97	22.72
5	-0.06	6.90	12.61	19.35	20.25
5.5	-2.27	4.57	9.84	16.92	17.94
6	-4.46	2.26	7.45	14.51	15.35
6.5	-6.63	-0.04	5.06	12.11	12.92
7	-8.79	-2.31	2.70	9.74	10.50
7.5	-10.93	-4.56	0.36	7.37	8.08
8	-13.05	-6.8	-1.97	5.02	5.66
Average Life	0.58	0.88	1.42	12.15	24.80

Let's assume the security was being offered at a 12.61 percent yield currently, assuming a 5 percent prime and 325 percent PSA rate. The security would perform poorly under two conditions—either an increasing prime rate or an increasing prepayment rate. As prepayment increases, the security is subject to call risk, even a decreasing prime does not help much.

In order for the security's performance to increase, we would need to have falling prepayment rates. If the prime was to also decline, we would get a double benefit. This would have to be a fairly unusual yield-curve movement. Long rates would have to be rising, while short rates would be falling.

One way to evaluate the sensitivity of the inverse-to-parallel yield curve movements would be to trace out the yield profile as we move along the diagonal of the matrix. This would require that we keep our changes in the index and prepayment rates in sequence. That is, if we were to use our five percent prime and 325 percent PSA, then a 4.5 percent prime would have to correspond with the 500 percent PSA (which would be the forecast under a 50 bps decline).

Income

Many financial institutions rely on measures of income that assume that all yield-curve movements are parallel. The methods described in this section can be used to develop methods of analysis that will allow institutions to evaluate the impact of changing yield-curve shapes on their income. For example, a bank may seek to fund a mortgage asset. The key rate duration approach may provide insight into which maturity liabilities would be the most appropriate in order to produce stable earnings. Alternatively, a manager who is managing against an index may use the shift, twist, and flex method to determine if the value of his holdings have the same total return characteristics as the index. The earnings and value of leveraged financial institutions such as banks and insurance companies are very sensitive to the relative costs of funds for different points on the yield curve. Failure to adequately analyze the impact of changes in the shape of the yield curve may lead to serious problems as the yield curve undergoes its gyrations.

■ CONCLUSION

In previous chapters, we saw how changes in the yield curve affect MBS value and performance. This chapter focuses sharply on the relationship between the yield curve and MBS cash flows. By exploring the relationship between forward rates and cash flows, we get a glimpse behind some of the factors at work in the OAS approach. This aids our understanding of both the characteristics of the underlying securities and the valuation processes.

This chapter went further, examining the relationship between MBS value and the various sectors of the yield curve. Tools such as the key rate duration give us a measure on how to relate changes in the shape of the curve to MBS value. We have also found ways to characterize the ways that the yield curve moves, looking at methods for parallel and nonparallel shifts. Understanding the relationship between MBS performance and nonparallel movements is useful because of the discounting effects and the relationship between the prepayment models and the shape of the curve.

In the next chapter, we carry this yield-curve sensitivity further by looking at the sensitivity of MBS to paths of interest rates. This extends our methodology of scenario analysis by developing fairly complex interest-rate shifts and OAS by looking at the relationship between paths and the risk/return relationship.

CHAPTER TEN

Whipsaw and Path-Dependence Risk

What's a good test for the durability of a car? Perhaps you might think giving it a grueling workout on the test track, putting it into wind tunnels, and that sort of thing. Really, one of the best tests would be to use the car as a taxi in New York City. This would give the car the best test of its durability, given the combination of bumpy roads and erratic driving. The same sort of analogy extends over to MBS. One of the best ways to know about the bond you are considering is to put it under some stress. In the parlance of MBS, we call this type of testing whipsaw analysis. While it may not have a strong underpinning in financial theory, it is often an invaluable tool in learning about what you are purchasing.

In the previous chapters, we have considered two methods for analyzing the risk and return of MBS: scenario analysis and OAS. Both of these methods have proper applications, but like all models they have limitations. In fact, the existence of multiple approaches implies that no one model is absolutely correct. But given the application or need, some models may be more appropriate.

The scenario analysis model gives us a method to understand the general price and risk profiles for a security. These profiles can be an invaluable tool to know how a bond will react under differing interest-rate scenarios. Our choice of scenarios can be a limiting factor. Rarely does the world move in a manner suggested by the pristine world of scenario analysis. As a result, we may be getting only a partial picture of how a security will behave under differing rate scenarios.

We cannot predict accurately how future interest rates will evolve. One thing we do know, they will probably not move in the simple ramped manner described by most implementations of scenario analysis. The scenario-analysis approach still remains useful, but it can be augmented through the creation of more dynamic scenarios.

OAS uses a lot of scenarios, but too many to look at individually. One of the major limitations of the OAS approach is the reliance on a single output, the spread. In the process of estimating this number we must make numerous assumptions and calculate a great deal of information. Much of this information provides further insight to the performance characteristics of the security. Unfortunately, we usually discard the information.

What we really need to do is extend our models somewhat. Through the scenario-analysis method, we will look to add other types of interest-rate scenarios. We will try and capture the wealth of information generated in the OAS model. We need to consider these extensions because of the particular attributes of MBS. Unlike most fixed-income securities, the performance of an MBS depends on the path of interest rates. In addition, the security will keep on changing characteristics over time as borrowers leave the pool. We need to use the methods described in this chapter to learn about how the securities will evolve.

Our method for examining whipsaw risk analysis will be consistent with our other chapters. We will divide our examination into four stages, as described in Table 10-1.

Table 10-1 Chapter Overview

Environment	Prepayments	Cash Flow	Analysis
• Interest rate paths	• Burnout	• Scheduled securities	• Scenario analysis
• Different directions	• Path dependency	• Bucket analysis	• Income

| Environment | Prepayment | Cash Flow | Analysis |

■ ENVIRONMENT

Our interest-rate environment will be characterized by the use of interest-rate paths. This is an extension of the ramped interest-rate approach we used in the scenario-analysis chapter. Through the creation of some more robust interest-rate scenarios, we will be able to learn more about how MBS respond to shocks.

Our analysis will try and uncover the stress limits for a security. In some ways, this will resemble the infamous stress interviews that were used long ago in business schools. These were the ones where the interviewee would be asked to do things like open windows that had been glued shut and move chairs closer that had been nailed to the floor.

Paths

Our first type of environmental concern will be interest-rate paths. Under typical scenario analysis, we will be concerned with the final change in interest rates. Using a path approach, we will also look at the effects of how we arrive at a particular scenario.

We are concerned with the path of interest rates for two major reasons: First, the prepayment characteristics of an MBS will be different depending upon the way interest rates change; second, for structured products like CMOs, the paths of interest rates will lead to differing amounts of amortization for the classes. This could have a material effect on the prepayment protection embedded in PAC bonds.

To understand the path effect, let's set up a sample interest-rate scenario. Our sample scenario will be the up 100 basis points over 12 months. We will consider three possible ways of getting there, as seen in Figure 10-1.

Figure 10-1

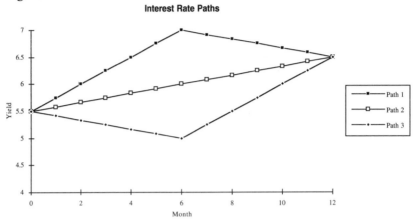

The typical scenario analysis would only consider the up-100-basis-point scenario. This mode of analysis can be expanded to consider many ways of reaching this scenario. In Figure 10-1, we have shown three paths, which all result in the final up-100 scenario. Path 1 would be a scenario where rates rose initially then fell, with the result being an overall rise of 100 basis points over one year. The second scenario would be the standard approach, rates rising linearly over the holding period. Path 3 is the mirror image of the first path, it considers a scenario in which rates would initially fall, then rise. Because of the unique properties of MBS, all three paths would result in a security that after 12 months had slightly different characteristics. A CMO investor would likewise have a deal with differing characteristics.

The analysis we presented in Figure 10-1 considers the movement of the yield curve to be parallel along all of the maturities. We could present our path analysis along a slightly different dimension; considering interim changes in the shape of the curve. Suppose the current difference between the two and 10 year was 180 basis points. As an additional type of scenario analysis, this slope could be assumed to change over time. An example of these scenarios can be seen in Figure 10-2.

Figure 10-2

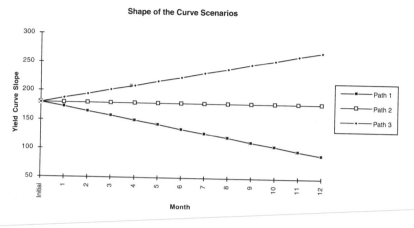

The interest-rate scenarios consider three ways in which the slope of the curve could change. In the first path, the curve would have steepened by 90 basis points over the holding period. This would lead to slightly higher prepayments over the scenario and would affect the implied forward rates used in any OAS horizon pricing model. The second path has no change over the scenario. The third path has the curve flattening over the horizon, this will lead to changes in expected prepayments and in the terminal pricing.

Changes in the slope of the curve could be paired with the scenarios presented in Figure 10-1. At some point, we start to be overwhelmed by the number of scenarios. If we start with a simple scenario analysis of up and down 200 basis points by 100 basis points we would have five scenarios. If each of these scenarios were to have three possible paths, then our total number of scenarios would grow to 15 (5 x 3). Should we layer on top of this change in the slope of the curve, say three curve-shape assumptions for each scenario, then we would wind up with a total of 45 scenarios (5 x 3 x 3).

Taken to extremes, we would soon find the method impractical. Investors would be interested in knowing what types of paths most affect the securities. The method of creating paths may not be most useful in looking rigorously at each path, rather it would be useful when learning about the general performance characteristics of the securities.

Whipsaw Scenarios

Another way of extending the scenario analysis approach would be through the creation differing types of scenarios. Unlike the path approach, we do not want to concentrate on the outcome and look at differing paths. In whipsaw analysis we want to really shake up the rate scenarios, looking at more cases of oscillating rates. Going back to our automobile analogy, we want to put our car on the bumpiest road (Hudson Street if we keep in practice of our New York taxi experiment) and see what shakes loose. A sample whipsaw scenario can be seen in Figure 10-3.

Figure 10-3

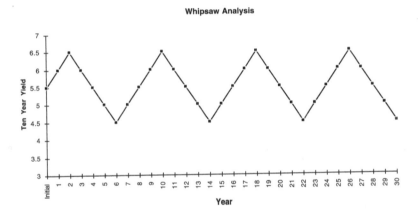

In the whipsaw analysis, we look at oscillations in the yield curve over time. Our case looks at a consistent up and down movement, rates rising then falling. The method for developing scenarios is not standard, there is a reason that the shocks must be symmetrical along the time dimension or along the size of interest rate shocks. Other types of whipsaw scenarios can be seen in Figure 10-4.

Figure 10-4

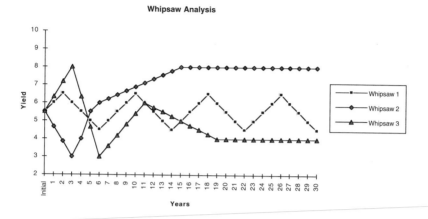

In Figure 10-4, we repeat our initial whipsaw case (number 1) and we add two additional cases. Whipsaw case two looks at a situation where rates fall then rise over time. The third whipsaw case has successive cycles of rising then falling rates, with a long term decline.

Creation of whipsaw scenarios is a somewhat arbitrary method. We generally look to find scenarios that really put a CMO structure under stress. In some cases, we may be looking to set up scenarios that try to give us some idea where a bond begins to fall apart. That is, we may try to set up cases to look at a PAC bond. Using a whipsaw approach, we could see how the effective PAC collars are shifting over time. For another security, say an inverse floater, the whipsaw analysis could be used to see how much rates would need to rise and for how long the rate rise would have to persist before the yields on the security began to deteriorate substantially.

Environment	Prepayment	Cash Flow	Analysis

■ PREPAYMENT

Up to now, our discussion of interest-rate scenarios has made the case that we need to consider the paths and whipsaw conditions because of their effects on MBS. In the next two sections, prepayment and cash flow, we will link the whipsaw and path-dependent analysis with the performance of the securities. Our investigation follows along two parts. First, we will investigate how the paths affect the behavior of the underlying passthrough security. This will be analyzed in the prepayment section. In the cash-flow section, we take this one step further in the discussion of whipsaw risk for structured MBS products.

For prepayment analysis, we will investigate two related features: burnout and path dependency. Many relative-value analyses rely upon arguments related to these factors when looking at the MBS performance characteristics. To illustrate the burnout effect, we will use the interest-rate paths developed in the environment section. To look at the path-dependency effects, we will use the whipsaw analysis.

Burnout

In our investigation of MBS prepayments, we presented some of the data related to the burnout effect. In the present analysis, we will explore the implications of burnout in the analysis of securities. Before we begin our investigation, let's try and be precise about the definition of burnout.

The MBS pool contains a finite group of borrowers. These borrowers may not have much in common other than the fact they got their loans about the same time or went to the same lender. They may differ greatly in their financial resources and demographic characteristics. As a result, they may have different predispositions toward moving and refinancing.

Each time a borrower exits from the MBS pool, the aggregate characteristics shift. With respect to refinancing, our working hypothesis states that borrowers with the greatest predisposition prepay first. Over time, we would expect the pool to be comprised of borrowers with less of an incentive to refinance their loans. As a result, we might expect prepayment rates to decline as interest rates remained constant.

Burnout is the decline in prepayment rates experienced as the level of interest rates remains constant. Evidence shows that the prepayment rates do not go to zero as rates remain constant. So, even though the pool may be more and more comprised of less prepayment-sensitive individuals, there is some change in the characteristics. We suspect that some of the borrowers become more predisposed to prepaying their loans, thus prepayment rates do decline indefinitely. In our modeling efforts, we use an adjusted factor to examine the burnout effect. This adjusted factor uses the actual pool factor as the starting point and then allows for some reversion as we move through time. The reversion moves the pool closer to its original characteristics.

The burnout effect will be different for securities depending on the underlying age of the loans and the factor. It will be much more prevalent for loans in which the borrowers have an incentive to refinance. For current coupon and discount securities, the prepayment-sensitive borrowers may not have had an opportunity to refinance yet.

To show some of the implications for burnout on MBS, let's consider an interest-rate path that has a final shift of no change. We will consider five ways of getting to this point, as seen in Figure 10-5. At the end of the horizon, interest rates are assumed to remain constant. To examine the effect on an MBS, we will calculate relevant measures, including the long term PSA and average life at the horizon.[1]

Figure 10-5

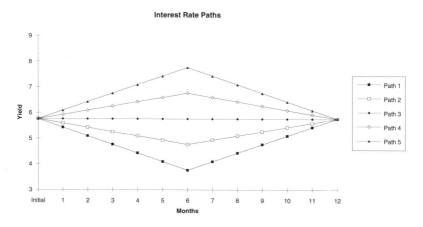

[1]The long-term prepayment speed is determined by taking the monthly payment projections and finding the single PSA rate that gives the same average life. This has been described more fully in Chapter 7.

Our analysis will focus on a slight-premium MBS, with a remaining term of 325 months, and a .70 factor. For each path, we have calculated the horizon characteristics, as seen in Table 10-2.

Table 10-2

Path	Horizon WAL	Horizon PSA
1—Rates -200 at 6 months	6.55	202
2—Rates -100 at 6 months	6.50	204
3—Rates stable	6.28	213
4—Rates +100 at 6 months	5.87	232
5—Rates +200 at 6 months	5.57	246

From the table, we see some interesting results. The horizon characteristics are different depending upon the path of interest rates. As interest rates drop, prepayment rates increase, as seen in paths 1 and 2. However, the burnout effect makes rates decline as we go into the future. For these two paths, the MBS would actually have a longer average life and long-term PSA[2] than the paths where interest rates rose. The burnout effect depresses the future prepayment rates for paths 1 and 2, making them less susceptible to future prepayments, even though the interest rates remain constant along all the paths from the horizon to the remaining term of the MBS. For the security we are examining, the difference in average life is in the range of one year depending upon the path of interest rates.

Path Dependency

As we mentioned before, the mortgage pool begins its existence with a fixed set of borrowers. These borrowers have very different tendencies toward prepaying or refinancing their mortgages. When borrowers leave the pool, the aggregate characteristics of the remaining borrowers changes, and the pool can be assumed to be more composed of less prepayment-sensitive individuals.

---

[2] The long-term PSA and average life are based on forward rates.

The major implication of a mortgage pool with changing characteristics is the varying prepayment behavior over time. As we go through various interest-rate cycles, the prepayment rates of the pool will change. If we had an interest-rate scenario where rates fell then rose and then fell again, we would expect differing prepayment rates on the second interest-rate decline. The borrowers with the most sensitivity toward prepayments got out on the first cycle. We call this phenomenon path dependency.

In the presence of path dependency, our projections of future prepayment rates must be conditional on the past behavior of rates. During interest-rate declines, we cannot expect rates to peak at levels similar to the previous rate decline. This compounds the challenge of prepayment forecasting, making it less reliable to look at long-term prepayment estimates to know how an MBS would prepay over a short horizon.

The notion of path dependency is not exactly the same as burnout. Although both work from a similar framework—that is, the changing prepayment sensitivity of an MBS pool, there is a fundamental difference. When considering burnout, we are looking at analysis that holds interest rates constant and looks at the declining prepayment rates. With path dependency, we are letting interest rates fluctuate. For any given level of interest rates, our prepayment rate will depend on the path of previous rates.

To consider path dependency, let's compare a path of interest rates that follows a regular cycle. Rates periodically follow a rising and falling sequence. We will plot out the corresponding prepayment rates, along the path of interest rates. This relationship can be seen in Figure 10-6.

In Figure 10-6, we have plotted the CPR versus the path of the 10-year Treasury yields. Our MBS was chosen to be a premium security with a low age. We plotted prepayment rates for the first 120 months. The yields follow a regular cycle, rising then falling. Along the cycles, the MBS exhibits differing prepayment characteristics. In the beginning, the aging effect keeps prepayments low. As we get past the first year, we see prepayment rates peaking with the decline in yields. Moving through the next rate cycle, we see that prepayment rates do again increase, but not to the levels seen in the first rate decline. This continues with each successive rate decline, although the effect becomes less pronounced.

Figure 10-6

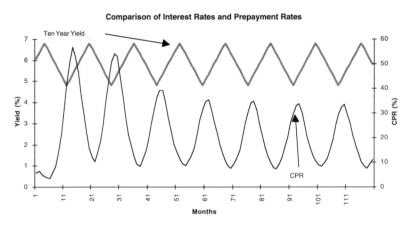

Comparison of Interest Rates and Prepayment Rates

By the time we get out past five years, the changes in each interest-rate cycle become very small. The pool continues to contain some prepayment-sensitive borrowers, but the prepayment rates peak consistently around the 35 percent CPR level. This regular behavior is probably due to our assumed reversion properties of the MBS pool.

As we move through time, our prepayment model builds in an effect that pushes the pool closer to its origination characteristics. We assume that some of the borrowers with less proclivity towards prepayment become a little bit more prepayment sensitive. This may occur due to changes in economic conditions (more income, higher property values) or because of demographic considerations (family size increasing, divorces). We relate this reversion property to the observation that pool prepayment rates do not go to zero and that pools for which the prepayment options are in the money do show increases in prepayment rates as yields drop.

Path Dependency

■ CASH FLOW

In our consideration of prepayments, we have concentrated on the characteristics of the underlying mortgage pool. We have seen that the pool shows varying sensitivities to interest rates because of burnout and path dependency. These effects have a direct relationship to the cash flows of an MBS because of the resulting declines in prepayment rates.

As we move away from the standard analysis of passthroughs and into structured MBS products, like CMOs, our considerations change. Under an analytical framework such as whipsaw analysis, we will have differing cash flows at the pool level. However, when looking at CMOs, the effect of fluctuating interest rates will be a change in the underlying structure of the deal.

Changes in the underlying structure of the CMO and the resulting change in cash flows are not really an effect of burnout. Rather, the deal will be changing its characteristics as the more prepayment-sensitive classes are retired. As we go through continual interest-rate cycles, the absence of the support classes makes the scheduled classes (PACs, TACs) more exposed to average life variability.

The performance of a CMO under varying interest rates is a result of the effect of prepayments on the underlying mortgages and the effect on the structure of the CMO deal. For the moment, we will concentrate on the effect of prepayments on deal structure, leaving aside the more complicated impact on the mortgages. Instead, we will focus exclusively on the relationship between interest-rate fluctuations and deal structure. Throughout this analysis, we will try and apply whipsaw scenarios to test the viability of PAC bonds. Our two bonds for consideration are shown in Table 10-3.

Table 10-3

Security	Collateral	WAL/PSA	PAC Collar
FHLMC 1527 E	FHLMC GOLD 30 7.5%	4.85 @ 260%	110-331
FN93-75 D	FNMA 30 7.5%	5.79 @260%	110-260

Under the rules of the CMO analysis game, both securities would be called five-year PAC bonds. Both bonds came from the same type of 30-year conventional collateral and were priced near the same time.[3] The FH1527 E had some PAC protection while the FN93-75 D traded at the outer end of the PAC collar.

Using some whipsaw analysis, we can compare the overall stability of the two PAC bonds. First, we may want to look at the basic average life versus PSA for the two bonds, as seen in Figure 10-7.

Figure 10-7

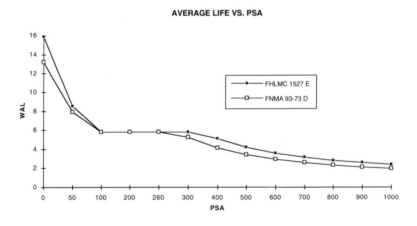

A comparison of the basic sensitivity to interest rates would suggest that the securities share somewhat the same exposure to prepayment risk. The FHLMC 1527 E has a bit more protection from the upper PAC collar. However, it does extend more than the FNMA 93-73 D as prepayment rates slow down. Looking at the whipsaw risk provides a way to distinguish the risks of the securities.

---

[3]The analysis was performed as of July 1993.

As part of the analysis we will look at the overall integrity of the PAC structures under a whipsaw analysis. Before running the whipsaw analysis we should take a look at the built-in drift of the PAC bonds. This tells us the implied PAC collars as other PAC securities and support bonds pay down. Based on a constant speed of 260 PSA, the two bonds would have the following PAC collars, as seen in Figure 10-8.

Figure 10-8

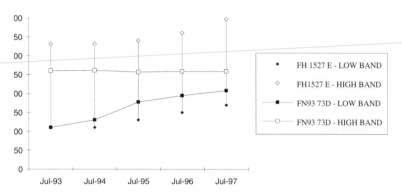

In the figure, we have compared the collars of the two bonds on the same scale. The effective PAC collars for the FHLMC 1527 E have been plotted using the vertical lines. For the FN93-73 D, the collars have been shown based on the two horizontal lines. PAC collars were computed at 12-month intervals, assuming the deal had been paying at 260 PSA throughout time.

The low end of the PAC collars for both bonds rises over time. This suggests that as the other classes of the deal pay off, there are less support bonds to absorb the extension risk. The FN93-73 D has a much greater contraction over time. It is interesting that the upper collar rises for the FHLMC 1527 E. This may indicate that there are adequate amounts of long-support bonds in the deal. The long supports probably have little room to extend, hence the increase in the lower end of the PAC collar.

For our whipsaw analysis, we will consider a scenario where PSA speeds move above the PAC band and then return back to the original long-term forecast. This whipsaw scenario can be seen in Figure 10-9.

Figure 10-9

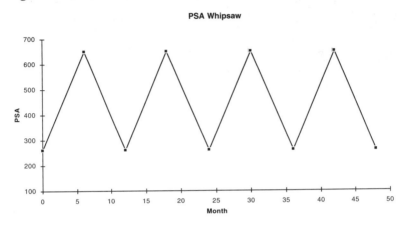

We will evaluate the PAC bonds again in 12-month intervals. Thus we will be stopping our whipsaw every year and measuring the PAC collars in existence at that time. We can then compare the overall drift from the whipsaw scenario to the base case to see the effect of breaking down the deal's structures. This is shown in Figure 10-10.

Figure 10-10

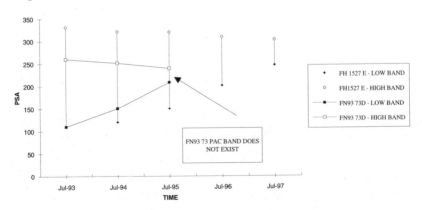

Our classification scheme remains the same for the two bonds. Unlike our original analysis, we see that the whipsaw analysis leads to significant changes in the PAC securities. For the FN93-73 D, the bond would become a broken PAC by year two and no further PAC collar would exist. The FHLMC 1527 E, by comparison, fares much better, although the collars do contract.

What we draw from this investigation is the idea that not all 5-year PAC bonds are the same, even though they may come from similar collateral. Deal structure plays a large role in the overall stability of securities over time. We saw that one bond had an effective collar with the high end at the long-term prepayment estimate. Both bonds were expected to see changes in their effective collars, even under a stable prepayment environment. As we applied the whipsaw analysis, it became apparent that one of the securities displayed significantly better characteristics than another.

| Environment | Prepayment | Cash Flow | Analysis |

■ ANALYSIS
Value

The effect of whipsaw scenarios and interest-rate paths will be reflected in our measures of relative security performance and value. As an example of the relationship between interest-rate paths and total return, let's consider the interest-rate paths shown in Figure 10-5. In this case, we had five interest-rate paths, all of which lead to the same horizon point. In Table 10-4 we have the total return and horizon price for a premium MBS.

The effects of interest-rate paths on total return is rather interesting. Our analysis considered a seasoned 8.5 percent conventional 30-year mortgage. We valued the security originally at 100 basis points OAS, and then determined the horizon price at this constant OAS. We see that total returns, prices, and yields vary along each scenario.

Table 10-4

Scenario	Total Return (%)	Horizon Price ($)	Horizon Yield (%)
1—Rates -200 at 6 months	4.73	107.92	6.86
2—Rates -100 at 6 months	5.04	107.87	6.85
3—Rates stable	5.63	107.70	6.84
4—Rates +100 at 6 months	6.41	107.35	6.81
5—Rates +200 at 6 months	6.91	107.04	6.79

What is most interesting is the pattern between interest rates and value results. The paths in which we did best are those which had interest rates rising over the holding period. This occurred because we experienced a decline in the prepayment rates. Less of our money came back at par to be reinvested at low rates.

However, we see a different story when it comes to the exit price. Here our terminal price rises in scenarios that experienced an interest-rate decline. This occurs because of the burnout effect. After going though an interest-rate decline, the pool has slower prepayment rates compared with scenarios where interest rates remained constant or rose. As a result, our premium mortgage becomes more valuable in this scenario relative to the others.

At first glance, it may appear incongruous that the scenarios with the highest terminal price had the lowest total rate of return. We must keep in mind that there is less principal outstanding in scenarios 1 and 2. Even though our price may be highest, we have less of an outstanding balance to which it can be applied. By the time we try to reap the fruits of burnout, there is not enough of the security left to give us a significant improvement in performance.

This is an important lesson to those who look to purchase an MBS with knowledge that prepayments may be fast during an initial period but will slow down at some future point. By the time prepayments slow down, the balances may be so low that the price gain becomes irrelevant. In the case of IOs, you may have a nice coupon but no principal.

When considering the effects of whipsaws on value, we must be mindful of the amount by which rates move and the time period of the interest-rate cycle.

Risk

Profile analysis

As part of the profile-analysis section, we will examine how interest-rate paths may influence the risk and return characteristics of a CMO. Our investigation will center on the analysis of a support bond, FHLMC 1527 PA. This security is part of an REMIC collateralized by 30-year FHLMC 7.5 percent gold securities. Long-term prepayment estimates for the collateral expected a 260 PSA rate, this would lead to a security with a 3.33 weighted average life. The support bond we have chosen is somewhat sensitive to prepayment rates, as seen in Figure 10-11.

Figure 10-11

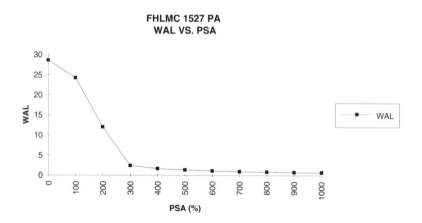

The support bond has significant exposure to changes in average life. As prepayment speeds move from 200 PSA to 300 PSA, the average life declines from 11.99 years to 2.39 years.

As part of our analysis, we will again consider the role interest rate paths play in combination with scenario analysis. Our base scenario will consider interest rates rising 50 basis points over one year. Around this base path, we will create a set of interest-rate paths, representing interim shifts of 50, 100, and 200 basis points each. The corresponding prepayment speeds for the paths can be seen in Figure 10-12.

Figure 10-12

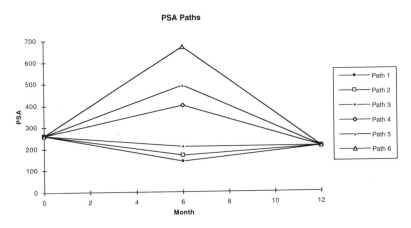

Past month twelve, the security is expected to prepay at a constant rate of 210 PSA. To see the impact of the interest-rate paths, we have determined profiles for the average life and modified duration for the support bond, as seen in Table 10-5.

Table 10-5

Path	WAL	Modified Duration
1	9.53	6.54
2	9.29	6.41
3	8.78	6.15
4	7.38	5.37
5	6.43	4.83
6	4.31	3.56

Profile Analysis

Path 3 represents the base case, which has interest rates rising 50 basis points over the 12 months. The average life extends from our current base case estimate of 3.33 years to 8.78 years. The average life is very dependent on the potential paths of interest rates. Should rates fall initially and then rise (paths 4-6), the support bond would have a shorter average life. On the other hand, if rates initially rose, we would see some extension of the security. Even changes in PSA that are over a limited duration have a significant effect on the long-term effects on the support bond.

Bucket Analysis

Typically we use the OAS model to calculate spreads, values or interest-rate measures. For these purposes, the OAS model grinds through many calculations. The information used in calculating the OAS gets discarded. However, we can make use of preliminary OAS model results in understanding the path-dependency risk of MBS.

Using a technique known as bucket analysis, we can gather and present information about the MBS path-dependency risk.[4] This analysis gives us an extension of the scenario-analysis based path dependency and whipsaw techniques presented earlier. When using the OAS model to analyze path dependency, we can look at a much richer set of interest-rate scenarios.

In the OAS calculation process, we compute a present value for each simulation process. When solving for the OAS, we find the spread, which makes the average of the present values equal to the current market price. Along our simulation trials, we have a rich set of information, which tells us how MBS would perform based on many types of interest rate paths.

The method of bucket analysis looks at the individual paths of the OAS process, but with a unique method for summarizing the data. Given the large number of interest rate simulations used to calculate an OAS, it

---

[4]The method of bucket analysis can be explored further in "Analyzing the Path Dependence of MBS," *The Handbook of MBS*, Third Edition, Frank Fabozzi, Ed., Probus Publishing.

would be futile to look at each path individually. In our classification method, we group similar paths together in buckets.

The classification method uses two ideas to group rates, windows, and buckets. A bucket would be characterized by a specific time period and a range of interest rates. To consider the path-dependency aspect, we look at another time period, and group rates into windows. We are specifically interested in knowing the value of the MBS, assuming that interest rates pass through the window that defines the bucket. To illustrate this concept of windows and buckets, let's look at some simulated interest-rate scenarios based on the OAS model in Figure 10-13. Our bucket will be based on interest rates rising 100 basis points over four years.

Figure 10-13

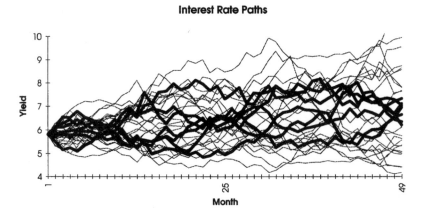

The interest-rate scenarios in Figure 10-13 consider the path of the long-term Treasury rate simulated by the OAS model. All of the interest paths we will consider reflect the path of the ten-year Treasury. Rates falling into the up-100-basis-point bucket have been put into bold lines. This up-100-basis-point bucket represents the change in rates relative to the implied forward rate. Price sensitivity from rising-rate buckets would be compared to that of falling-rate buckets in order to get a better perspective on the relative riskiness of the security. To see how this notion would work, let's look at the a comparison of two Treasury securities: the seven year and 30 year. Our price profile graph has been plotted in Figure 10-14.

Figure 10-14

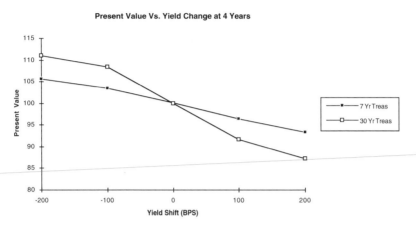

Present Value Vs. Yield Change at 4 Years

The interest rates in Figure 10-14 have been grouped into interest-rate buckets in a 100 basis point range. We have chosen four years to be our sampling point for the buckets. In the graph we see that the 30-year Treasury shows more price sensitivity than the seven-year Treasury. For both securities, we get an expected relationship that values rise when interest rates fall and decrease as interest rates rise. This essentially shows that the method of setting paths into buckets is consistent with general measures related to duration and convexity.

To consider the path-dependence aspect, we associate a window with each bucket. The window may be based on an earlier time period. In the context of our previous example, we would focus on a specific bucket and look at the ways by which we reach this end result.

For measuring path dependence we would look at the present values of the MBS, assuming that interest rates passed through a specific window, which defines a specific bucket. We can see the idea of the window through a further partitioning of the paths seen in Figure 10-15. Now we add an interest-rate window of up 50 basis points at two years. Our paths in the graph represent the scenarios where rates rise 50 basis points in two years and 100 basis points in four years.

Figure 10-15

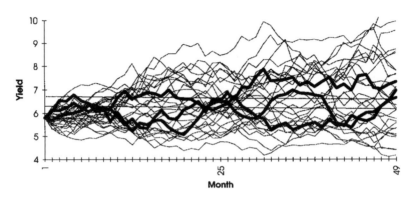

The two horizontal lines in Figure 10-15 represent the up-50-basis-point window at two years. All of the paths in bold now represent the case where we are up 50 basis points in two years and up 100 basis points in five years. Our paths in Figures 10-14 and 10-15 only represent a subset of all of the interest-rate paths we would use in an OAS calculation. If we plotted them all, the graph would be illegible.

Through the windows and buckets, we get to create standard interest rate paths. This is similar to the interest-rate paths that we have been looking at previously but with the benefit of many added scenarios. When considering the impact of path dependence, we are examining the relative price performance based on interest rates fluctuating. For a security with no path dependence, like a Treasury, the method by which interest reaches a certain destination should have a minimal impact on the valuation. Paths will be of some importance because they impact the valuation of coupon payments. However, there is no change in cash flows, unlike MBS.

We have set up average present values for three securities, a seven-year Treasury and two passthrough MBS, a current coupon and a 50-basis-point premium. To normalize the present values, we have normalized the scenario prices around the base case. The path-dependent present values can be seen in Figure 10-16.

Bucket Analysis

Figure 10-16

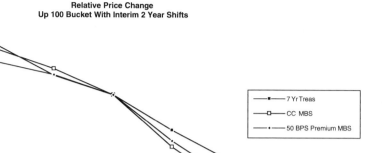

Relative Price Change
Up 100 Bucket With Interim 2 Year Shifts

For the Treasury security, we see some effect of path dependency, in cases where interest rates initially fell (the -200 and -100 cases), the average present values increase. The two MBS have slightly different behaviors. Recall that all of the points reflect a scenario in which interest rates wind up with the same end result. The degree to which the MBS curves diverge from the MBS provides some reflection of the impact on path dependency.

In the case of paths where interest rates rose initially (up 100 and up 200), we see that the overall present value dropped dramatically. This reflects the impact from a sudden lengthening of the securities. On the other hand, if interest rates first fell then rose, we see some impact on the securities; the 50-basis-point premium MBS actually does quite well in the down 200 at-two-year scenario. Whipsaw may be working to the benefit of this security because of the burnout effect.

To see a more extreme example of path dependency, let's consider three securities: a current coupon MBS and its IO and PO. The average present values can be seen in Figure 10-17.

The IO and PO show extreme cases of path dependency. In fact, the passthrough MBS now looks nearly linear. The IO value increases as we get more immediate rate increases. On the other hand, the IO decreases significantly for paths that immediately fall at two years. The PO has the opposite effect. Between the two types of paths, the cases where interest rates initially fall then rise show more extreme present-value effects than the rising-rate paths.

Figure 10-17

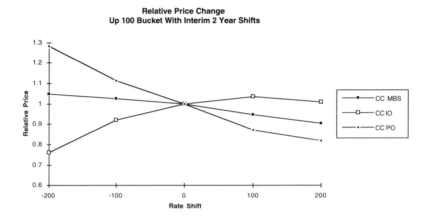

The impact of bucket analysis gives us ways to examine the path-dependency attributes of securities. The major drawback is the arbitrary nature by which we form the buckets and windows. However, this type of analysis can be performed for all types of MBS. By exploiting the information in the OAS model, we can get a systematic way of calibrating the level of path sensitivity.

Income

Whipsaws and Income

When considering the relationship between whipsaw analysis and the income aspect, we are extending our measures away from the traditional measures of value and risk. In particular, the income considerations will relate more to asset/liability considerations. The area of asset/liability analysis remains a very wide domain for analysis and consideration. We will briefly touch on the considerations of putting the whipsaws into an asset/liability framework.

For income measures, we are really more suited to consider the entire portfolio and not to concentrate so much on the bond-by-bond analysis followed up to now. Consideration of the entire portfolio assumes that there is some exposure to a portfolio system capable of looking at asset and liability analysis across interest-rate scenarios and paths. Scenarios would then be set up to measure the earnings exposure across scenarios. Earnings would represent the asset income minus liability expense.

Income analysis will involve two types of measures. First we need to consider the stability of earnings across scenarios. We would be trying to keep a stable interest rate spread between the assets and liabilities. In addition, we may have to keep some limitation of mark-to-market risk. This would be an import consideration for portfolio managers looking to keep a stable relationship between the asset and liability durations.

The second consideration would be putting some floor on the income expectations. That is, we would be making a tradeoff between a higher expected spread in order to ensure that along any scenario, the interest rate spread did not fall below a certain level.

Interest-rate paths and whipsaw analysis present an additional way to look at the income measures. By using whipsaws, we can take into account the mismatch of asset and liability reset. That is, if we were looking at a depository institution, which had short-term liabilities, the reset levels of the liabilities would be subject to path risk. To the degree that liabilities reset at different frequencies than assets, the more effective the use of whipsaw analysis.

Coming up with standard measures for whipsaw exposure may not be an easy task. One approach would be to use something like the path analysis to develop measures of income volatility and then to modify the asset and liability structure until the risk was brought down to a suitable level. In another approach, we would use the whipsaws to isolate the types of scenarios that may cause problems for the portfolio. The portfolio manager may not be able or may not want to take any immediate action. The analysis may lead to the development of contingency plans for managing the risk.

At a higher analytical level, optimization technology could be employed to find the right balance of liabilities for a given set of assets. This would give us a systematic way to achieve a specific objective while keeping risk within tolerable limits. Objectives could encompass ways to maximize income or to minimize the variance of income. Our risk constraints could be put in terms of minimal acceptable income levels.

Regulatory Considerations and Income

FFEIC

As part of safe and soundness tests for financial institutions, various regulatory bodies have been devising tests to examine the overall riskiness of MBS. These measures of risk do not relate directly to the credit component. Rather, more stress is placed on the cash flow and price stability of the securities. In this section, we briefly touch on some of the current regulatory perspectives and relate them to the measures of risk we have been developing.

As part of developing policies of safety and soundness, the Federal Financial Institutions Examining Council (FFEIC) has developed a set of guidelines to determine the riskiness of MBS. Depository institutions who hold "risky" securities may do so in order to reduce the overall interest-rate exposure of the institution. However, the securities must be reported as part of the trading account based on market value. Alternatively, the securities may be booked as assets held for sale marked at the lower of cost or market.

The FFEIC guidelines are an attempt to put a break on the outright speculation taken on by the purchase of higher-risk CMOs. However, institutions may wish to purchase derivative securities, which fall under the FFEIC unsuitable category, for quite legitimate reasons. For instance, an institution that has asset duration longer than liability duration may want to shorten the duration of their overall portfolio through the purchase of negative-duration securities (such as IOs or IO-like products). To the degree that the other assets of the institution are not marked to market or valued in a similar manner as the "risky" MBS, the higher is the accounting earnings volatility of the firm. While the true economic position of the firm may be enhanced through the use of the derivative securities, the fund manager must make the decision to take on more earnings variability.

As part of the tests for CMO suitability, the FFEIC has proposed three testing criteria, as listed in Table 10-6. Any bond that fails any of the FFEIC tests falls into the risky category.

Table 10-6

FFEIC Risk Tests
• **Base Cash Average Life:** Average life of the CMO cannot exceed 10 years.
• **Average Life Sensitivity:** CMO cannot extend more than 4 years or shorten more than 6 years based upon an instantaneous shift of the yield curve of +/ 300 basis points.
• **Price Sensitivity:** The value of the CMO cannot change by more than 17% for a yield curve change of +/ 300 basis points or any 100-basis-point incremental shift up to 300 basis points.

The tests look both at the cash-flow timing, stability, and price variability of the CMOs. By constraining the maximum average life, the test would generally discourage an institution from taking a large yield-curve bet. Likewise, the tests for average life variability and price risk are intended to prevent an institution from purchasing a CMO with a large amount of embedded option risk.

The FFEIC tests cover many of the major risk categories, which we have described up to now. They incorporate the notions of cash-flow stability, as well as duration and convexity. For many institutions, considering these factors is an important step in the measurement and control of risk.

Are the FFEIC tests perfect? No, but it would be hard to think up a set of criteria, which would be all encompassing and still give the depository institutions some latitude in making asset-allocation decisions. There is nothing magical about a ten year average life security or the average life changes stipulated by FFEIC. From a higher-level risk perspective, the

FFEIC tests do not consider the impacts of changing the shape of the yield curve. Measures such as the key rate duration and twist can be used to examine this type of risk.

One of the implications of developing cut-off rules will be that Wall Street will try to design the maximum number of CMOs, which just meet the testing levels. This may lead to large numbers of securities, which initially meet the tests, but soon fall outside the bounds of riskiness. Given supply and demand aspects, securities could show more price deterioration as they move to the edges of the risk tests.

Using the criteria of instantaneous interest-rate shifts may be a bit too conservative. Looking at volatility at this scale may not be realistic and could lead to the disqualification of securities, which are not truly risky. Still, using the instantaneous shift makes the test easier, as it may only require using a single prepayment speed for the new scenario.

In addition, the tests do not consider the impact of interest-rate paths. Whipsaw scenarios may cause a security, which ostensibly looks protected, to become vulnerable to cash-flow variability as the structure of the CMO changes.

Despite its faults, the FFEIC tests lead portfolio managers to look carefully at the risk profiles of the securities they purchase. By using the scenario-analysis approach, the portfolio manager can use the FFEIC criteria to examine the risk and return characteristics of the securities he or she owns or is contemplating purchasing.

Insurance Regulation and FLUX

The NAIC committee has been working to develop standards of MBS suitability for the insurance industry. Currently they are planning to use a measure called the Flow Uncertainty Index (FLUX)[5] for the determination of CMO risk. Using FLUX, securities will be scored based on a risk index with overall suitability being based on the risk score.

---

[5]A more in-depth discussion of FLUX can be found in "FLUX; Flow Uncertainly Index: A Measure of CMO Cash Flow Variability," *Quantitative Perspectives*, Andrew Davidson & Co., Inc., October 19, 1993, New York.

FLUX looks to combine the price sensitivity and cash-flow variability risk into a single index. The basic components of the index are in Table 10-7.

Table 10-7

NAIC CMO Flow Uncertainty Index (FLUX)
Price Sensitivity: The first component measures the magnitude of negative percentage changes in the present value relative to a base case scenario.
Cash-Flow Timing: The second term represents the timing risk of cash flows. It is calculated based on a period-by-period comparison of the cumulative present value of the cash flows of the bond relative to a base case.

The price sensitivity component captures the risk of premium MBS prepaying sooner than expected or discount MBS prepaying later than expected. Securities with large positive or negative durations would score high on this category. This would include standard products such as long PACs as well as derivative products such as IOs and POs.

The second component examines the change in cash flows for a specified scenario relative to some base case. By looking at the change in cash flows we can measure the potential reinvestment risk or asset/liability mismatch. MBS with high cash-flow variability, such as support bonds would receive high scores across this category.

The FLUX method builds a general framework for categorizing securities. Scenarios can be used, which look at both the parallel rate shift cases as well as the whipsaw scenarios. The measure could be applied at both the security level and the portfolio level. By running analysis at the portfolio level, products that serve as hedge securities to another could be analyzed more as a whole instead of as two potentially risky parts.

■ CONCLUSION

MBS have exposure to the path of interest rates for two main reasons: First, the prepayment characteristics of an MBS pool will depend upon the manner in which interest rates move. Because a pool contains a finite group of borrowers, the pool's prepayment characteristics will change as the more interest-rate sensitive individuals prepay their loans.

The second dependence of MBS value on the path of interest rates comes through the CMO sector of the market. The manner in which interest rates move will affect the structure of a deal and the relative performance of the classes. In this chapter, we examined how to use the method of whipsaw analysis to judge the characteristics of various CMO securities. These methods give us a viewpoint to compare how well a deal is constructed and how to compare two relatively similar classes.

We have further examined how to extract path-related information from the OAS model. This gives us an opportunity to exploit the vast amount of information generated in the course of a typical OAS analysis. The bucket analysis categorizes the relative present value of an MBS based upon the paths the interest-rate simulator creates.

The techniques of whipsaw analysis bring us full circle in our methods for analyzing MBS. After examining the static environment, scenario analysis, OAS, and path-dependence risk, we need to step back and consider the relationships between the methods and the best ways they are utilized. In the following chapter we consider the various analytic techniques.

CHAPTER ELEVEN

Comparison of Approaches

Anyone who has ever had the misfortune to go into the hospital or spend time in an emergency room can commiserate with the experience of endless medical exams. It would seem that the health-care profession has more types of tests than Wall Street has models. Sometimes these tests serve differing purposes. At other times, they may be used to get related information about the same condition. Tests may also be repeated to check for false readings. Whatever the case, we put up with a lot of probing and poking on our way to getting healthy. Like the medical tests, our models can teach as much as possible about the securities we wish to purchase. Used improperly, we just waste time and money with no insurance company to bear the costs.

Up to now, our discussion of MBS has covered a wide variety of topics. We have looked extensively at the properties of the securities. In our effort to understand the behavior of the securities, we have looked at various methods for security analysis. These methods have covered both methods for relative value and risk analysis.

Along both the relative value and risk-analysis dimensions, we have looked at models with varying degrees of complexity. From the portfolio manager's point of view, there may seem to be an endless choice of alternatives, each requiring various assumptions and decisions. Pairing the methods with the securities may seem to be a daunting challenge and could lead to frustration or misapplication.

In this chapter we try and synthesize some of the topics covered previously. In doing so, we set up some guideposts to consider when looking at different approaches. The overriding theme will be the mapping of the problem onto the solution.

When using models and analytics we may see ourselves as searching for the ultimate truth. However, in the world of MBS, there can be no absolute truth. There are just too many unknowns. Much relies upon human behavior, which can be modeled but not fully and perfectly predicted.

We must make choices and decisions in this search. One could spend unlimited amounts of time and money in search of the "right" answer. This may lead to more and more OAS simulations or increasing complexity of models. At some point, the cost of getting more information outweighs any benefits of having the data. From another perspective, we could be searching for fruitless information. That is, we may be over-analyzing a security. This may be the case where we apply an options-based model to a security with little option risk, like running an OAS for a very deeply discounted passthrough.

In developing a comparison of alternatives, we will look at the general types of problems encountered in analyzing securities. Then we will move on to discussing the accuracy, insights, and costs of using differing types of approaches. The chapter finishes with some thoughts on integrating the models with internally developed systems.

■ APPROPRIATENESS TO THE PROBLEM

Like the carpenter on a job, the portfolio manager needs to find the right tool for the job. A carpenter does not approach the task by laying out the tools and then applying each one sequentially until the task is completed. Instead, the job drives the tool that will be needed. Likewise, the portfolio manager must know about the problem before initiating the solution.

By properly categorizing the problem, we can consider the alternative approaches. Depending upon the approach taken, we may have to make further decisions. These decisions will be driven by the constraints placed upon time, cost, and accuracy. The two general types of problems we consider are bond evaluation and portfolio strategy.

Bond Evaluation

The day-to-day decisions of the portfolio manager necessitate choices about which securities to sell and which to purchase. One of the standard ways to go through the bond-evaluation decision is to look at some measure related to the yield or spread of the security. This measure gives a quick synopsis of value and can be compared across securities.

However, consideration of relative value requires some tradeoff between risk and return. That is, the decision to purchase a three-year PAC bond at 80 basis points to the three year versus a three-year support bond trading at 250 to the curve. Extra spread does not come for free. Applying the models we have discussed earlier can give some idea about the potential benefits from taking on additional risk.

Our measures of risk cover the traditional categories of general interest-rate risk: duration and convexity. This may be expanded further to cover other measures, notably basis and liquidity risk. Basis risk covers the potential for yield-spread relationships between market sectors to change. For example, whole-loan CMOs have wide spreads relative to agency CMOs. In some cases, basis risk may not be something that can be hedged. Exposure may at least be calculated. Liquidity risk may also be considered in our list of categories. In the cases of derivative products, the bid/ask spread may be sufficiently wide to cause a serious loss in value when looking to reverse a transaction. This loss of value does not require a sophisticated options model.

In terms of the relative value measures, we can define our measures into those that consider long-term value and those with some intermediate time frame. A long-term type of value measure means we extract the relative benefit over the life of the security. This will generally involve measures of yield and spread. A brief overview of the long-term types of measures can be found in Table 11-1. More intermediate measures of value look at the gains from holding a security over some specified period. At the end of the period, the security may or may not be sold.

Table 11-1 Long-Term Relative-Value Measures

Value Measures	Calculation Difficulty	Critical Assumptions	Option Risk Addressed
Yield	Easy	Prepayment	No
Spread to Benchmark	Easy	Prepayment	No
Spread to Curve	Moderate	Prepayment Base Case Curve	Somewhat
Option-Adjusted Spread	Difficult	Prepayment Volatility	Yes

Our measures of long-term relative value assume that we purchase a security and then hold it until the final cash flow. Value will typically be quoted in terms of yield or spread to the benchmark. These types of measures simply require access to a bond calculator, a price, and a prepayment projection. This prepayment projection could be a simple long-term speed, a vector of changing speeds, or a prepayment model.

If we want to extend the analysis a bit further, we can consider the spread to the entire yield curve. By doing so, we get a better match between the monthly paying MBS and a yield curve, which may not be perfectly flat. Our critical assumption will be the prepayment projection, which could be one of the choices described above. In the case where we want to use a prepayment model, some further choices can be made about the base case yield curve. That is, whether or not to allow the current yield curve to persist into the future to allow rates to follow along the implied forward yields. By using the implied forward yields, we start to bring in some measures of option risk.

Unfortunately, these long-term measures do not consider the full option dynamics that make MBS complicated. They tell the potential investor nothing about the decision to purchase the PAC or the support bond. Or even less stark, they do not show how to compare two PAC bonds with the same average life but with one backed up by premium collateral and the other backed up by current coupon collateral. Consider the choice in Table 11-2; which bond offers the best value?

Table 11-2

	Bond 1	Bond 2	Bond 3	Bond 4
Security	5-Year PAC, 8% Collateral	5-Year PAC, 8% Collateral	5-Year Support, 7% Collateral	5-Year PAC, 7% Collateral
Nominal Spread	95 bps	100 bps	225 bps	80 bps

We could draw some preliminary conclusions between the bonds. It would appear that Bond 2 offers better value than Bond 1 because it trades at a somewhat wider spread. We would probably want to know something about the relative PAC bands between the securities. In the absence of some other confounding information, we would not really need to run any further analysis if the choice was only between these two securities.

For choosing between the other alternatives, it can be a little like Monte Hall asking the investor to choose the magic door containing the cheap security. Without some way of looking at the underlying option risk, there is no clear way of determining which security has the best value.

Applying Static Spread

Looking at current measures of spread may be a way of determining the security to select, given a menu of alternatives. At other times, we may want to compare various segments in the MBS market. By comparing segments, we may get some idea of the relative value ebb and flow. It may be useful to look for sectors, which move from fair value to good value. Situations like this may occur when various supply and demand factors temporarily move spreads in specific sectors. For example, if we kept examining the spread relationships in Figure 11-1, we might draw some preliminary conclusions between current relative value.

Figure 11-1

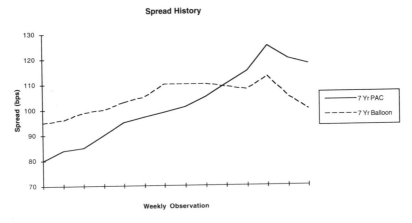

Spread History

In Figure 11-1 we show a representative time series of nominal spreads. It compares the spread of a new-issue seven-year PAC bond with a seven-year balloon passthrough. Looking at the graph, one could surmise that spreads on PACs had widened significantly, moving beyond the spreads for balloons. Spreads for balloons had recently tightened, but PAC spreads had not tightened very much. Does this make a good case for PACs over balloons? Maybe. The change in nominal spread could reflect some increased option cost for the balloons, perhaps reflecting increased option risk. Still, looking at longer-term spread relationships may give us some clues about where to start looking for relative value.

Applying OAS

Until now, it would seem that the OAS approach is the answer to all of our problems. It gives us a flexible way to look at the long-term spread measures while fully accounting for the option risk. However, applying the OAS model may not be always the most effective way of deciding between securities.

Before making a choice based on the OAS model, the investor should be comfortable with the overall risk characteristics of the security. Purchasing MBS solely based on OAS ignores the decisions about the desired duration and convexity of the security under consideration. Just like the portfolio manager who does not buy the Treasury security with the highest yield, purchasers of MBS should not always look for the highest OAS bond.

While the OAS procedure corrects for duration and convexity differences among securities, the portfolio manager must still make the duration call. After deciding the duration range of the securities to consider, OAS can be used to look for the security with the highest spread. Determination of duration and convexity could be done using either a method that varies spread and prepayment speed, or using a constant OAS pricing model for duration. The choice may be determined based upon the amount of time needed to perform the calculations and the range of securities to consider.

The OAS approach serves as the best method for looking at value net of option risk, but the model has its limitations. OAS relies very heavily on the assumed prepayment function and on the estimate of volatility used to drive the interest-rate process. Because prepayment models will differ across dealers, it is very difficult to get matching OAS results for the same security. Thus, it is never clear what the real OAS may be.

From the portfolio manager's perspective, relying on OAS requires getting comfortable with a couple of firms' models. By tracking a model over time, the reliability and consistency of a model can be verified. When comparing across firms, it may not be as important to get the same exact OAS levels as it is to get some consistency of ranking. Consider the securities we had in Table 11-2. If two models said that Bond 4 had the highest OAS, then we would have greater comfort about the overall relative value of this security.

The OAS model relies on averaging procedures for estimating the spread. In coming up with the solution, we use the average present value when solving for the OAS. This average has a certain distribution, implying that we really could form some confidence intervals for our OAS measure. By thinking about the confidence interval, we suggest that there is a certain tolerance for the OAS results. This suggests that making investment decisions based on a few basis points of OAS may not be too reliable.

Scenario Analysis

From the investor's perspective, measures related to spread can give guidance about the benefits from holding the security until the last cash flow. There may be times when the investment may need to be evaluated over a shorter period. This may be true for institutions who have to mark to market and look at their investments on a total-return basis. The decision to purchase a security may be driven by the expected returns.

For bond-evaluation purposes, a security that outperforms another in all scenarios will probably be a preferred investment. If this security does not also trade at a wider OAS, then there must be some conflicting information, which may mean that model assumptions need to be checked. In most cases, a security will not dominate in all scenarios, reflecting differences in duration and convexity. When this occurs, the investor may rely on averaging procedures to get the best probability-weighted return or purchase a security, which has a return profile in line with the needs of the portfolio.

When going through an evaluation of various investment alternatives, scenario analysis may prove useful to compare the expected performance. The decision to use scenario analysis will require other choices regarding the way to implement the method. An overview of choices can be seen in Table 11-3.

Table 11-3

Decision Variable	Alternatives
Prepayment assumption	Single speed, vector, model
Horizon pricing method	Speed/spread, OAS model
Reinvestment	Short-term rate, yield of security
Rate shift-timing	Immediate, gradual
Rate shift-method	Parallel, yield curve twists, paths

Implementing scenario analysis leads to various choices over the level of detail contained in the model. These choices may be driven by the need to get a result and the desired level of accuracy. Our listing of alternatives, in some cases, ranges from the simple to the more complex. This is the case with the prepayment and pricing methods. The most common applications of the model would be to use a single speed and some method for using a horizon price driven off a matrix type approach.

Using a prepayment vector would be more appropriate in cases when one would expect the long-term prepayment estimate to be different from some short term numbers. This may be the case after a decline in interest rates. The short-term outlook may be significantly higher than the long term. When looking at very prepayment-sensitive instruments, using a vector may be more meaningful. At the highest end of the analytical methods, one may use a prepayment function. This may not always be a viable alternative given the cost and effort needed to create a model.

From the pricing perspective, one normally has to choose between using some sort of matrix approach or a pricing model. In many cases, a matrix-type approach may be suitable. This would be the case when there may be a reasonable understanding or consensus about how a security would trade in a particular scenario. For more complicated securities, the matrix approach may be difficult or misleading to implement.

The reinvestment decision does not really range in terms of sophistication as much as it does in terms of degrees of aggressiveness. Reinvesting at the short-term rate plus some spread represents a more conservative approach to looking at total return. Dealers may sometimes assume that proceeds from interim principal and interest will be reinvested in a similar yielding security to the one being analyzed. Raising the reinvestment rate will help out the total return. This may be a realistic assumption, but the investor must be sure that any proceeds being reinvested at the yield of the MBS have price risk at the horizon. Otherwise they are assuming that the funds get reinvested in a money market account with the yield of an MBS but no price risk. If we could all make this type of investment, there would be little need for sophisticated models.

Methods for shifting the interest rates will usually be decided depending upon either the tools available to the investor or some external needs. We have discussed the merits of gradual interest-rate movements relative to immediate shifts. However, as pointed out in the description of regulatory-risk measures, immediate rate shifts may be required for certain cases.

The types of shifts required will depend upon the need for the analysis. Most common applications will be the parallel yield curve shifts. Securities with significant yield-curve exposure should be examined under cases of changing the slope of the curve. When looking at these types of scenarios, we may have to modify other choices of model implementation. In particular, deciding to look at a nonparallel yield-curve twist may necessitate the use of a prepayment function and an options-based horizon-pricing model. For securities with the potential for high path-dependency risk, looking at interest-rate paths may be the most appropriate implementation of the model.

While not mentioned above, the choice of horizon will have a material impact on the results. The standard approach uses a 12-month horizon for the model. Using shorter horizons puts great emphasis on the horizon-pricing assumption. Extending the horizon puts greater weight on the reinvestment decision. Although a security may be expected to be held for longer than 12 months, using this as a nominal horizon may be a more prudent way to look at the expected return.

Combining Approaches

In the decision to look for the bond offering the superior relative value, there are really no limitations on the combinations of relative value tools. From the investor's perspective, the first issue may be finding the sector offering overall better value. This may come from the investigation of current trends in value, looking for areas currently out of favor.

Along this type of inquiry, one may look across different product sectors, agencies, and sections of the yield curve.

The second question will be to find the security offering the best value within a specific sector. This may involve some ranking according to a spread measure. By using the spread comparison first you may be able to put some minimum thresholds on expected return. From there, it may be advisable to compare the expected return and risk profiles of the security. This certainly gives some guidance about the behavior under differing interest-rate scenarios. Profiles can also be developed to look at the extension and call risk of the securities.

In some cases, securities will appear to offer value according to both spread measures and total return. This makes the decision-making process more straightforward. When there may not be a clear-cut answer, some tradeoffs may have to be made. For institutions that have to mark to market, there may be a bias toward relying more on total-return measures. This would lead toward investments that provide sufficient returns over a variety of interest rate scenarios. The result may be a somewhat more conservative investment strategy, but should lead to a disciplined investment strategy.

Those investors who rely heavily on OAS-based results for the investment decision should feel comfortable for the stability of the model. This may lead to looking at sensitivity to changes in OAS assumptions. In particular, it may be useful to see the change in OAS levels for changes in the prepayment model.

Even with the general ideas of total return and OAS, certain classes of securities may be better suited to some specific types of analysis. Bonds with values that depend heavily on the shape of the yield curve should be analyzed based on some basic curve twists. These twists would cover both steepenings and flattenings, from changes in both the short end and long end of the curve.

For securities such as inverse floaters and inverse IOs, the methods of analysis may be a bit more specialized. First, with bonds offered at such high yields, the investors should be clued in that there will be significant performance declines under changing scenarios. It becomes important to know what these scenarios would be. One initial way to look at scenarios would be to compute yields based on some range of yield scenarios from rates not changing to rates moving exactly along the expected forward rate curve. An example of this can be seen in Table 11-4.

Table 11-4

Scenario	Yield
Unchanged	31.2%
25% of Forward Curve	22.3%
50% of Forward Curve	10.3%
75% of Forward Curve	8.4%
100% of Forward Curve	5.3%

A multiple of the forward curve is formed in the following manner. First, we compute the vector of implied short-term forward rates. We would look at the difference between the forward rate and the current rate to come up with the projection. For example, suppose current short-term LIBOR rates were 3 percent and, in one year, the implied forward LIBOR rate was 4 percent. Moving along at 25 percent of the forward rate would mean using 3.25 percent as the rate in year; 75 percent of the forward rate would mean that we would use 3.75 percent as the projection in one year. Using a method such as this combines the spread method with scenario analysis. Its basic objective will be to see how much the yield of a security depends upon the forward-rate expectations. Also, one could use the method of examining the yield of an inverse floater relative to changes in both prepayment speeds and LIBOR rates as described in the risk section of Chapter 9.

Portfolio Analysis

From the perspective of analyzing the entire portfolio, we take on a different set of objectives than deciding about the purchase of a specific security. At the portfolio level, we are more concerned with the overall characteristics of the portfolio rather than the focus on relative value used in the bond-evaluation decision. In looking at the portfolio, our focus will be both on the actual recorded characteristics as well as the relation of the portfolio to some established benchmark.

The use of a benchmark provides a valuable guide for the portfolio manager. In many cases, the performance of the portfolio relative to the benchmark plays a large role in compensation and the ability to attract additional funds. Comparison to a benchmark provides a source of discipline to the fund manager and gives a way to evaluate risk positions and investment decisions.

When setting up the comparison to the benchmark, the most important questions may concern the relative interest-rate exposure. This may involve calculating duration or price profiles of the portfolio relative to the benchmark. In addition, some accommodation must be made for measuring the exposure to yield-curve changes and basis risk. The consideration of basis risk will occur when a portfolio has used alternative securities to replicate the benchmark. An example would be holdings of whole loan product for a portfolio compared to an agency index.

The choice of model to apply depends upon the scope of the problem, the size of the portfolio, and any constraints related to the cost of computations or the time needed to reach a solution. The general decision of the portfolio manager will be to look at the level of return relative to the degree of risk taken. For example, consider the portfolio in Figure 11-2.

Figure 11-2

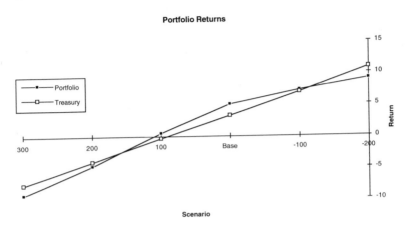

The portfolio shown in Figure 11-2 may be representative of an insurance company, which uses a seven-year Treasury as the benchmark. The return strategy implicit in the portfolio could be described as purchasing higher-yielding MBS and taking on some convexity risk. That is, the portfolio seems to have sold options. This causes the base case scenario to outperform the Treasury by a significant margin. However, as we move across differing scenarios, the portfolio begins to underperform the Treasury. This underperformance occurs in both directions—an indication of more negative convexity in the portfolio than the benchmark.

To derive the information from Figure 11-2, some choices must be made about the method of computing scenario returns. The various choices have been described in Table 11-3. In considering the comparisons to the benchmark, it would be useful to know how its descriptive statistics are calculated. If the benchmark were an MBS index, the decision may be influenced by the manner in which the MBS returns are computed. In other words, if the index returns were formed using a matrix pricing method and our portfolio returns were computed on a constant OAS basis, any comparison may contain some bias.

Portfolio Analysis

Portfolio analysis will focus on two types of issues, coming up with descriptive statistics and developing the relative performance information. We have laid out some of the motivations for the performance information and described the methods to derive the information. For the descriptive statistics we would look at factors related to both the relative value and risk. A summary of descriptive types of portfolio information can be seen in Table 11-5 below.

Table 11-5

Value Measures	Considerations
Yield, spread	Calculate portfolio yield
Yield profiles	Calculate portfolio yield
Expected return	Scenario analysis
Horizon price	Matrix pricing vs. OAS model
Risk	
Duration, convexity	Spread/speed vs. OAS model
Curve exposure	Spread to curve vs. OAS model
Volatility sensitivity	OAS based
Average life profile	Prepayment expectation
Basis exposure	Inter-sector yield volatility

The most important consideration to the portfolio manager will be the various value and risk measures. Deriving these results will fall into the Considerations column. As indicated in this column, there may be several ways to derive the same type of information, each with slightly different levels of accuracy and complexity.

For some of the measures, notably those related to yield, there exists only one correct way to calculate the result. When dealing with portfolio yield, the only proper way to perform the calculation is to lump all of the cash flows together and treat the portfolio as one synthetic security. Other methods, which involve averaging the yields of the component securities, provide approximations, not the actual yields. In some cases, portfolio models have been known to arithmetically average the yields of the underlying securities in order to come up with a portfolio yield.

Unfortunately, yields are not linear functions, so simple averaging does not give accurate results. At other times, yields may be averaged based on some duration weighting scheme. While this may be a better approximation, it is still an approximation and should only be undertaken when no other method exists to determine the portfolio yield.

Spread numbers could be the simple yield of the portfolio minus the yield of a benchmark or the method of developing a spread to the curve. Solving for a spread to the curve would require creating the synthetic security out of the entire portfolio.

Expected return profiles and price profiles appear as the output of scenario-analysis programs. We have elaborated at length about the various ways of implementing these models. When dealing at the entire portfolio level, simplifying the calculations may be the only way to get results in a reasonable amount of time.

Duration and convexity are fairly important risk parameters for the entire portfolio. They may serve as the best indicator of the potential deviation of portfolio return from the benchmark. These numbers could be derived along with other scenario-analysis results. However, the scenario analysis would look at profiles based upon the horizon. Duration and convexity should be based off of instantaneous shifts in rates.

Exposure to the curve is something not often considered in the examination of MBS portfolios. This is not because the results are unimportant but because of the difficulty in calculating the exposure. One less onerous way to calculate the exposure would be to determine the overall spread to the curve. This spread could then be held constant as the yield curve shifts. The bonds in the portfolio could then be priced off of this spread in the yield-twist scenario. Some assumption must also be made about prepayments, a forecast table may be appropriate, but access to a prepayment model would be the best way to consider the effects of the changing curve. At a more complex level, a curve shift could be evaluated based on OAS pricing technology.

Sensitivity to volatility derives from the options exposure of the portfolio. Measuring this requires an OAS-type model. Determining the volatility exposure, or vega in option parlance, would be done through calculating the price of the portfolio by holding OAS constant and then moving volatility up and down a discrete amount, such as 100 basis points.

Measures related to average life exposure look at the potential for the extension or call risk of the portfolio. This is useful because it gives some indication about the amount by which the payback schedule for the portfolio begins to differ from the benchmark. This may lead to differing strategies for selling or purchasing securities as the yield curve changes. The critical choice for looking at the average life sensitivity will be the type of prepayment forecast used.

Basis risk would be used to look at the exposure to differing market sectors relative to the benchmark. This risk measure is static based, it can be driven off of a price/yield calculator. Determination of basis risk may be taken by finding various groupings for the securities, such as agency or issuer and then looking at the price sensitivity to changes in yield.

■ ACCURACY

In the best of all worlds, we would be able to expend unlimited resources in our search for the best analytical solutions. But in reality, some compromises must be made in order to have enough information in order to make a reasoned investment decision. In considering the issues of bond evaluation and portfolio analysis, we look to apply pricing methods and risk models, which give answers commensurate with the needed level of accuracy.

What do we mean by accurate results? We are not suggesting sloppy or questionable analysis. Rather, we look at how to get a sufficient amount of information in order to make a reasoned decision. For example, using a matrix pricing model and scenario-dependent PSA prepayment forecasts, we may be able to derive the effective duration of a portfolio, which differs from the OAS-derived number by a reasonably small amount, say less 0.5 or less. If it took us 15 minutes to compute the duration using the simple method, and three hours using the OAS, which would we prefer? This depends upon the need for the information. If we were running an end-of-the day portfolio update, then time may not matter. However, if we needed to update the portfolio during the middle of a volatile trading day, then it may be more effective to go with a slightly less accurate method. Less accurate may be better than no answer.

In examining the duration issue, we may explore other alternatives. For example, assume that the constant OAS duration and convexity could be run on an overnight batch process. During the trading day, the duration could be updated using information about the change in the yield curve and the convexity.

Questions of accuracy arise when running OAS analysis. If we use the method of simulating future interest rates, we have to make a decision about the number of simulation trials. To minimize the amount of potential statistical error, we could run enormous amounts of simulations. However, this would be foolish. In an ideal implementation, we would run a sufficient number of trials so that our potential error was within the range of the bid/ask spread. That is, there may be no reason to be accurate to the nearest penny for an MBS when the bid/ask spread is half a point or more.

If we were making an investment in a highly volatile mortgage derivative, we would want greater accuracy than if we were examining a PAC bond. Likewise, if we were deriving the constant OAS duration for the portfolio, we may be willing to use fewer simulations if this means getting results in time to take action.

When calculating the OAS for a CMO, we may make some simplifying assumptions about the underlying collateral. In some cases, we may find that our results are sufficiently accurate when grouping the collateral of the CMO deal into a single set of descriptive characteristics. We would then run the OAS on the CMO as if its cash flows depended on a single pool of MBS.

Issues related to accuracy are more likely to occur when considering portfolio-level analysis. On the bond-evaluation level, accuracy may be paramount because results may lead to direct buy/sell decisions. At the portfolio level, the number of the holdings may make it difficult to run level at the highest level of detail.

A Question of Accuracy

We were asked to evaluate the MBS holdings of a commercial bank. The bank had assets split between CMOs and passthrough MBS. The passthroughs totaled over a thousand pools. Analyzing each one would have proven to be an unneeded task, and it was unlikely that the analysis could have been completed in a time satisfactory to the client. In a case like that, we found ways to group the pools by coupon and aging category in order to create aggregate holdings. This leads to almost no change in results, but a significant decrease in the time needed to compute results.

■ INSIGHT

Our choice of tool may be influenced by the type of insights we are looking to gain from the analysis. In the evaluation of single securities, we are usually trying to determine if any higher expected yields are consistent with the increased level of risk taken on. When the critical factor is the risk-versus-return issue, we need to be confident with our measure of return, which may be spread or scenario-analysis driven, and with the risk measures we are deriving.

Understanding the level of option risk embedded in a security requires using some sort of options approach. However, if the need is to understand the cash-flow patterns of a security, setting up simple profiles of average life versus PSA may be in order. At other times, we may have to come up with some hybrid type of analytical method, such as using a multiple of the forward curve when looking at inverse floaters.

As users of analytical models, we should look for tools that provide flexibility. By flexible, we are concerned with the types of securities capable of being analyzed by a model and the ability of a model to have its assumptions and structure changed. One of the constant factors of the MBS market is change. The market has experienced a proliferation of new mortgage contracts and CMO types. Tools should be designed to be adaptable and handle new securities.

Scenario analysis and OAS models have shown tremendous robustness in their ability to be adopted across a wide range of MBS products. The greater the flexibility of a model, the more likely it is to have some complications in regard to the level of assumptions or model structure.

■ COST/TIME

Static measures related to price, yield, and cash flow come cheap. Many prebuilt calculators exist and are easily accessible to investors. There may be a need to develop pricing calculators for new types of products. Some of these could be as simple as developing some functions within a spreadsheet type of program.

Our experience has taught us that the relative cost and time needed to perform calculations directly influences the type of analysis performed. This will be related to the issue of accuracy. While OAS-type models may provide significant insights into security behavior, they are very costly to build, support, and run. We should look for ways of improving the computation time of calculations without sacrificing too much accuracy.

When we choose to put all the bells and whistles on a scenario-analysis model, we may wind up with a tool too weighted down to be effective. Running constant OAS total return may be a fine analytical tool, but if its costs are prohibitively high, we may want to limit the number of times we require updates, and perhaps look for a scaled down way of determining results between OAS runs.

■ INTEGRATION WITH INTERNAL SYSTEMS

The trend in model development has been going in two directions. On the one track, many institutional investors have been putting time and effort into developing internal systems. These systems try and link up analytics with the tasks of portfolio management, including the trading and settlement of securities. The trade-related software portions are generally familiar to the systems staff, but the expertise for analytical development is less widespread. This may lead investors to seriously consider purchasing analytical software rather than trying to develop the models in-house.

On the other track, the number of software vendors has increased and now there are many companies who provide sophisticated MBS analytical services.[1] In some cases, these analytics come as part of a general bundle of services, such as the CMO functions provided on Bloomberg. However, some vendors of analytical portfolio models market the cash-flow generators for the securities. This provides a critical tool for those institutions looking to develop their own internal systems. Having access to the cash-flow generators provides the basic building block for all types of value and risk analytics. It is this type of development that will make it easier for firms to have their own analytics.

This may mean that, in the future, portfolio managers may rely less on getting hard copy output of pricing and prepayment models from dealers. Instead, more time may be spent in integrating modules into internal systems. Much of this will be driven by the decreasing cost of computing power. As a tribute to this, all of the OAS results in this book were derived from a model coded on a PC running with a 486 processor. Years ago, OAS models were being run on Cray supercomputers, out of the reach of most investors. Now the results can be obtained by a computer, which fits into a briefcase.

■ CONCLUSION

The MBS investor faces a daunting task. Bonds will often be offered with yields and spreads, which seem fairly attractive, but which may not be realistic. Like peeling away the layers of the onion, the task becomes

---

[1] Oddly enough, perhaps the greatest catalyst in the availability of CMO analytics was the demise of Drexel, Burnham Lambert. During the liquidation of the firm, its CMO database and cash-flow routines were sold to various parties. Many of the firms that now provide CMO analytical services to institutional investors purchased this software.

one of uncovering the true value of the security. To do this, we must consider the assumptions on which the yield and spread quotes are founded.

Moving further, we may need to know the degree to which the quoted spreads reflect an option component. The greater the option exposure, the larger the quoted spread. There is nothing really new about this, it boils down to the risk and return relationship. We have explored a variety of techniques to analyze MBS. These techniques can be applied in conjunction with another depending upon the need.

The time and desire to determine the MBS value, net of the options component, will be driven by the need for having the information and the available tools. Many Wall Street dealers will supply analytics to support their contention that a bond looks rich or cheap. Investors can accept or reject this "free" service. Declining costs for computer hardware, combined with increased supply of software modules bring the development of analytical techniques into the realm of the investment manager. In the following chapter we consider some of the issues related to developing your own tools.

CHAPTER TWELVE

■
Building Your Own Tools
■

Susan Spring calls the investment committee meeting to order. It has been a year since they instituted the mortgage-backed securities investment plan. Using internal resources and third-party tools, they have developed a good approach to analyzing mortgages. There have been ups and downs. Prepayments moved unexpectedly at times, and a new product was analyzed incorrectly. Nevertheless, the portfolio has beaten its benchmark consistently. Moreover, the development of new risk measures has helped in the understanding of the company's liabilities and the investment benchmarks. Challenges still lie ahead, but the venture into mortgage-backed securities has proven to be interesting and rewarding.

■ SETTING AN INVESTMENT STRATEGY

The first step in building your own tools has nothing to do with the tools. The first step is to identify your investment objectives. Throughout the earlier chapters we have stressed the importance of identifying the purpose of a model before applying it. Until there is a universal model, which we do not expect soon, portfolio managers and analysts must still make all the hard choices. Identifying your investment objectives requires that you evaluate the goals of the portfolio. Are you interested in total return, or do you have specific liabilities? Are you targeting an index or a duration target? How important is liquidity? How much risk can you bear? An important question to address is: How aggressive are your goals?

After assessing your goals, you can begin to develop an investment strategy and determine the role of analytics within that strategy. In developing a strategy, the complexity and aggressiveness of the strategy, the analytical requirements, and the cost of implementation must be considered together. Complex strategies may require sophisticated analytical tools. Sophisticated tools usually require an investment in hardware, software, and people. As the cost of analysis rises, the investment objectives become harder to meet.

How much should you spend on analytics? There is no specific answer; but here is a way of analyzing the problem. Mortgage-backed securities generally offer option-adjusted returns of 50 basis points or more over Treasuries. That 50-basis-point advantage can be quickly erased if the investment strategy is implemented poorly. Clearly, you need to spend enough to keep that advantage from eroding. MBS also pose other operational obstacles that lead to back-office costs that could cost you up to 10 basis points, depending on the size of your operation. (Sophisticated investors can turn operational complexities into profit opportunities.) Furthermore, just beating Treasuries usually isn't sufficient. There are usually high-grade corporate obligations that offer 20 to 30 basis points in excess of Treasuries. That only leaves about a 10 to 20 basis points advantage, of which only a portion could be spent on analysis. For a billion dollar portfolio, 5 basis points translates into an annual budget of $500,000. While that seems like a lot to spend, expenditures for software, hardware, data, and people could easily exceed that budget.

Another strategy is to use analytics to expand the advantage of the portfolio over alternative investments. While MBS generically offer a 50-basis-point advantage of Treasuries, the market offers many opportunities to make substantially more. These opportunities often result from situations that others have overlooked; situations where regulatory or other changes are forcing a realignment of portfolios, or when others are not willing to take risk. Taking advantage of these opportunities usually involves the ability to see the market differently than others, and therefore, usually requires additional analytical capabilities.

The cost of additional analytical power (and insight) must be weighted against the investment gains. Superior tools must produce more than marginal investment gains; they must pay their own way. In the first type of investing, where tools are used to preserve the inherent advantage of mortgages, portfolio size is an advantage. Larger portfolios can produce greater income and justify greater expenses. In the second strategy, the portfolio manager is looking for unique opportunities to improve return through the use of analytical tools. In this, strategy size is only an advantage up to a point. Extremely large portfolios may not be able to find enough "special" opportunities to make significant improvements in portfolio results. For these portfolios, careful analysis of portfolio goals and integration of the portfolio into the larger objectives of the firm (especially for financial institutions) may be the most appropriate allocation of resources.

■ THE WALL STREET ALTERNATIVE

The primary alternative to building an internal analytical capability is to rely on Wall Street for analytical resources. Given our experience in developing tools for the Street, we are in a good position to describe the strengths and weakness of using Wall Street analytical tools. Wall Street tools have one major advantage: they're free. At least in the sense that usually there is no direct cost. A firm is usually willing to provide quite a bit of analysis as part of the sales process. Sometimes, all this free service has a hidden cost, as Wall Street firms try to extract value from their client relationships. The second advantage of the Wall Street analytical efforts is their access to data. Wall Street firms have the best pricing data, and prices are the key to accurate analysis. The Wall Street firms have also invested heavily in databases and most have extremely good databases of security indicatives, price history, and prepayment data. This wealth of data enhances the analytics process. The third advantage of the Wall Street firms is their access to markets and information. Wall Street analysts have excellent access to traders and market information. This information can be used to refine models. Often, important components of security performance are not readily discernible from the outside. Wall Street models are also subject to the discipline of the market. Models that fail to produce valuable results are quickly weeded out.

With all these advantages, it would seem that buy side firms would have little basis to compete and would always be at a severe disadvantage in trading. However, Wall Street models generally have two major disadvantages. Wall Street firms tend to concentrate on trades, should I buy security A or security B? Moreover most Wall Street traders are operating within relatively narrow markets. Because of these institutional factors, Wall Street modelers tend to concentrate on relatively short-term investment horizons (minutes, hours, days), rather than the longer horizons of most portfolio managers (weeks, months, years). Furthermore, the narrow focus means that Wall Street models may be good for distinguishing the value of two similar bonds, but they won't usually address the issue of how the bonds should work together.

A simple analogy might clarify this issue. Think of your portfolio as a football team. As the coach, you need to figure out an overall game plan and make sure you have the necessary talent to win the game. Wall Street can tell you who are the best receivers, and how much you'll have to pay. They can tell you how fast each player can run, and how well they catch the ball. Suppose that you have decided to concentrate on the running game. The *best* receiver may not be the most valuable for you. What you need is a receiver who can and will block. You might see value in a player that Wall Street views as too slow to be counted among the best. On a player-by-player basis, he's not the best, but for your team he adds the most value.

Similarly, Wall Street analysts and traders, focused on their narrow markets and short time horizons, may favor bonds that don't fit into your investment strategy. Wall Street traders concentrate on finding value among reasonably similar securities. They tend to understand value between securities that fit within the sector of the market that they trade actively. Their focus is on buying securities that they can resell quickly at a higher price. Thus, the tools that Wall Street develops are not always appropriate for portfolio investments that span broad markets and are intended for long-term holding periods.

Another reason to limit reliance on Wall Street is because you may not be able to rely on long-term continuation of the supply of reliable analysis from Wall Street. Priorities change at Wall Street firms, leading to increased or decreased emphasis on analytical tools and providing support to clients. Moreover, even analysis provided for free often comes with a hidden charge. Wall Street firms provide analytical support in exchange for insight into your investment process and preference in execution. At times, that support is worth the cost, especially in situations that require very sophisticated support on a one-time basis. For example, if a pension plan is being defeased or restructured, building tools internally for a single transaction would be expensive and would unnecessarily delay implementation.

■ THE ADVANTAGES OF IN-HOUSE ANALYTICS

In-house analytical capabilities can lead to competitive advantages for the firm, given the complex investment environment and the complex requirements placed on portfolio managers. Flexible tools, which allow the investment manager to assess how well the portfolio addresses the wide variety of competing requirements can make the investment process more efficient. If these management tools are integrated with sophisticated valuation tools, then the investment manager can make portfolio decisions that enhance the economic and other requirements of the portfolio simultaneously.

Regulatory and accounting requirements are undergoing a period of rapid change. New requirements may lead to substantial shifts in portfolio composition. In-house analytical systems that can address the institutions' unique requirements, while taking into account market opportunities, can help institutions not only survive change, but also benefit from regulatory realignment. Institutions that lead in the realignment of their investments are likely to benefit from better pricing and execution than those who follow the crowd.

Another major advantage to using in-house tools is that it fosters development of insight into the workings of the securities and securities markets. In developing tools to analyze mortgage-backed securities, a large number of decisions need to made about which factors to emphasize and what modeling assumptions to choose. One point that we have emphasized is that there is a substantial component of judgment in these models. Therefore, none of these models is a definitive statement of truth. These models are merely one possible approach to the problem. When tools are developed internally, you gain greater insight into the strengths and weaknesses of the approaches you have used. Furthermore, with in-house models you have greater flexibility to change the assumptions or use the model as conditions change.

One extremely important area of insight is prepayments. All mortgage models depend crucially on the prepayment phase of the analysis. Only internal tools give you the opportunity to develop an in-depth understanding of prepayment dynamics and the ability to assess the impact of varying prepayment assumptions on portfolio strategies. The investment process is far more than implementing the output of a model. Investing involves tempering the model output with judgment. Better understanding of the tools, leads to better judgment. Understanding the strengths and weaknesses of the tools you use will allow you to concentrate on the areas where your judgment can be used to produce the greatest improvement in performance.

Because prepayment models tend to be based on historical data, they tend to be one step behind the forces that are influencing prepayments. Understanding of what factors are imbedded in your prepayment models and what factors are left out, provides the opportunity to identify value where the model sees none. These additional insights can be used to create superior performance.

■ BUILDING YOUR OWN TOOLS

Firms that decide to build in-house tools must decide on building from scratch or using prepackaged tools. This choice will depend on a wide number of factors. The most important considerations involve the needs of the organization for specialized tools and the people available for development. For most firms, internal analytical tools are pieced together from a variety of sources. Analytical capabilities represent a blending of hardware, software, data, and analysis, with a variety of skills required to develop and maintain a working system.

Analytical tools come in a variety of sizes and shapes, capabilities, and platforms. Before embarking on an internal development effort, it is advisable to explore third-party solutions. These third-party tools include integrated systems, prepackaged calculation routines, general purpose development tools, and databases. The decision of whether to build or not is a trade-off between cost and speed of development versus customization and flexibility. In-house tools offer the advantage that they can be modified to meet changing internal requirements. On the other hand, internal tools require a larger commitment to systems staffing. Given the rapid pace of development in computer technology, it is difficult for internally developed systems to keep pace with vendor software.

A third alternative avoids the choice between internal and external systems, and instead relies on some packaged routines and some custom routines to develop a system of proprietary tools based on purchased components. In the modern computing environment, a blended approach makes the most sense for all but the largest and smallest firms. The benefits of third-party software are so great that even large Wall Street firms with tremendous systems resources have turned to third-party analytical tools as a cost-effective means of supporting their requirements.

■ DATA REQUIREMENTS OF ANALYTICAL TOOLS

For all analytical tools, access to data is a crucial issue. Without good data, security analytics is a purely academic exercise. Analytical tools are only a way of transforming data and information into a form that facilitates the investment manager's decision-making process. It may be possible to manage a portfolio without analytics, but it is impossible to manage a portfolio without data. MBS evaluation is particularly data intensive, and good analytical tools need to be supplied with sufficient data.

Analytical tools require several different types of data. The more successful tools have automated input of the most important data. Automated data feeds increase the usefulness of the system and reduce the risk of data-entry errors. Data requirements include market data, bond indicatives, portfolio position data, and historical data.

Good market data is the key ingredient to any trading analytics. The valuation tools we have described in this book are primarily relative value tools. That is, they indicate whether one security has better potential for future performance relative to another security. These measures typically rely on choosing a base set of securities to outperform. In most cases, the on-the-run Treasury curve provides the initial basis for comparison. It is essential that the data used to construct the foundation of the analysis be of the highest quality. In addition, trading decisions should be made using real prices. Frequently, bonds seem cheap based on overnight analysis of vendor supplied prices. However, when executable prices are included and the real bid-ask spread is included these "fly-by-night" deals often vanish under the harsh light of day-time trading reality.

Fortunately for analytics developers, the quality of trading data available in machine readable form is rising rapidly. Bloomberg was responsible for much of the availability of real price information on a wide variety of fixed-income securities. However, Bloomberg's "closed" architecture made integration of this data difficult for all but the simplest applications. The availability of the Bloomberg data, however, has led other data vendors to improve their offerings on more open systems. Various pricing services provide end-of-day prices on a wide variety of fixed-income securities. These services are used primarily for pricing of mutual funds and other regulatory requirements, but can also be used to feed analytical systems.

Another favorable development for investors in general, and analytics developers in particular, is the growing availability of real-time price data on open systems. Knight-Ridders windows product is the current leader in this field but there are other entrants. Intraday updates of key variables can provide valuable insight into relative value during rapidly changing markets. Avoiding time-consuming and frequently inaccurate hand updating of market data can lead to quicker response in dynamic markets. Of course, as with overnight data, care should be taken to assure that prices used for analysis represent real levels where transactions can occur. In rapidly changing markets, advanced analytical tools can provide the greatest benefit is also the time when they pose the greatest risk.

Indicative data, the information needed to describe a security, is a far more complex requirement. For investors with relatively small, stable portfolios of simple products, indicative data can be gathered by hand. However, most mortgage portfolios are neither simple nor small. Even portfolios of passthroughs, which generally require little indicative data for each security, often contain hundreds of pools. When it comes to CMOs, indicative data is almost a misnomer. Indicative data, the data that describes the priority of cash flows in the deal, must be combined with a cash-flow generator in order to produce usable results. Here also, numerous solutions are available, all coming at a cost. Merrill Lynch and Bloomberg provide CMO data on Bloomberg. Their offerings are continually growing in breadth and depth, and provide the standard for the industry for trading. Unfortunately as with the price data on Bloomberg, the closed nature of the system limits the flexibility of the use of the data.

More recently, other vendors have closed the gap and now offer CMO cash-flow generators that come in various forms including user-friendly interfaces or C-language subroutines. These tools allow portfolio managers to combine CMOs into their in-house analytics without the expense and burden of reverse engineering all CMO deals themselves. Vendors include INTEX, GAT, Wall Street Analytics, and BARRA. While these vendors strive for the highest level of accuracy, investors are urged to be cautious of the results especially for the more complex CMO tranches.

The next type of data requirement is position data, that is, what securities you own. The major requirement for gathering and maintaining this data is discipline. There are really two choices. Portfolio data for analytics can be maintained by hand or it can be fed directly from the firms' accounting systems. We highly recommend an automated link. Hand-updated systems are subject to error, and cumbersome updating procedures may reduce the use of portfolio systems. Moreover, with improving communications tools between computer platforms linking disparate systems is not the Herculean task that it was a few years ago.

The most difficult type of data to obtain and maintain is historical data. Most forms of sophisticated analysis will require at least some historical data. Back testing an investment strategy requires historical price data. Evaluating spread histories requires past spreads. Building a prepayment model requires historical prepayments. Unfortunately, this data is not readily available. Bloomberg and the other data services provide the best source for historical data. Bloomberg allows some manipulation of the data, but you cannot download the data for other purposes. Generally, other data sources are either quite expensive or not very reliable. Even the alternative of building your own databases can be very expensive and often does not produce the desired results.

For historical price data, the best choice is to make do with whatever is easily accessible. Some historical time series can be bought at reasonable prices and with reasonably good quality. These include-on-the-run treasuries and exchange traded futures. Most MBS pricing (except current coupon), CMO prices, corporate, and swap market pricing is unreliable. Key data that directly impacts your operations should be collected on a regular basis and stored in a database.

Prepayment data also poses a problem. While it is possible to buy raw factor data at the pool level, converting this data to a usable form can be quite time consuming and expensive. Other vendors sell prepayment data, and a decent database can be constructed at a reasonable price.

Maintaining a historical prepayment database still represents a significant investment. For investors who engage in complex mortgage strategies, the development of an in-house prepayment database might still be worthwhile. Wall Street published prepayment histories are not complete enough to provide a full picture of potential prepayment patterns. Investors with large holdings of whole loans or large servicing portfolios should construct and maintain prepayment histories on their portfolios. While developing these databases may be complex and time consuming, it is almost impossible to value unique portfolios without performing prepayment analysis on the specific loans. Such analysis will be crucial in valuing, hedging, and selling the portfolio.

■ DESIGNING INTERNAL ANALYTICS

There are three general approaches to developing your own analytics tools. One, you can purchase an integrated system from an analytics vendor and add some custom capabilities. Two, you can develop your own analytical structure and use productivity tools such as spread sheet and database programs and prepackaged calculation routines. Three, you can develop a hybrid system where the integrated system is one component of your overall analytical structure. Table 12-1 delineates these choices.

Table 12-1 Comparison of Development Approaches

Method	Advantages	Disadvantages
Build own system	Designed to needs Can be enhanced	Requires systems skills Uncertain development time
Use integrated system	Known capabilities Known cost Experts approach	May not fit needs exactly Hard to customize
Combine integrated system with internal development	Advantages of integrated system with potential for customization	Requires systems skills May be inflexible and expensive

Integrated systems offer the advantage of turnkey operation. They can be set up quickly and begin to offer value almost immediately. These systems vary greatly in instrument coverage, functionality, systems platforms, and cost. The chief advantage of these systems is that they work and offer a broader range of capabilities than one firm could develop at anywhere near the same cost. Generally, the cost of these systems ranges from the cost of one to three analysts. Systems thatprovide position-management risk analysis, security valuation, and scenario analysis are readily available. The main shortcoming of these systems is that you are generally locked into a specific view of the market. Each system represents a view of how securities should be valued and managed. If you agree with the viewpoint of the developers, the system has value. If you disagree, you will be frustrated by a system that does not produce the results, which you feel are valuable. The systems also differ in how much flexibility they offer in changing underlying assumptions such as yield curves, interest-rate processes, prepayment model, and security spreads.

It is important to choose a system that matches your needs. There are basically two types of portfolio systems. One type evaluates the performance of the portfolio on a total rate of return basis, typically comparing the portfolio to a benchmark portfolio. This type of system is obviously appropriate for money managers who are trying to beat a benchmark or maximize total return over time. Asset/Liability systems are the other type. These systems concentrate on producing income and balance-sheet information, and are more appropriate for financial institutions managing a portfolio of assets and liabilities. Over time, these two approaches will become more integrated. For example, asset/liability systems now have flexible-scenario and option-adjusted spread capabilities, tools that previously were only available in the total-return systems.

If integrated systems don't meet your needs, you need to build your own tools. Fortunately, you don't need to start from scratch. With the rapid increases in computing power and falling cost of computing and memory, many tools have been developed to help you to develop custom applications. The first step is to determine your needs. Choose a computation platform—PCs, networked PCs, workstations, minis, or mainframes—that is more than sufficient for your tasks. Due to the availability of extremely powerful productivity tools for PCs and workstations, we feel that these are the platforms of choice. On these platforms, a database program and a spread sheet program can form the core of your application. More sophisticated programmers can use programming languages linked with screen design packages to produce professional-quality tools. We strongly recommend that these types of productivity tools be used as the core of your system. They speed development and allow you to concentrate on the analytical content of the system rather than the development of systems tools.

In addition to these development tools. there are also prepackaged calculation routines available for financial instruments. A number of tools have been developed particularly for mortgage-backed securities. The easiest prepackaged calculation routines to use are spread sheet add-ins. These act like ordinary functions in your spread sheet, but allow you to calculate security cash flows, yields, balances, duration, and a variety of other statistics. For simple applications, they speed development and reduce the risk of programming error.

The other type of tool is calculation subroutines: These are routines that can be combined into larger programs and can speed the development process. These routines are commonly programmed in C and are available for a variety of computer platforms. As mentioned above, several vendors offer routines that produce CMO cash flows. These routines are combined with a database of CMO deals. By using these routines and databases, you can rent a "reverse engineering" team and leverage your analytical tools. Without these routines, the cost of developing a CMO analysis capability can be prohibitive.

Interest-rate generator and prepayment model subroutines are not commonly available now, but with the growing number of firms developing their own custom tools, these types of subroutines will be more commonly available in the future. Currently, it is possible to contract with an analytics vendor or Wall Street firm to acquire these tools.

A third alternative is to combine an integrated system with custom tools. A typical example is to use an integrated system to analyze a portfolio, and then do additional analysis and reporting using customized tools. It is possible to run several different analyses on the integrated system and then combine the results to produce a summary. Or you can take components of the analysis on the integrated system and recombine the results to give you another view of the portfolio. This approach is very effective for developing a broad capability in a short time. However, there is one extremely important caveat. Integrated systems generally do not give you the capability to make any change you like. It is important to determine in advance that the data you will need to perform your additional analysis is available to you. In particular, it is important the data can be stored and transferred to your custom system. If not, the process can become extremely frustrating. Also, it is important to determine that you can actually vary the parameters that interest you. Suppose you have developed a prepayment model for your portfolio. If the system does not handle the variables in your model, or does not allow the user to specify his or her own prepayment function, your integrated capability may fall far short of your needs.

In designing and selecting analytical tools, the four-step-analysis process provides a good framework for thinking about your system needs. For each step, you can determine your needs and construct an overall capability. Environment reflects your market data needs. Prepayment reflects your security data and historical analysis needs. Cash Flow reflects your computation needs and Analysis is the section where you put it all together.

Analyzing of mortgage-backed securities is a complex process. We have provided a road map of the steps involved in the process. In analyzing MBS there are hundreds of decisions that you can make. Or if you buy an analysis system, hundreds of decisions that have already been made for you. Whether you are buying or building, always keep in mind that every system has limitations. If you think through those limitations and test results for potential errors you will be a better investor.

■ CONCLUSION

Mortgage-backed securities present rewards and pitfalls to fixed income investors. Because the mortgage market is a large liquid market of high quality assets, fixed income investors can not sidestep this market. Investors also like the almost limitless variety of bonds that can be created through the mechanism of the CMO. Despite these attractions, investment in MBS is complicated by the prepayment option granted to the borrower and imbedded in every MBS. Borrower prepayments, the sizzle on the steak of MBS, are driven by economic and demographic factors and are not completely predictable. This human element to mortgage-backed securities means that investment performance can not be forecasted precisely.

As framework for evaluating mortgage-backed securities, we have developed a four phase process. The **Environment** phase sets the boundaries and parameters of the evaluation. The **Prepayment** phase determines the prepayment assumptions. The **Cash Flow** phase produces the security performance. The **Analysis** phase summarizes the results of the prior three phases and provides the decision tool to the investor. This four phase approach can be applied to simple analysis such as yield calculation, more complex scenario analysis, or to sophisticated Monte Carlo analysis of the impact of yield curve fluctuations on CMOs.

This framework provides the starting point for profitable investing in this exciting and complex market. To avoid risk and extract value in the ever-changing mortgage-backed securities market, investors must continually question, challenge and innovate.

INDEX

O

Obligation, *see* Collateralized
On-the-run Treasury, 47, 183
  curve, 272
  note, 196
Optimization methods, 15
Option(s)
  see Black, Embedded, Prepayment
  approach, *see* Terminal
  market, 56
  pricing approaches, 63
  risk, 244, 246-249
    see Embedded
Option-adjusted spread (OAS), 14, 149-177
  analysis, 15, 16, 173-177, 197, 242, 260
  application, 248-250
  approach, 200, 209, 212, 248
  assumptions, 253
  bond, 249
  calculation, 151, 154, 174, 175, 199, 234
    process, 231
  capabilities, 276
  convexity, 260
  duration, 260
  effective duration, 141
  framework, 167
  horizon pricing model, 215
  levels, 249, 253
  methodology, 161
  model, 132, 141, 149-152, 154, 156, 160,
    163, 164, 166, 168-171, 174, 175,
    177, 188-190, 193, 197, 202, 231,
    232, 236, 242, 248
    process, 151-152
  OAS-based model, 160
  OAS-derived number, 259
  OAS-type model, 150-151, 155, 187, 259,
    262
  path, 157
  pricing, 130, 131, 206
    methods, 163-164
    model, 130, 249
    technology, 258
  results, 150
  scenario analysis, 130
  simulation, 158, 244
    path, 157
    trials, 155, 161
  simulator, 152
  technology, 149, 150
  users, 165
  variables, 154

Option-exposure risk, 125
Option-pricing
  approaches, 127
  models, 155
Options-based
  analysis, 161
  horizon-pricing model, 252
  model, 244
Origination, 4, 74
Originators, *see* Mortgage
Over-the-counter market, 187

P

PAC, *see* Planned
Parallel
  interest-rate movements, 120
  shift, 121, 209
  yield-curve shifts, 199, 252
Passthrough(s), 201
  change, 97
  MBS, 234, 261
  securities, 129, 218
  trader, *see* Mortgage-backed
Path(s), 213-215
  see Forward, Implied, Interest, Interest-
    rate, Option-adjusted, Simulation
  dependency, 218, 220-222, 235
  risk, 237
  sensitivity, 236
Path-dependence risk, 211-242, 252
  see Mortgage-backed
  analysis, 227-241
Pay, *see* Interest, Principal
Payment
  see Coupon, Fixed-interest, Prepayment,
    Repayment
  types, *see* Interest-only, Principal-only
Peak CPR, 78
Pension funds, 9
Performance, *see* Financial
Planned amortization class (PAC)
  see Coupon, Sequential
  band(s), 107-109, 225, 226, 227, 247
    security, 130
    speeds, 106
  bonds, 71, 99, 105-108, 129, 130, 213,
    217, 223-227, 245, 246, 248
  cash flow, 105, 217
  class, 109
  collars, 217, 224-227
  products, 241
  protection, 224

measure, 126
model, 78, 96
prepayment assumption, 37
prepayment curve, 29, 34, 37, 50, 81, 83, 125
prepayment model, 32
rate, 208, 229
scenario, 105
speed, 145, 191, 226
Purchaser, *see* Mortgage-backed

R

Random process, control, 161
Rate shift, 123-125
Real Estate Mortgage Investment Conduit (REMIC), 93, 170, 229
see Collateralized
rules, 103
Refinancing, 66
costs, 83
opportunities, 74
Threshold Pricing (RTP) model, 68
Regulatory considerations, income relationship, 238-240
Regulatory-risk measures, 252
Reinvestment
decision, 252
rate, 119-120
strategy, 119
REMIC, *see* Collateralized, Real
Repayment, *see* Mortgage-backed
Reset loans, 3
Residual
see Collateralized
interest, 93
Return
see Expected
profile, 250
sensitivity, 144
Return on equity, 146
Reverse engineering, 277
Reversion, *see* Mean
Risk, 12, 15, 47-49, 102, 138-140, 199-208, 229-236
see Basis, Call, Collateralized, Convexity, Credit, Default, Duration, Embedded, Extension, Interest-rate, Liquidity, Mortgage-backed, Option, Option-exposure, Path, Path-dependence, Path-dependency, Prepayment, Price, Whipsaw, Yield-curve

analysis, 65, 173
see Mortgage-backed, Position-management
analytics, 263
calculation, 175
characteristics, 201
measures, 23, 174-175, 257
models, 259
profiles, 147
Risk-analysis dimension, 243
Riskless profits, 187
Rocket scientists, 82
RTP, *see* Refinancing

S

S&L, *see* Savings
Savings and Loan (S&L), 4, 9
Scenario(s)
see Expected, Interest-rate, Multiple, Planned, Single, Whipsaw, Yield, Yield-twist
creation, 120-125
Scenario analysis, 16, 115-148, 163, 188, 211, 250-252, 254
see Option-adjustedd
motivation, 115-117
Scheduled
bonds, 105-108
principal, 37
Seasonality, 80
Securities, *see* Adjustable-rate, Average, Benchmark, Collateralized, Corporate, Coupon, Derivative, Fixed-income, Floater, Government, Interest-only, Inverse, Mortgage-backed, Passthrough, Planned, Premium, Prepayment-sensitive, Principal-only, Secondary, Synthetic, U.S., Warm-blooded
Securitization
see Mortgage
rate, 6
Senior/subordinated structures, 112-113
Separate Trading of Registered Interest and Principal Securities (STRIPS), 55
see Interest-only, Principal-only, U.S., Zero-coupon
Sequential
bonds, 99, 102, 105, 109
CMOs, 100-102
PACs, 109-110